WOLF

TERRY M. DUNN

Volume Five of the DANEBURY series

Daneburyverse books

Cover Picture: The Ring Stone, Avebury.

visit
Daneburyverse books
at
tmdunn.co.uk
or
daneburyverse.com

Printed by Book Printing UK
Remus House,
Coltsfoot Drive,
Peterborough,
PE2 9BF
ISBN: 978-1-9162657-5-2

DANNU'S LAND

Winter 3,504-3 BC

3,504 BC

1

It had been more than two years since the tragedy and drama of his people's involvement with the lost village on the Isle of Wight. There had been upheaval, violence and deaths but Parrish never ceased to marvel at his people's ability to bounce back from severe events and tragedies and reclaim their normal, contented existence.

It was a bit of a cliché now for the Chieftain of Danebury, but he had to admit, things really were going along as they should. Surveying his domain from his favoured vantage point atop the highest point of Danebury hillfort, he found himself smiling.

Children were running about between the huts below him. Their movements seemed haphazard but they were no doubt doing something important to them at that moment. Women worked at tasks around the open hearths outside many of the dwelling huts, although he understood this would not happen for much longer. Autumn was in full swing. The leaves had all turned and the trees were now shedding their auburn cloaks and beginning to cover the forest floor in a rustling, pastel hued carpet. Soon the cold weather would come, but that was still a short while away. Some other women could be seen out beyond the confines of the hillfort, making their way either too or from the watering stream in the woods beyond the open pasture between the hillfort and the edge of the great forest. His warriors were also about their business. The odd cluster of men chatted, perhaps settling some minor dispute, while others tended their personal or families equipment. And somewhere down there, Parrish smiled, was the Holy one, probably inside the great shrine hut, doing a bit of religious tinkering or some such.

It all looked calm, peaceful and Parrish was quite happy to say to himself, for these Neolithic times, prosperous and productive.

And that was how the people themselves also saw things. Life was good in Dane-Bre. And they knew who they had to thank for it. In the many seasons since Parrish had arrived in the land of the young, the people knew there had been great things, both good and bad, done by his hand. But the overriding total effect of his presence here had been their good fortune. The people could not be sure how many seasons now, but it had in fact been just over seven years since the tall man had first appeared out of the wilderness, bringing the warm summer sun with him. The tall man. He who watches and waits. Parrish of Dane-bre. Their great Chieftain and Dannu's Man.

They all knew he was watching, even now. But they were not concerned. Everyone knew they were not being watched, but being watched over. Dannu the Earth Goddess always smiled on him and so the people of the village, *his* village, were all grateful to feel her benevolence through him.

In an almost unbelievable run, every summer season since his arrival had been a great season. The sheep had lambed well. The crops had grown in rich abundance and the harvests had been the best since anyone could remember. All the underground storage pits/silos were full to bursting. This was something that did not happen that often, and twice there had been so much excess grain that great summer bakes had been held to make use of the spare grain. Sometimes there was even enough grain left for the people to still be enjoying fresh bread well into the following year. Yes, for the village as a whole, times have been good for Dane-bre.

Occasionally a villager would glance up at the tall, cross-legged sitter atop the mound towards the rear of the hillfort and a discreet, wry smile would cross his or her lips.

Not knowing this himself, but enjoying the same satisfaction, Parrish continued to gaze fondly down on his people. He could see they were happy, healthy and well fed. It not only increased their general wellbeing, but unknown to them he knew it would also increase their longevity. A good diet, enough food and a healthy lifestyle would naturally gift them several more years of life upon Dannu's land.

Parrish had the right to feel satisfied with his lot, and of those under his charge. He looked up into the cloud scudded autumn sky. Beneath it the great forest was rust, gold and red. The air was not yet cold but already fresh, and he knew winter was not too far off. But, barring any major catastrophes, his people were as ready as they could be for the winter season. As the Chieftain himself had been known to say from time to time, not bad, not bad at all.

*

The very next day, late in the afternoon, although Parrish only knew that because the sun was getting low in the sky, he was called out of his cabin into the fresh, cool air. Stepping out into the sunlight, with a smile on his face he nodded to Tomps and simply raised an eyebrow.

Tomps bowed formally to his Chieftain then, straightening up, smiled back at his tall friend.

"Please come." He asked. "Someone comes from the north. Klud is watching and thinks you might be interested." The warrior looked on expectantly.

Parrish's first thought was that his good friend Klud was getting a bit more diplomatic in his old age. He had to stop himself from actually laughing out loud. Of course he would come. Lone travellers were virtually unheard of in these wild times. If the mystery man had been the travelling minstrel and friend to Danebury, Cor-teer, he would have been welcomed with open arms. So, this other person then must be a stranger. So, what could he want or need? Parrish's interest was naturally piqued.

"Sounds like fun." was his unexpected reply. "Lead on, my young friend. Let us see what we shall see!"

Tomps smiled again to be called his Chieftain's friend, hiding his light bafflement at the tall man's odd phrase. How could you not see what you see? He mentally shrugged and fell in beside his tall mentor and together they set off back down the slope towards where the main gate was set into the palisade wall that enclosed the hillfort.

Juli had appeared in the cabin doorway just as they started off. She had clearly heard the conversation from inside.

As the two men walked away, the tall twentieth century man and the short Neolithic warrior side by side, she smiled. It was acceptable for a woman to smile if no warriors were watching. Abruptly, without looking back, Parrish raised one arm and waved backwards at his wife. She smiled again to know that he knew she was, as ever, right behind him, then turned and went back to work inside cabin.

Klud and several other warriors were up on the parapet to the left of the great gate. They were all armed. The warriors bowed to Parrish while Klud just looked up into his tall friend's face.

Parrish gave the fierce looking Neolithic man with the brutish tattoos, the single slash of hair across his face that was his full complement of eyebrows and the badly broken nose beneath it, the merest of nods. He smiled.

"Hey-ho, matey. What's up then?" he said in his native tongue.

Klud grinned back. The other, slightly intimidated warriors frowned in puzzlement but Klud and Parrish were as one. They had known each other since Parrish's first day at Danebury. They had fought together, experienced triumph and tragedy together and carried a deep personal connection to each other. It mattered not what Parrish said, even if it was in that strange, incomprehensible gobbledy-gook that the man called 'English'. One always knew what the other meant.

"An odd thing, my Chieftain." Klud replied, using his friend's formal title for the benefit of the warriors standing behind him. He pointed off over Parrish's shoulder, towards the north. "A single person. Hard to say what or who at this distance."

“OK.” Another English phrase. Reverting to the language of the people, he added. “Let us see what he does. But we will keep an eye out in other directions just in case he is not alone. Send a man or two to different points along the wall. Just as lookouts. To make sure we are safe.” He didn’t really doubt that they were. The defences of Danebury were impressive, almost impenetrable and always kept in good order. But it was a wise chieftain who covered every eventuality.

Klud nodded, spun to the men behind him and in seconds several had sprinted off to take up positions around the parapet of the encampment.

Parrish nodded his satisfaction and looked down at the two men who was greatest friends.

“Right. Now we wait, and see what he wants, yes?”

Tomps and Klud nodded. As one the three turned and leaned on the top of the palisade wall, eager eyes looking out to the lone figure in the distance.

The young mystery man at the centre of everyone’s attention came on at a jog and as he closed, became aware of the warriors behind the hillfort wall watching him intently. He gulped back a wave of anxiety and pulled up at the beginning of the well-worn chalk pathway that led up to the entrance gate. Ensuring he was still well out of arrow range, he put his hands on his thighs and leaned forward, gasping to catch his breath but not taking his eyes off the watchers above him.

Parrish could see, even at the mid distance, that the lone mystery man was no more than a teenager, but couldn’t be more exact. The lad was wiry in stature but that was no surprise. There were no fat people in the land of the young. He had to agree though that the lad looked particularly built for speed. And it didn’t take a genius to figure out that he had travelled some distance. There was only one other village nearby and he had come from the opposite direction to that. Plus, he looked a bit dusty, dishevelled and decidedly tired.

"The lad looks cream crackered!" He said almost to himself in English then turned to Klud, again reverting to the language of the people. "He looks very tired. I do not think he is any sort of threat. My friend." He paused. "Being careful, go and see what he wants." Probably some food, drink and a good kip, he thought but never said.

Klud nodded in acceptance of his instructions and, as if reading his Chieftain's mind said.

"Of course. Though how he looks now I do not think he could even fight off one of our sheep."

Several of the nearby warriors laughed at his joke.

"Yes." Agreed Parrish. "Bring the poor boy in and let us get to the bottom of this."

No one quite understood their Chieftain's last words but grasped the meaning of the phrase. Several men went ahead to open the gates before Klud strode manfully out to meet the youngster. Everyone there knew Klud could easily crush the youngster if it came to a fight, including the man himself, but he was wisely taking no chances. With one hand 'casually' resting on the war club tucked into his belt, the Neolithic warrior strode down to meet the young visitor.

The Danebury observers watched as the pair came face to face then exchanged a few words. The youngster nodded then Klud unexpectedly put one arm around the youngsters shoulder and began to guide him back up to the great gate.

There were several looks of surprise on the faces of the men as well as Parrish, and he said to no one in particular.

"Well, it looks like there is no immediate danger. This could prove to be interesting."

Everyone else there nodded at their Chieftain's wisdom and they all descended the parapet, gathering behind their Chieftain as he stood astride the pathway, just inside the gates ready to receive the unknown visitor.

The young stranger was tired from his recent exertions but braced up, ready for anything, as he was led into Danebury by the hard and brutal looking warrior at his side. The warm grin on the man's battered face seemed completely at odds with his fierce demeanour. Smile or no smile, the youngster felt that the warrior by his side could with very little effort snuff out his life in an instant if he so chose.

But worse, after he had been led meekly into the entrance, he was confronted by a band of unknown warriors each with blank expressionless faces, all staring at him. And at their head was the biggest man he had ever seen.

This giant towered above everyone else. His tattoos said much but everything about him struck the lad momentarily dumb. The huge physique. The raw power and energy he exuded. And those piercing eyes. It all stopped him in his tracks and he continued to stare dumbly up as the warrior at his side stepped away and moved to stand beside the giant. So this was the man he'd been sent to see. The Chieftain of Dane-bre. The man had been described to him and he had been forewarned that the Chieftain was quite impressive, but it still did not prepare him as he finally found himself standing before, and being studied in return by Dannu's man.

The tall man's voice shocked him back to the present moment.

"Well. We do not get all that many visitors here. And you are?" Parrish grinned a genuine, warm welcome and that too stunned the young warrior.

"I..." he gulped, took a deep breath and tried again. I... am Hew and I have been sent to speak to Dan... Chieftain Parri... You."

"Good to know! "The tall man's reply was not anything like the youngster expected. Again, he was momentarily lost for words. "Well, Hew. You look like you have run a marathon." Parrish continued. No one knew what a marathon was but no one was about to ask. "Some food, drink and a bit of a rest will put you right. Then you can tell me what this is all about." He then said to no one in particular. "Someone settle him into my stall in the shrine hut, rustle up some food and water. Then," he nodded to the young warrior. "In the morning Klud, Gant and I will hear what young Hew here has to say."

With that the giant turned away. Hew suddenly felt dismissed and several warriors sprang into action. Everyone else seemed instinctively to know the strange parley was over. Two men took Hew by the elbow and started to lead him away towards the centre of the Danebury compound whilst others turned to give instruction to the small number of women who had silently and unobtrusively gathered behind the group. And one man set off to recall the other lookouts.

2

Hew really was fatigued. He had covered the distance that might normally take up to three days, in less than one full day. He had been chosen to do this because he was known to be a fast runner, his Goddess given talent for fleetness of foot discovered during his first training/hunting sortie.

But the distance he had been tasked to go at speed he had never covered in one go before. In truth, he doubted if anyone had ever before done such a thing.

But he had accepted his task, and was proud to say that he had completed it. But it had been hard and had needed real effort and determination.

And so the great Chieftain of Dane-bre was right. At its finish he *was* hungry, thirsty and very tired.

Then, before he could even fully recover his breath he had been led into the village shrine hut to be allowed to rest and recover and settled into the most revered spot there, the double stall of the Chieftain's, right beside the statue of the Earth Goddess.

It had all happened so fast too. During his cross-country travel, as he approached his destination, he had not been sure what to expect on his arrival at Dane-bre. He did wonder if he might be killed on the spot. Or at least be rough handled and perhaps even tied up as an unknown stranger who might be dangerous?

And yet, he had been given the most prestigious stall in the shrine hut. Several women had treated him with great respect, even as an outsider. He had been fed, watered and offered a warm woollen cape as a blanket over his deep straw bedding. Then they had left him to his solitude.

Night had fallen. A single woman whom he did not know but was eventually to discover was the Chieftain's wife, had visited him, informing him it was night. He did not dare to venture outside to see for himself. The woman said if he signalled that he was ready, she would douse almost all the tallow lamps in the hut and leave him to his rest.

He nodded dumbly, forgetting his natural right of power as a warrior over a mere female, even in this strange place. With a final bow the woman turned away, put out many of the lamps and quietly vanished through the entrance passageway, leaving him to his silence.

Settling down on the straw and pulling the cape up around his chin, the youngster looked respectfully, and if truth be told a little fearfully, around the great hut and then up at the great statue of the Goddess. It appeared to shimmer in the feeble light of the few remaining lamps. He couldn't help it, a shudder passed through him, his eyes darting about, peering into the dark corners of this strange place then back to the huge, bulbous statue. He found the whole recent sequence of events unnerving and unsettling. He was certain he would not sleep a single wink, no matter how tired he felt, and tried to settle back, steeling himself for a long night.

He was asleep in moments and enjoyed a peaceful, restful and reviving night's sleep right through to the next morning.

*

The same woman who had 'tucked him in' the night before was standing quietly to one side when he awoke.

The sudden sight of her, hovering silently beside the stall entrance made him snap harshly awake and he instinctively snatched his cape-cum-blanket against his chest in a childlike gesture of defence. He jerked into a bolt upright sitting position.

The woman jerked too in reaction to his. She bowed to him.

"I... I am sorry. I did not mean to startle you." She said apologetically.

"You... You did not." He pulled up his suddenly flagging spirits from where they currently languished, somewhere down near his ankles. "I was just... I ... I am ready."

Ready for what, he had no idea.

"Of course." There was a long pause. Then she took a deep breath. "My husband has sent me to see if you were awake. He says that when you are, I am to give you some food, ask if you are well, then also to ask if, in a short while, you will be ready to speak with him."

Only then did Hew see the food and water bag in a small heap at her feet. He certainly would not bow to a woman, even if she was the Chieftain's wife, but it once more impressed him that Chieftain Parrish did seem to think of everything.

"Tell the Chieftain, thank you. I accept the food and say that I'm ready to see him whenever he chooses."

The woman nodded.

"I will tell him. I think that he will be along shortly."

Hew's thought was that that was a bold and almost disrespectful thing for a mere woman to say, to try and foresee the actions of a warrior, but all he did was nod back.

With open hands Juli offered the food and drink on the ground before her, bowed again to the young warrior and spun on her heels. In moments Hew again found himself alone.

After taking a deep breath he jumped up and began brushing bits of straw from himself. He had better eat up and make himself as presentable as he could.

The great Chieftain of Dane-bre was about to pay him a visit.

*

Hew jumped to his feet again as the Chieftain of the village emerged into the shrine hut. He was flanked by two men to his left, and one to his right. As they crossed the hut floor, circling around the large central hearth, the youngster studied the men intently as they approached.

To the Chieftains right was the man who had been his very first contact at Dane-bre. His eyebrows and smashed nose prominent but the previous warm smile was glaringly absent. A matter-of-fact, almost grim expression was on his face. He walked boldly and proudly beside his tall Chieftain. So too did the pair to the tall man's left. The warrior nearest him did not look too many seasons older than Hew, but the straight gaze and assured way he handled himself was unmistakable. The man almost seemed to flow across the floor as he moved and the hard confidence in his eyes said that this warrior was not the sort of man to mess with.

The last man he could only describe as calm and steady. He gave off the air of someone who knew what was going on about him and he had an almost serene confidence. Then Hew noticed the limp and glanced down at the man's legs. His jaw dropped open. Not legs, leg! One of the man's lower limbs looked normal and was moccasin shod, but the other was just a thick wooden peg.

The four closed and Hew recovered from his shock, briefly noting the hard eye of the one-legged man on him. He quickly darted his own gaze away and concentrated on the tall man as the group stepped up to face him.

Parrish crossed his arms over his chest, looking down at the clearly intimidated young warrior, who bowed deeply to him. That'll do, he thought, and smiled.

"I am Chieftain Parrish of Dane-bre." He announced formally, "And these are my trusted friends." Parrish indicated the man with the broken nose. "Klud you have already met. He is my right hand." Hew bowed to him and got a curt nod in return. "This young fire eater here is Tomps." The dangerous looking one nodded too and also received a bow. "And the man on the end there is Gant. He is my left hand." Hew hesitated to look directly at the third man, then managed a nod/half bow. The man in question appeared completely unmoved. Then Hew couldn't help himself. His eyes darted briefly to the man's legs. After all, he had never seen anything like it.

"Yes." said Gant evenly, as if reading the young man's thought and answering the unspoken question. "I have one leg.

Dannu has the other, but I still live, thanks to Parrish." He smiled at his Chieftain.

Astounded by this sudden revelation, and wondering at the power of Dannu's man, his gaze returned to the tall man. Hew bowed again.

"I am honoured to meet you all, especially the great Chieftain of Dane-bre." He did manage to prevent himself from blurting out 'and Dannu's man' also. There was awe in his voice.

Parrish stifled a chuckle and nodded at the compliment.

"Thank you. But I am not *your* Chieftain so, at least among friends, I am happy just to be called Parrish." He received another bow, being hastily converted into an exaggerated half nod as the lad remembered the now informal nature of the gathering. Parrish again smothered a chuckle and continued. "Right! Now we are all known one to another, let us get down to business. So, tell me young Hew, what exactly brings you all the way to Dane-bre at a full run?"

Everyone from Dane-bre perked up, intensely curious to hear the young stranger's next words.

Hew nodded. Now for the second, most vital part of his task. He drew in a long breath.

"I have come from the holy village beyond the stones at the great temple."

The three Danebury warriors eyed each other. Suddenly, this was Dannu's work. Parrish just nodded.

"Thought so." he said almost to himself. "Ah..." he continued, more audibly. "Carry on."

"Well," Hew paused, girding himself up to launch into his most important task. The reason why he had been sent to Dane-bre. And yet he felt a brief explanation was needed. "The Wisest of the Wise Ones has sent me to you with a message. He said that he hoped it would interest you enough for you to act on his words. I... had to commit his words to my mind exactly as he said them." Hew nodded at the tall man to make the point.

Parrish understood completely and he looked intently into the youngster's eyes.

"OK" he said quietly. Now the lad had his undivided attention. "Take your time, recall the words fully and speak when you are ready. As if the wisest one himself was talking only to me."

Hew understood and there was a long moment of heavy silence as he locked his eyes to Parrish's piercing gaze, and took a deep breath and started to speak. His voice flattened in tone. It was as if he were unconsciously trying to duplicate the old one's rustling, parchment dry sound.

"Hello my good friend. I send this message to you because a strange thing has happened. I know how you like to know things. So, I now ask if you would like to find out about this strange thing so that we here at the great temple will know things too." Hew paused. Parrish gave the briefest of nods, the pair still locked eye to eye.

"You are doing well. Go on." He urged.

"We noticed that a small number of villages were not present at the last solstice gathering. And now a strange tale has come from the north. This too is the area where the missing villages come from. It is an odd thing, and I feel it is not a good thing. If you will come to us, I will tell you more, that is if you are curious? I hope you are and that I will see you as soon as you can get here. And look after the boy we have sent to you. If you are hearing this message, I would think that he has done well. Be well, Chieftain Parrish of Dane-bre. Take care, my son. Go with Dannu."

Hew exhaled forcibly, releasing his concentration and glad to get the message off his chest. He had learned the message parrot fashion back in Avebury, but now he was face to face with Dannu's man, the words suddenly had a powerful resonance and urgency.

Parrish was still staring into his face but his eyes had gone out of focus. The tall man's mind was now somewhere else.

A quiet whisper between the three Danebury warriors broke the hushed spell.

"Dannu calls." said Klud.

"And Parrish must go." agreed Gant.

Parrish stiffened his back at those last words, the spell now broken for him too.

"We must indeed go." He stopped the others dead. "I must think on this."

And with that he simply turned and stalked away, back towards the entrance passageway, and was soon gone from sight.

Even Hew knew that the meeting had finished and the four Neolithic men momentarily stared at one another.

Klud took charge. A hardened, concerned look had settled on his face. He well remembered unpleasant events of the past.

"Parrish will let us know his decision when he is ready. We must wait. You," he looked at Hew. "You are free to go where you please, but do not leave the village. As the carrier of the message, I am sure Parrish will want to speak with you again."

"Yes." said Tomps, the first word he had spoken. "There is much more to this message than we just heard, but Parrish will know what to do. He always does. But where he goes, I go."

"Agreed." said his companions as one. Almost in unison, they nodded to Hew, turned and followed in Parrish's footsteps.

Once again, Hew found himself alone in the shrine hut, and as much in the dark as ever.

3

Hew spent a while wandering around the shrine hut. He examined many of the trophy skulls hanging in the stalls, but he had no intention of going too near the statue. An earlier peek from his angled position at the entrance to the Chieftain's stall told him that there were holy effects behind it and he had no intention of going uninvited into that religious space. He did wonder where the village holy man was, but he did not intend to ask, even if there had been anyone nearby *to* ask.

So, eventually he found himself at the entrance passageway, took the plunge, walked through and stepped gingerly out into the day. Drawing in a deep, reviving breath of the fresh crisp air he looked about.

The sky was grey, but quite bright through the thin cloud cover. He could see people moving about at their tasks, but no one paid him much attention. It seemed the occasional brief glance in his direction was all he warranted. Word had got about of Klud's direction and so they let the lad be. There were to be no challenges or threats against him unless he took stupid liberties.

Hew decided it would be a good thing to stretch his stiff legs and so spent the next few hours exploring the village. He walked the full inside perimeter of Dane-bre. Then he did the same, only up on the parapet, this time looking out across the Neolithic landscape with a practised eye. It was a very different view from that of his own village's ramparts of course, no more so because the view from the holy village where he lived held the spectacle of its massive shrine house that dominated the western aspect of Avebury village. Yet, he could see that Danebury was clearly in a good position within the landscape. Its vistas were pleasing to the eye as well as giving clear views of anyone who might be approaching. One odd thing. He saw what looked like another village off in the distance, on high ground away to the east. He puzzled over this and couldn't decide if it were either abandoned or of no consequence. He could not see any movement out there and there was very little if any smoke rising from the mysterious village site.

Turning back to look at the interior of Dane-bre, it was clear to see from anywhere in the village that this place had its own unusual, unique feature. On the highest point of the hillfort, towards the northwest quadrant of the village enclosure, was a dark, brooding, timber built structure. It was unmistakable not just because of its position, but also its shape. Roughly the size of all the other main dwelling huts, but square!

After he had looked at the mouths of the sealed grain storage pits, then watched some women baking at one of the clay ovens and even stood and admired the flint knapper at his work, his attention was drawn back to the square hut on the high ground.

He plucked up his courage and walked slowly up to investigate, but had barely started his upward climb when he heard voices behind him and spun in alert to see.

The men he knew as Klud, Tomps and Gant were approaching, having emerged from between some 'normal' huts. With them was another slightly shorter man, easily identified as a holy one. Hew bowed to the three warriors then bowed deeply to the holy man, who cocked an eyebrow.

"So, this is our young runner, eh? I hear that you can go from the temple of Dannu to Dane-bre in a single day. Very impressive."

Hew was at a loss for words as the little man just nodded in admiration, but then dismissed the praise with a sudden change of subject.

"You are here now, anyway. This is good. I was about to send someone to fetch you. Parrish has called a meeting and he wants you there."

"Oh. Really? What sort of meeting?" blurted the youngster.

All four men looked at him with flat, expressionless faces.

"We do not try to think Parrish's thoughts." said Klud with a hint of annoyance. "He knows things no one else knows. We just go to him when he calls and, if he is feeling generous, he will explain." Hew bowed his head in apology but then the fierce warrior stepped up, put a hand on the lads shoulder and grinned. "Do not think on it, my young friend. You were not to know. It is just the way of things here with Dannu's man." Hew's head came up to see them all nodding. Without a word he fell in beside them and they all continued on up towards the square wooden structure on the brow of the hill.

Parrish appeared in the cabin doorway just as the four Neolithic men reached the top of the rise. They all stopped respectfully short and looked up at him as he briefly scanned the horizon before looking directly at them.

"A pleasant enough day." he said. "Shall we sit outside?"

A Chieftains request is a warrior's order. They nodded and as one they dropped into a squat, forming an open circle before the cabin. Parrish stepped into the gap and as he lowered himself to the ground looked directly at the holy man.

"How is our man?"

"Good." came the shaman's reply. "I sat with him through the night. His fever has broken. With the goodwill of Dannu I believe he will recover."

"Good man." smiled the Chieftain. "Now, my friends, to business. Hew, can you tell me the wise ones words again, please."

Hew responded instantly to the demand and in the same steady tone as before, repeated the high priest of the Earth Goddess's words. Parrish listened again intently and nodded when the lad had finished, as did the others. They were all trying hard to somehow read between the lines to grasp some deeper, hidden meaning there.

So engrossed were they all that it was only when Hew had finished and a silence fell, they became aware of people behind them.

Juli had appeared carrying some foodstuffs and was waiting patiently to catch the men's attention. Beside her was a young boy. Everyone from Dane-bre knew Parrish's son was almost six summers old but he was already almost four feet tall, reaching his mothers shoulder in height. Hew only had a mere inkling that something about the boy was unusual but he could not help notice the oddity. He looked so young yet still older. And he had his father's eyes.

As the youngster moved around offering clay pots of water to the seated men, Parrish smiled.

"Good idea, son."

The lad smiled.

The others took the offered drinks and each a slice of cold meat from Juli's wooden platter, as much not to offend as for accepting free food.

Woman and boy then bowed to them all, intending to leave.

Hew caught Parrish winking at his wife before she turned away to return to the cabin. He had of course recognized the woman from earlier. It was she who had been there when he'd awoken.

As her parting gaze passed over him, he couldn't help himself. Perhaps it was simply because she was kind. Perhaps it was because he had spotted Parrish covertly acknowledging her, or perhaps it was because she was close to Dannu's man, but Hew felt the sudden need to give her the almost imperceptible, smallest of nods. Yet Juli saw, and even though she gave no sign of reciprocating, she momentary paused, pleasantly surprised to get a completely unexpected acknowledgement. Then, as she turned her back and moved away, was there the slightest sideways inclining of her head for him?

Hew drew a sudden feeling of warmth from it, smiled to himself and pulled his attention back to the meeting before him, only to find Parrish gazing directly at him. There was no expression on the big man's face, but he realized that what had been said about Parrish was true. Dannu's man missed nothing!

Then Parrish called the meeting to order.

"I am sure you all want to know what happens next." He smiled, seeing the fierce curiosity bright on the faces before him. "Well, I have been thinking and paying heed to the words the Wisest of the Wise Ones has sent to me." An acknowledging nod to Hew then. The Danebury trio tried not to look too keen, but the Chieftain was about to explain which in itself was a gift, and it usually meant that they would be astounded by some great revelation. "That man is a crafty so and so." The English phrase was lost on them as Parrish continued with a wry smile. "He gives just enough for me to want to know, without giving away too much. I believe he wants me to go on a scouting trip for *their* benefit, to find out what is happening away to the north, beyond the great stone circle. And of course, he knows I will go. The Wise One as always is right. He hopes I am curious enough, but he knows that his words are a request from Dannu's temple, so how could I refuse."

There were nods of agreement. Parrish looked to the holy man.

"You are a man of the Goddess's great shrine hut, my friend. Tell me, if I would go north of her great temple, are there holy men at the temple I could call upon to go with me and to guide me? I have no knowledge of the lands beyond the great stone circle. I simply would not know where to go."

The shaman nodded. Now was not the time to keep secrets from Dannu's man.

"Yes. He agreed. "Holy men from the temple travel to all the different villages of Dannu's land every now and then. Yes, there will be at least one servant of Dannu that will know the way to the north and the villages there."

"Outstanding!" said Parrish, using a word he had picked up from the American soldiers who were on an exchange visit to the Second Battalion Light Infantry regiment in Winchester when he had been stationed there in what now seemed millennia ago. Seeing the confusion on his companion's faces he hastily added. "Good. Now that issue is cleared up, onto the next thing. I think it is also clear that once I have reached the holy village by the great stones, I will be asked, no, *expected*, to go on and try to make sense of this mystery of the missing villages." The men were now stiff backed and leaning forward, listening with great intent. "And I will not go alone." This was more like what they wanted to hear. Wide grins appeared on the faces of those around him. Parrish laughed. "Not so fast, my eager friends. Not all of you will be going with me."

"But, my Chieftain ..." Tomps blurted.

"Hold on." Parrish halted his friend with a raised palm. "I will give my reasons. If afterwards you have any questions, any of you, I will listen."

Everyone relaxed slightly and leant back into a more comfortable sitting position.

"Better. Right. I think that if we go north into the unknown, it is possible, even likely, that we may get into the odd scrap."

This was greeted again with uncomprehending frowns.

"Er ... a fight." Parrish explained. "So, at the very least I would want good men, like Klud and Tomps, by my side."

There were grins from the two men named.

"But Parrish..." Gant, immediately offended at being left out, made to jump to his feet but was of course hindered by his false leg. No words needed to be said. The Chieftain's point was obviously and instantly made.

"My friend." Parrish addressed him quietly. "It is clear that long distance travel will be difficult for you. Never mind the chance of going into battle." He again put up his hand to quell any protest. "But that is not the reason why you will not be travelling with me. I need someone I can trust. Not just trust with my life, but with something much more valuable than that."

"Huh?" came more ignorant grunts.

"Klud will be with me so who else can I rely on to take care of Dane-bre when I am not here?" He fixed Gant with a heavy stare. "My friend, I offer you the village until I return. Will being Chieftain of Dane-bre satisfy you enough to get over not travelling north with me?"

"I... I am honoured. If you think I..."

"I can think of no one better. So, my friend, I put the safety of my village into your hands."

Both men were now still, as they looked deep into each other's eyes. Then Gant broke into a grin.

"How could I refuse such an honour. And you are right of course. I must admit the travelling a fair distance might cause me some discomfort." He waggled his false leg.

Parrish just bowed in acknowledgement and the diplomacy of the statement. When his head came back up, he looked to Klud and Tomps.

"You two will come along with me. That is if you have nothing better to do?"

Huge grins were their answer. Klud clapped Tomps on the back and the men nodded vigorously to each other. Parrish's voice brought everyone back to the moment. He looked again at the holy man.

"If you could honestly say you know the northern lands, I would welcome you to join us. But if you cannot, I do not want to put you in unneeded danger. I am sure Dannu would not be too pleased with me if I let one of her loyal servants be possibly injured or even killed, if it was not necessary. So I ask you to stay here in Dane-bre, as is your proper place."

"Of course." If the shaman was disappointed, his face did not show it. He just offered the tall man a seated bow. Parrish finally turned to Hew.

"You are a free person, my young friend. You can stay in Dane-bre if you so wish and wait until I and my warriors return. It is a fine place to be. Or you can come along with us. Wherever we may go after, our first stop will be at the holy village. And that is your home is it not?"

Hugh just nodded, but he looked a little concerned.

"Do not worry too much. We will travel there at a good pace, but trust me, no one will be running!"

There were laughs from the others and Hew grinned widely.

"Then I would be happy to join you, Chief... Parrish."

"Good man." The Chieftain of Dane-bre looked around at those before him. "Now, any questions?" There was complete silence. "OK, rest or whatever you must do for the rest of the day. Then sort out your equipment and be ready for an early start tomorrow morning. I will meet you all at the gate shortly after sunrise."

As he started to rise to his feet everyone else knew the meeting was over and clambered to their feet too. They all bowed deeply to the Chieftain. He bowed just as deeply back, eyed them solemnly for a long moment then turned away.

The four Neolithic men watched him go then looked at each other in silence before Klud said to no one in particular.

"Well, It looks like there will be some exciting times ahead."

4

The skies had cleared during the night and the dawn revealed a soft, glittery frost covered Danebury and its environs. However, around the inside of the gate area of the hillfort the crisp whiteness was being trodden into oblivion by all of the village's inhabitants there, awaiting the arrival of their Chieftain.

The women stood respectfully at the rear, but they had ensured their men at the centre of the gathering, were ready. Klud and Tomps were pointedly not looking at their wives. They had been chosen by their Chieftain and needed to look worthy of the honour. Everyone knew there had been personal and fond goodbyes in the privacy of their houses, so no one mistook the aloofness as a sign of not caring. Karin and Klud's first wife were shoulder to shoulder, silently bathing in the reflected glory of their men folk.

The two men in question stood before the great gate ready and awaiting their leader. They wore warm clothing and their woollen capes. Each had a slung water bag over one shoulder and a bag of foodstuffs over the other, the carry straps crossing their chests like bandoliers. Tucked into their belts were the ubiquitous flint headed daggers. Klud also had a war club there alongside his knife. Tomps held his war hammer at his side, the butt of the long handled shaft resting on the ground. Across their backs were birch bark quivers, each one holding a fist full of arrows and, unstrung, a bow, one end of it sticking out the top.

Hew stood beside them. He too was wrapped up against the chill as best as he could be, and also had a dagger tucked into his belt but other than that, he was unarmed.

All heads turned at the sound of an approach and the crowd parted to allow Parrish passage through to his friends. Even without really trying he looked a figure of authority and also of menace.

His camouflage jacket was glaringly out of character with everything around it. Strapped over the multi coloured garment was his green Army webbing. The rear kidney pouches were stuffed with supplies and the one litre water bottle at his right hip his only water supply. Opposite that on his left hip was strapped the black bladed knife everyone recognised and that had been used to deadly effect in the past. His extra-long cape hung unevenly down over his back because of the bulky webbing belt pouches. Across his shoulders was slung the big leather quiver Oona had made for him. Everyone could see the ends of the arrow shafts, all fletched with the black feathers of the sky spirits. In one hand he held, unstrung, his great bow, made for him by a now dead friend. It was as tall as the tall man himself and was so powerful no one could draw it but him.

Behind him walked Juli and Chris. As the tall man reached the edge of the crowd Juli increased her pace slightly and closed with her husband. She briefly placed her palm on his back before peeling away to join Klud's wife and Karin. As she stepped up to the two ladies Gants wife Teri join them. They all nodded in the shared knowledge of their suppressed feelings.

Parrish smiled briefly at his wife's touch but did not turn and continued towards his waiting friends. Gant stepped out of the crowd to join them. Parrish walked up, came to a halt and there was an expectant silence. Everyone waited for the Chieftain's words.

Klud eyed his Chieftain, nodding his agreement and suddenly wondering if somewhere amongst his clothing, tucked safely away out of sight, was that terrible black death giver. The grim gift from Dannu that sometimes Parrish had used to take men's lives even while they were well beyond the man's reach. He might have wondered, but he had no intention of asking though.

Hew stood slightly off to one side of the group, still close, but alone among all the people. He knew virtually no one and had no real idea how the people of Dane-bre truly were. So, he kept his peace and quietly watched.

Parrish stood before the men who were set to leave. He was about to speak when he felt a hand on his arm. Turning, to his surprise he found a delegation of 'his' girls at his side. Karin and Teri at the rear, Klud's wife and Juli beside him, and Anna at their head. It was Juli who had attracted his attention. Anyone else interrupting the Chieftain would have risked dire consequences, so Parrish just raised an eyebrow. In answer Juli pushed Anna forward. The girl looked quite terrified as she sought her Chieftain's permission with a quick glance then a bow. Seeing what she held in her arms, the tall man smiled and nodded back.

To everyone's surprise she stepped up to Hew. The pair were both suddenly aware of every eye on them. Anna bowed to the young warrior and held out her gift. In truth it was a gift from *all* the women of Dane-bre. Anna offered out what she held. Hew was stunned and momentarily froze.

"I... I was once an outsider too." Anna blurted in explanation. "But the people here at Dana-bre are good and kind and I am proud to be called one of their own now. We all know you are about to go across country again, so it is felt that you might need these."

Again, she held out her arms. Hew looked down at the easily identified water bag, but that rested on top of what appeared to be some folds of woollen cloth. He looked to Parrish and the Chieftain nodded. Plucking up the water bag by it strap, he slung it over one shoulder then took the folded woollen cloth from Anna. Holding it out before him, it dropped down curtain like from his hands, unfolding to reveal itself as a woollen cape.

"Er..., thank you." was all he could say, remembering at the last moment not to bow to a woman. A nod would do. Seeing everyone about him wearing capes, he swept it behind him, settled it across his shoulders and hooked the loop and toggle clasp together at his throat.

"It will keep you warm and dry." Parrish explained rather unnecessarily. "And of course, you know it is a good blanket."

"Yes. Thank you again." This time he bowed to the people.

There were grins all around then.

Parrish laid a gentle hand on Anna's shoulder.

"Well done, girl." He knew full well all 'his' girls had had a hand in this. Anna bowed deeply to the Chieftain then hurried back to join the other wives.

“Right.” Parrish snapped, getting everyone’s attention. “We shall leave now. I do not know how long we will be gone. We could be away for many days. Just know this. We *will* return. And until then, I leave Gant here in charge. He is wise, fair and, more important, sensible. He understands me and Dane-bre, so treat him as you would me. I trust him completely to do good by the village. Respect him and he will respect you. Until I return, he is your Chieftain.”

There was a sea of nods and Gant’s heart felt that it might burst out of his chest, so full was he with his Chieftain’s praise.

“Look after my people, my friend.” Parrish clapped his hand on Gant’s shoulder. The stern look in his eye dimming the feeling of pride slightly as the unspoken words impressed upon Gant how seriously Parrish took the decision of the burden he was now passing on to his friend.

“On my honour.”

“Good enough!” Parrish looked back up at his friends. “Ready for the off then? All goodbyes been said? Good! Then let us be away.”

Some warriors swung the great gate wide, and with Parrish at the head of the little troop, Klud, Tomps and Hew all set off down the well-worn chalk path, their way somehow highlighted in its cold, frosted dressing.

*

The four men set off towards the northwest, Salisbury Plain and Avebury. This was a journey that the people of Danebury as a whole would take three days to complete, even with their upbeat mindset. They would be on their way to a meeting with Dannu at the solstice before three more days of barter, exchange and friendship.

This trip was entirely different. Parrish was quite aware of the undercurrent of urgency in the message brought by Hew and although he allowed a full day for the youngster to recover from his run, and for his people to prepare for their Chieftain to leave the village, he wanted to get to the holy village as soon as possible. There would be no marathon running this time though. The distance Parrish knew to be approximately thirty five miles or about fifty five kilometres. He set a good pace, using the tried and tested military method to cover distance but still being fit for battle at the end of it. Yomping was simply using the rate of twelve steps in five seconds, or one hundred and forty four paces to the minute. Essentially double marching. The route was over open ground and everyone knew the way, so it was not quite as difficult as it sounded. He did have to remind himself that his strides were so much bigger than those of his companions. So even though the Neolithic men with him were moving very quickly and efficiently across Dannu's land, Parrish was still slightly holding back. He permitted himself a small smile, though making sure his expression was flat whenever he looked around to check his men's condition and positions.

The three smaller men were finding the pace required some exertion, but they would not fall behind to show either weakness in their bodies or to fail the Chieftain. But Parrish was not merciless. Several times during the day they would stop, take on some water and around the middle of the day there was a break for food and rest. But not too long.

The early frost and overall coolness of the day was a boon. Even Parrish had to admit that yomping across the untamed wilderness of Southern England for more than a day in mid summer heat would have been really punishing. As it was, the group made good time away from the Test valley that was home to Danebury and on up over the slightly more hilly, heavily wooded ground that would one day be crossed by the A303 trunk road. Then on through an undulating area of ground Parrish knew in his past as the Army town of Tidworth before the land rose up to become the open landscape of Salisbury Plain.

It was at this point that the migrating village would have pulled off into the wooded hinterland of the Plain as the sun set low, and set up a discreet camp for the night in the relative protection of the ancient woods.

But Parrish's pace was good. He kept an eye on his companions and, though there was no talk as they saved their breath for their exertions of the yomp, they continued to match their leader. They easily passed the place where the village would have camped, and the four were well across the Plain and starting down into the deeply wooded Vale of Pewsey before nightfall. And this distance still covered considering that the days now, at the edge of winter, were several hours shorter than when the village of Danebury made the same journey at the height of the summer sun.

When he called a halt, in the dimming half light of dusk, the men slumped to the ground. Parrish was also exhausted but tried not to show it. He laughed.

"Phew. I can truly say that was a good stretch of the legs." He exclaimed. The men smiled but no one spoke. "Good work troops. We have all done very well. I think we are not too far from the great temple and will arrive there before the high of the sun tomorrow. So the worst is over. How is that?"

Tomps grinned and nodded. Klud just nodded. He would be glad to get there. He wouldn't admit it but he had found the exertion of the day very hard. Parrish caught his eye and there was a brief moment before his tall friend nodded. Klud knew that Parrish knew, and he also understood that his efforts have been appreciated. Then the warrior smiled.

Hew cocked his head to one side for a moment, listening to his body. He too felt the effort of the day but realised he was nowhere near as exhausted as when he had run the whole way in a single day. Admittedly, there was still some small distance to go in the morning but he personally felt that would be no big effort. Young, healthy and with his fitness at its peak he looked up at Parrish.

"I have learned a thing this day. By not running but fast walking, with short stops along the way, it is possible to go great distances without too great an effort." A look of awe came over him. "Thank you, my Chief... Parrish. It is a great thing."

"Do not get too excited, my young friend. Tell too many people about this and the holy men of your village will have you running messages all over Dannu's Land. You will not get a minutes peace." The English phrase was lost on Hew but he understood the tall man's message.

"You are right, of course. Thank you."

"No problem." came the cheery reply. "Right. Camp here. No fires. Early start in the morning, yes?"

There was a chorus of tired nods.

*

Everyone was awake with the dawn. No one had slept well. The night sky had again been clear and even though there were some remaining leaves on the great trees around them, the frost had settled on the men as well as everything else.

They ate a small amount of food from their packs and cleared away the more obvious marks on the ground that would show where they had camped. Swinging their still frosted capes onto their shoulders, the three Neolithic men looked to their Chieftain. He clasped his own cape at his neck, ran his fingers through his hair and rubbed his face vigorously with the palms of his hands. Looking back at the trio he smiled a slightly tired smile.

"I bet you were glad of that cape last night." He nodded at Hew. "Come on, not too much further now." He estimated that only a few more hours of fast travel but he couldn't tell the men that. It did not matter. They all naturally took him at his word and all bowed slightly and as Parrish set off through the trees, they fell in behind him.

They had not been travelling more than an hour in Parrish's estimation when Hew jogged up alongside the tall man and, grasping his arm, said quietly.

"I think I hear voices."

Parrish instantly signalled a halt. Klud and Tomps gathered round and they all stood in silence, listening intently. Sure enough, after a few moments very faint, indistinct voices could be heard carrying through the bare trees. Parrish did wonder if, only being at a few hours distant from Avebury and not more than three or four miles south of the river Kennet and the gathering point, the approaching strangers might be from the great temple. Hew might know but Parrish was taking no chances.

He quietly told his men to lay low in the undergrowth behind the large trees and make no sound. To do nothing unless at his signal. The men complied and settled down into the landscape, all crouching behind the bulging root ball at the base of a truly huge and ancient oak tree. It was actually large enough to conceal all four men as long as they stayed low to the ground. They watched in tense silence as the owners of the voices slowly approached through the woods.

It was a small hunting party.

There were three men and the same number of young boys. Two men had a large deer suspended beneath a pole carried across their shoulders. The third man was speaking to the attendant lads. Two boys were quite young and one was very young.

Parrish realized it was more a training exercise than a full blown hunt. Then he noticed Tomps, Klud and even Hew tensing up and starting to reach for their weapons. To them they saw two men burdened with dead meat and one teaching the boys, all distracted from the area around them. Here was an easy chance for trophies. They were in a position to surprise the group and strike them down before they could retaliate. If the unknown men were not quick off the mark with their wits, or fast on their feet, they would be easy pickings. The hidden men looked to Parrish, who stared hard back and pushed his palm downwards against some invisible pressure, indicating that they should not move and stay where they were.

The Neolithic warriors at his side looked bitterly disappointed but did as they were bid. And so the unsuspecting little hunting party passed them by, totally oblivious that their sudden and bloody deaths were potentially but a few silent feet away.

The Danebury group held their hidden position, silent and still, until the unknown group were gone from sight and its sounds had faded away to silence.

Parrish stood up and looked down at his men. They too rose to their feet, still silent but their feelings were plain on their faces. Not quite so much for Klud and Tomps though. They knew their Chieftain and he would always have a reason for his actions, but Hew could not understand the reluctance to attack. It was not the way of a warrior to hide when there could be a battle and the chance of honour and trophies. Without a word Parrish simply turned and led off. Again the three fell in behind.

"I ... I do not understand." Hew said quietly to his Neolithic companions. "Warriors do not hide from a fight, especially when there are trophies for the taking. Yet Parrish made us stay hidden, like frightened children. Why?"

If you really want to know, you can ask him." said Klud bluntly. "I will not."

"Nor I." said Tomps. "Parrish knows. He always knows. That is how it is."

"But…" Hew's confusion was plain.

The three looked at their leader's back in time to see his broad shoulders tense up. He had heard the exchange.

Without stopping or turning to face the men, he said in a growly, annoyance edged voice to no one in particular.

"We are on a task for Dannu. No matter how easy the chance looked to take trophies, I do not doubt those warriors would not go down without a fight. I would expect no less from my own men. So there was also a fair chance that if we attacked, at least one of you would have been injured or killed. Less men beside me would make the coming task for the Goddess more difficult, so I let them pass by. There is a much greater task ahead to be completed. That is our aim. Not to risk injury or death for an easy skull. Now, no more talk." He finished gruffly and with that picked up the pace.

As the three warriors increased their own pace to keep up with their leader, Klud turned to Hew.

"Now we know also." He said flatly. "But if I were you, I would not make it a regular thing to ask Parrish to explain." The warning was plain in his voice.

And once more silence fell as the group marched on, ever nearer to Avebury.

5

Parrish's squad reached the holy village, as predicted, well before the high of the sun. The Neolithic men were by now grasping the meanings of one or two of his unintelligible words of English. Once they were translated into something they could grasp, they were happy to use the terms in his presence, such as referring to the high of the sun as 'noon'.

The travellers had first passed respectfully along the edge of the great stone circle before wending their tired way northwards up towards the sprawling double village at the crest of the rise.

Their approach had been noticed and as they entered the village, the gate already opened, a small welcome committee stood ready.

A little phalanx of holy men stood centre stage with several warriors and women either side. Everyone bowed as Parrish led in through the portal. He quickly scanned the small gathered throng and, off to one side, he noticed a woman and a small girl stood well back behind the others. Their eyes never left Hew. Parrish thought he detected a flash of relief on the woman's face, but it was gone before he could be sure.

"Greetings, Chieftain Parrish." said the lead holy man as the tall man pulled to a stop. "The Wisest of the Wise Ones is expecting you but says that first you must rest. He knows you must be tired. If you will follow me, I will show you to your hut. There you will find food and warmth for you and your men."

Parrish bowed in return.

"Thank you, and please pass on my thanks to the Wise One." As the holy man turned away, about to lead off, Parrish ignored him and turned to his young companion. "Hew. Go to your family. I am sure they have been waiting and will be glad of your return." He rested a hand on the lad's shoulder and patted it as he added. "You have done well. I am proud to call you my friend."

Klud and Tomps nodded in agreement and all three bowed to the youngster, even though protocol said there was no need.

"Thank... thank you, Parrish." Hew stuttered. It was true he thought, Dannu's man knows all. "It has been my greatest honour to be of some service. And if you ever need me again, for anything, I am yours to command."

Klud and Tomps smiled. They heard the sincerity and commitment in the voice and glanced knowingly at one another. Another convert and follower of Parrish. The tall man just nodded.

"Well said, and I thank you for it. Now, be off. Say hello to your family. You can run there if you like." he grinned. Everyone smiled and Hew raised a hand to his Dane-bre friends, turned and headed off towards the two more happy looking females at the back of the spectating group.

"Now," Parrish addressed the holy one again, ignoring the little man's barely concealed annoyance at being interrupted. "Lead on."

A smile crossed Parrish's features as they were shown to one of the many non-descript huts in the village compound. For a simple, basic shelter, it was a most welcome sight.

They ducked inside and it was deliciously warm. A small but hot fire burned in the centre of the floor. Rattan mats covered the remainder of the ground around it and there were the correct number of beds laid out. To one side of the hearth was also laid out a selection of food and some water bags.

To keep face and not admit that they were all fatigued, the men tried to hide their pleasure at the sight but Klud and Tomps sighed as they settled down on to the mats.

It was only then that Parrish noticed the young woman, stood motionless at the back of the otherwise empty space, almost invisible in her dun coloured clothes and the half-light.

Klud had obviously seen her though. He beckoned her forward with a casual wave of his hand and she leapt into action, immediately coming forward into the firelight and reaching for the foodstuffs.

Parrish had to bite his tongue at the ease with which Klud controlled her, and her total subjugation to his command. The twentieth century man had known and bore witness to this since his first days in the times he now lived, but for him the last twenty four hours had been just lads out on patrol. He did so love basic soldiering and it had unknowingly dropped his guard to the way of the world here.

The woman of course served Parrish first. He helped himself to some welcome food then said without looking directly at her.

"See to my men then you are free to go. We need to rest." It was the best he could do to somehow release her from this instance of servitude. It helped ease his conscience a little. "Tell the holy man outside we do not wish to be disturbed." He looked to his friends, who could only nod. "We sleep till we wake. Then we will see the Wise One."

The girl goggled at this tall man who was basically dictating to the high priest of the Earth Goddess. To the most powerful man on Dannu's land. But all she could do was bow in acknowledgement and turned to serve the other two men. In moments she had completed her task. She bowed again and moved away. Parrish smiled once more as she exited the hut. He thought she would have run out if she could, had it not have shown disrespect. Klud and Tomps were still sitting, open mouthed in amazement at their Chieftain.

This time Parrish laughed out loud.

"Do not look so shocked. will not disrespect the Wisest of the Wise Ones. He knows we are tired and I know we will not sleep too long." He nodded to the food, momentarily forgotten in their hands. "Get stuck into that. Food and a good kip in the warm and we will be fresh as daisies and up for seeing the CO."

Klud and Tomps didn't grasp half of the words Parrish had said but they understood enough to know his intentions were good, and that was enough.

As one they started to eat. Parrish chuckled. He had rather enjoyed his short burst of 'Army' speak, enjoyment enhanced by the bafflement of his friends. And he was really looking forward to some sleep.

Fed, watered and warm, the men slept undisturbed for the rest of the afternoon, Parrish coming to as the sun was getting low in the sky, although he did not know that. He rolled over and saw his companions already awake.

"How long have I been asleep?"

"It is still daylight." answered Klud in a, for him, non-specific away.

"Oh." Parrish sat up, ran his fingers through his hair and, realizing that they had been waiting on him, added. "I hope you are both well rested and have not been waiting too long for me?"

There were just shakes of the head.

Parrish understood, gave a wry smile and climbed to his feet. "OK then." He wasn't about to apologise even though he felt he ought to. "Let us see what is what then."

Klud and Tomps followed their Chieftain outside, where they found a holy man waiting patiently. They all wondered if the man had been stood there since they had arrived, but no one asked. Parrish smothered a second smile. Perhaps his little vigil might teach the man some humility. He doubted it though. Not bothering to bow in acknowledgment he simply said.

"Lead on."

The silent holy man showed his annoyance by not bowing either, turned and led off into the centre of the village.

Yet the holy man didn't lead them all that far. Just to another hut, but this one was very close to the mouth of the raised causeway that linked the main village to the great shrine house and the personal habitats of all the holy men.

Parrish genuinely thought they were going to traverse the causeway and go into the massive temple hut but was surprised when their guide turned sharp left just before the causeway and ducked into a hut there. Outwardly, a hut just like all the other 'standard' huts.

The Dane-bre trio also ducked in, unsighted as they entered and, on coming back upright inside, stopped dead in their tracks.

Seated on the ground just beyond the central hearth, well illuminated by lots of hanging tallow lamps and the glow from the fire before him, was the Wisest of the Wise Ones.

He looked unchanged from the last time Parrish had seen him, with the frail body, the unruly locks of grey hair and the twinkling, sharply intelligent eyes. He was flanked as usual by two holy men standing either side and just to the rear of him.

The three warriors bowed deeply, and Parrish looked into the old man's eyes, only to receive a slightly quizzical look in return. He suddenly understood that this old man, the great high priest of the Earth Goddess, had probably been kept waiting just as Klud and Tomps had been. Now he really felt that he should apologise. But before he could speak, he saw the understanding of his position become clear in the wise one's eyes. A brief grin creased the old man's face before he raised a deeply lined palm, held it for a second then gestured Parrish and his men to sit. The tall man had been read like a book, admonished and then forgiven all in that glance.

Grateful, Parrish sunk to the floor. His two friends, completely overawed by suddenly being confronted by the holiest of the holy men, dropped immediately to the floor just a pace behind their Chieftain, combined looks of awe and trepidation on their features.

"Welcome, my friends." The old one said in that rustling, parchment dry voice. He eyed Parrish directly. "I hope you are all rested?"

Parrish coughed uncomfortably at the veiled remark but rallied.

"I thought we would be speaking in the shrine hut." He hastily changed the unspoken subject.

"No. Not today. That is a place of worship, and I am afraid this may be a council of war." He looked at the men before him and decided now was not the time to mince words. He took a deep breath, sighed and spoke quietly.

"Unclear messages and half-truths have been coming from the north and none of them are good words."

“It is still going on? Since before the solstice?” Parrish asked although it sounded more like a statement. The two were now beyond petty notions and their eyes were locked together.

“Yes. That is why I sent a runner for you. The year grows short, and I feel sure if nothing is done until the spring, things will be much worse.”

Surprisingly, Klud broke the silence that followed.

“Er ... If ... if this is Dannu’s work, would you like us,” he indicated Tomps and himself. “to leave?”

“No.” said Parrish and the wise one together. Parrish bowed and let the old man continue.

“It is a problem that will need you to play your part in, so both Parrish and I feel you too should know what we know.”

“He is right.” agreed Parrish. “The more we all know, the better chance we have of somehow putting right whatever this problem is.”

The two Neolithic warriors nodded at the wise words.

“And yet we do not know much.” The wise one picked up his narrative again. “All that we have here is gossip and rumour. Tales brought back by the occasional hunting groups that have gone further north than usual.”

“Just rumour? Nothing else?” asked Parrish, suddenly shocked at the complete lack of concrete information.

“Yes. I have sent three holy envoys to visit the missing villages. We waited but none have returned. I waited as long as possible before sending for you, my friend. I fear perhaps now that I have waited too long. It grows colder. There are frosts and the start of the bitter winds. Soon the snows will come and then everything stops till the next spring. By then I fear much more damage will be done to Dannu and the people of her north land.”

“Please tell me what you do know then.” Parrish leaned forward, his attention was total. Now, this was a full-on mission briefing as far as he was concerned. He hoped his two friends were paying close heed also.

“There has been no actual contact from the silent villages since before the last solstice gathering. We have only heard whispers about an attack on Dannu as Goddess of this land, giver of our lives and provider for her people."

"Attack?"

"There is talk of wolves of some sort. I think that perhaps the people up there are either frightened, persuaded, or forced to a different worship or leader. I do not know. It is even stranger that no person has come down from the north to tell or even barter with us for anything. Not even the usual visitors, or passed on messages through the holy men in preparation for the solstice gathering or the coming winter. No one. All is silence."

"And so, you want us." Parrish indicated the men behind him. "To go up north to wherever and sort out whatever? I do not even know where these missing villages are or who lives there!"

"A holy man from here will accompany you on your journey. He knows all three villages and how to get there. They are almost at the northernmost limit of this part of Dannu's land that comes under the care of us here at the great temple."

Parrish's eyebrows shot up at that. Were there other great temples caring for other villages spiritual needs, in different parts of the country? He thought that only he, because he came from the twentieth century, knew that there was a huge mass of land, namely the rest of the British Isles, far to the north of Avebury. Far to the north of Central Southern England. Yet perhaps he wasn't the only one who knew that. These holy ones know a damned sight more than they are letting on. But now was not the time to press this. His attention returned to the wise ones words.

"All I ask is that you go and try to find out what is happening. Do what you can but at the very least we here would like to know just what is happening and how we can help bring these lost villages back into the fold."

"You do remember what happened the last time I tried that?" growled Parrish.

"Yes." There was a solemn pause. "But this time you do so with our blessing."

Parrish looked at the Wise One for several long silent moments. Klud and Tomps found themselves holding their breath. It was very likely the silently watching holy men were doing so as well. Parrish and the Wisest of the Wise Ones just stared intently into each other's eyes, trying to read the other's thoughts.

Finally, Parrish nodded. There were exhalations from behind him, which he ignored.

"Very well. I will go and see what I can see." He took a deep breath. "We will set off in the morning. Me and my men will need cold weather gear and a food supply. Please make sure that your holy man is ready too."

The wise one just nodded, but he never smiled.

"Parrish, know now that this is not something I would ask lightly, my friend." he said quietly, "But things are not clear to us now. Everything is cast in shadow. And you are the best man for this task. I would not trust it to anyone else."

"I understand." was all Parrish said in reply to the great complement he had just received.

"I know it is a trip into the unknown. But you will have a holy man with you and Dannu will help you wherever she can."

"I put my faith in my friends." Parrish growled and the pair behind him swelled with pride. "But I thank you for your offer, for Dannu's guidance as well, and for your holy man as guide."

"Then you have my greatest thanks in return. And my best wishes for a safe return, my son." The Wise One nodded.

Klud, Tomps and the surrounding holy men all heard the warmth, friendship and even love in the softly spoken words.

Parrish smiled then, bowed from the waist to the old man and rose effortlessly to his feet. Klud and Tomps followed suit.

"Thank you." Parrish was suddenly formal, but the two words were heartfelt. "Please have the winter clothing and supplies sent to our hut and be sure your holy man is kitted out the same *and* knows his way north. Tell him to be ready for a journey of many days. We will all be leaving early tomorrow morning, so he had better not be late." And with that he bowed again deeply from the waist, turned and ducked back out of the hut. Klud and Tomps followed at the double.

Once they had gone the old man just sat, staring at the door blanket as it fell back into place behind them. An ominous silence settled on him.

He knew he had gotten what he wanted and needed. But he was not happy about it. Not happy at all.

6

The morning broke cold and grey. The wind was light but had an edge to it. People were now beginning to wrap up. Bare skin chilled quickly in the open and though not bitterly cold yet, the edge of winter was now upon the land.

Parrish stepped out from the warmth of their hut and as was his usual practice, took a good look about. For the first time he noticed, as the chill smarted his cheeks, that all the trees he could see, way out beyond the confines of the village, were now bare. Acknowledging that he was now a good thirty plus miles north of Danebury, he understood that even those few miles had made a difference in the weather, which did not bode well for the imminent trip further north. He himself had done plenty of winter exercises with the Army and knew cold weather soldiering was a completely different proposition regarding travelling and personal care in the field.

But he had no real idea if the people around him had any concept of winter or snowbound travel or combat. The few years he had been here in these Neolithic times had only shown him that during the hard winter the people stayed close to their village, their families and their fires. He had not once heard of any winter travelling of any great distance.

Klud and Tomps stepped out beside him. They were well wrapped up just like their Chieftain, each sporting a coarse but windproof outer coat plus their capes. Baggy leather outer trousers and bigger footwear, similar to mukluks, completed the outfits. He knew that in their coat pockets were animal skin mittens and on their heads they wore skullcaps for hats.

Parrish had also been issued a hat and gloves. The people of the village had rushed through a coat for him, making one to fit his larger frame. The women had worked through the night and even though it looked rough and ready compared to his friends garments he too was grateful for its protection against the chill wind. Besides, he had his combat jacket on beneath it and he felt surprisingly well protected against the winter.

As the three stood and took in the scene, a group of holy men approached, the high priest at its head. He also wore a woollen hat and was enveloped in a huge cape that wrapped right around him, its hem dragging on the ground.

"You are ready then?" the old man asked unnecessarily. He smiled at his tall friend, who understood it was a warm gesture rather than simply stating the obvious.

Parrish bowed in acknowledgement.

"Yes. We await our guide, then we will be off."

The Wisest of the Wise Ones gestured with one arm like a US cavalry officer from a western movie. The crowd behind him parted and a single holy man stepped forward. He was dressed similarly to Parrish and his men but on his head he wore his ceremonial headdress rather than a functional hat. This was obviously a statement of his importance. A symbol to impress. Well, it didn't faze Parrish at all. He simply nodded at the food bag and water pouches slung at the man's sides.

"I see that you are ready. Good. You are sure you know the way to the northern villages?"

The holy man just scoffed. "Of course."

Parrish ignored the condescending tone and turned back to his old friend.

"Then I bid you farewell." He smiled. "I will not dishonour you. We will do what we can and return with what information we can gather."

The Wisest of the Wise Ones bowed to his tall friend, which raised many eyebrows. The high priest of the Earth Goddess bowed to no one.

"I know that you will do what is right, my son. I simply ask that you take care and be safe. I will add though that if it is your aim to return before the real winter snows arrive, I would not take too long. But that decision is in your hands."

Parrish nodded in acknowledgement and eyed his guide, who stepped up before him. Parrish's glance returned again to the old man.

"Then we had better get started. Be well, and we will see you as soon as it is possible."

He picked up his own supplies and slung them across his shoulders. Klud and Tomps followed suit, settling the straps across their chests, and picked up their weapons.

Everyone bowed then and Parrish, letting the holy man/guide have his big moment before the crowd, swept his palm across his body and said to him.

"Lead on."

The holy man nodded and with his head held high stalked past the three Danebury men and set off towards the main gate.

Parrish gave a final nod and grin to the old man, who smiled briefly back. Klud and Tomps fell in behind their Chieftain and in a silence only broken by the soft sigh of the chill breeze, they set off after him.

*

The four-man troop had been marching northward for only a few hours when Parrish, leading from the front, turned and looked over his shoulder just to check on his men.

Everything looked fine until he noticed that the bandolier straps of Klud and Tomps carry bags seemed to have increased in number. He called a sudden halt and moved closer to investigate.

"What is this?" He plucked at one of the additional straps across Klud's chest.

"It is the holy one's water bag." came the reply, Klud's tone implying that it was rather obvious.

"And I carry his foodstuffs." added Tomps.

As realization dawned, an angry look darkened Parrish's features. He turned to the holy one, who looked arrogantly back, as if there was nothing untoward. Clearly Parrish did not know that simple warriors did holy men's bidding, acknowledging to all that those of the religious order were superior.

Inside, Parrish was fulminating with rage at how with this simple gesture and the look the holy man gave, he had reduced his brave warriors and great friends to the status of meek servants and more or less being his pack animals. But the Chieftain of Dane-bre did not explode. He stalked slowly over to the smug man intent on setting the little shit straight, a representative of Dannu or not.

Tight lipped and with a growl in voice he stepped up to the holy man who, only as the tall man closed, registered that something might be amiss. Without looking at them, Parrish pointed to Klud and Tomps and said slowly.

"Take off the holy one's bags and put them on the ground."

The pair did not argue and did as they were told, staring on in silence. Clearly something had angered their Chieftain. As soon as Parrish heard the bags hit the ground he focused on the little man before him.

His voice was quiet, but the words were crystal clear.

"Listen closely now to what I have to say. And I warn you I will only say this once.

As far as I am concerned, this little journey is now a combat mission, ah, war party." he corrected. "And everyone here will pull his weight. One as much as any other. So unless or until your holy services are needed, you are just one more of this party." He let that sink in for a moment. "So, I expect you to do as I say. I expect you to obey any instructions or directions that Tomps, Klud or me give you. Your life and ours might depend on it, especially if there is a battle or any sort of fighting." He pointed to his friends, now watching open mouthed. "Their neck tattoos tell you all you need to know, as does your *bare* neck." He leaned in even closer. "Do as I say, or we will all return now to the holy village, and you can tell the Wisest of the Wise Ones why! This is how it is going to be. I lead, but every man here is equal and so does his equal share. That means me, Klud, Tomps and you, whatever your name is."

"We give up our names when we are taken into the temple." retorted the holy man. There was still a hint of arrogance that this tall man would not know such a simple thing. "We are simply servants of Dannu."

Parrish was slightly taken aback at that but did not let it show on his face.

"Then how do you know each other?"

"By our own look."

Parrish understood then that he meant by their features and clothing but used it to his advantage.

"Look? Look? Sounds like Luke. OK. So I say now, for as long as this mission lasts, you will be known as Luke." The holy man opened his mouth, but Parrish cut him short. "And, know this, Luke. Listen carefully, hear me and know. For as long as this trip lasts everyone here is equal. You will NOT take advantage of these two men. On this trip, especially if it comes to a fight, these men are your betters. But as I say, we are all equal here. And know this also." He gave the man a hard look. "If I see, hear or otherwise find out that you have ordered them about, made them do something that you could have done yourself, or if you have threatened them either physically or with the word of Dannu, I will take great pleasure in beating the shit out of you until you get my message." He grabbed the little man by his coat front, pulled him close and hissed into his face. "So, we are all equal. Yes?"

By now the terrified holy man just nodded dumbly.

Parrish released him and stepped back.

"OK then, Luke. Pick up your kit and let us get going."

With that he turned his back on the holy man and the silently still gaping pair of Danebury men, and set off in silence, once again heading towards the north.

The rest of the day was set in silence.

The men trooped on through the dense, bare woodland, Indian file. Parish led and Luke the holy man brought up the rear. No one wanted to intrude on or feel the wrath of the Chieftain's barely contained fury. Klud and Tomps kept their peace, knowing to let Parrish simmer down in his own time. They did feel uncomfortable leading before a holy one but dare not go against the Chieftain's wishes and give preference to their religious companion. The holy man himself felt some insult at being made to follow on at the rear like a lowly woman, but knew better than to demand priority over the warriors whose backs he now looked at. And he certainly did not wish to have 'the shit beaten out of him' by defying the tall man. For a while he fumed at his totally disrespectful treatment by Parrish but that did not mean that he himself was stupid enough to deny the reasoning behind it. It was true enough the warriors he travelled with were all seasoned fighters. He himself had killed nothing bigger than small game which he had hunted as a child before being taken into the realm of the religious order of Dannu. He had never even faced anything that might fight back. And much as it made him grit his teeth to think on it, Parrish was right. He *was* the least useful of anyone in the group, it just stung to have it brutally pointed out to everyone. And it was also true that if he used the warriors to his own selfish ends, and it came to a battle, his earlier actions could adversely affect the outcome of a fight. As he walked in silence, mulling over the tall man's wise words, he finally came to understand the sense of that earlier exchange. It was a fool who did not accept that wise words are wise words, no matter who says them.

In fact it was not that long after the heated exchange, as they all walked on, the sense of anger radiating from the holy one began to fade. Parrish had made his point forcibly, and enjoyed doing it, but it was a job that needed to be done. The little holy man stopped huffing and snorting and gradually settled before finally accepting the truth and fell in at the rear without objection. A broad grin softened Parrish's face as he had felt the man come around. He had no doubt he would, sooner or later. All the holy men he had ever met were a bit too full of themselves in his opinion, but they were also all good at heart and with the welfare of the people under their care paramount. And Parrish accepted the fact that it was very likely no holy man had ever been put in this one's particular situation. All things considered, Parrish thought the little religious so-and-so had fallen into line more easily than could have been expected. He enjoyed his private satisfaction but took care not to glance back and let his slightly smug smile be seen by his squad. As he had said before, it was a combat patrol as far as he was concerned and the chain of command had now been established. A good day's work.

So on went the day. With the winter solstice not all that far away, the nights they all knew fell much more quickly. With the watery sun nearing the horizon and the temperature dropping rapidly, Parrish called a halt. His estimate was perhaps twelve miles or so covered on this first day. Not bad, but he would pick up the pace a little tomorrow. Cocking an enquiring eye skyward, Parrish was still not that expert at reading the more long-range weather but even he felt the temperature shift. It was going to be a very cool night. He set everybody to gather firewood for the camp, and no one glanced at the holy man when Parrish said ‘everybody’.

*

The ever encroaching cold finally brought the sleeping men to wakefulness. It was no surprise. All those who spend time outside know that on cold wintry nights the temperature continues to drop and is at its lowest just before sunrise.

This decline was in parallel with the dying of the unattended campfire to embers just before the dawn. Parrish lay motionless, curled under his woollen cape and finally allowed his eyes to open. Moments before, at a sudden, unexpected sound, before the false dawn had fully lightened the sky, he had snapped instantly awake. Laying still and listening hard, he realised that someone was already up and bustling about as quietly as they could. Squinting through barely cracked eyelids he could see the little shaman, who was quietly stirring up the fires embers and with careful puffing, coaxing them back into a flame. It didn't take long at all to revive it to a small, hot fire. Next he draped strips of jerky over some small crossed twigs that had been thrust into the ground just at the edge the fire, and against other little crosses of sticks he propped some of the flat disc shapes of unleavened bread. It wasn't much in the way of a breakfast but Parrish could appreciate the effort.

He half faked a yawn and rose slowly into a sitting position. The tiny sounds of the crackling frost particles on the outside of his cape-cum-blanket sounded loud in the silence as the holy man spun to face the Chieftain.

Klud and Tomps both awoke too at that same moment. They also sat slowly up and Tomps somewhat theatrically rubbed his eyes.

Parrish did not know how astute the holy man was, but *he* was pretty sure his two friends had snapped awake the same moment as he, and they had also been feigning sleep until their Chieftain decided to act.

Parrish climbed to his feet, stretched tall then had a scratch before turning his attention to the holy man and the food items warming around the edge of the fire. He crossed the few paces to the flames, held out his palms to the warmth and briefly surveyed the scene. Slowly he turned to the holy man who just stood in silence, not knowing what to expect.

“Warm fire and food on the go.” Parrish said. “That will do.”

He turned away from the small man as Klud and Tomps approached. They both knew the holy man was trying to get on

Parrish's good side. They did not doubt Parrish knew that too, but they also thought that it would still be a good thing to do.

Parrish held the little group in silence for a few moments then smiled at the religious one and said the two words that all who knew Parrish hoped to hear from him. When they had done something well, and that the Chieftain approved of.

"Good man." This produced instant grins. He grinned back. "Some hot food and a warm fire to wake up to is a good start to any day."

The holy man bowed to Parrish.

"Thank you." he paused, briefly unwilling to immediately be the bearer of bad news. "But I must also say, this frost will be the last one for a while. There is a change in the air. More cold and heavy cloud is coming down from the north."

"S'OK." Parrish shrugged. "That is the very way we are going, cold or no cold. But you are sure? Been given the nod by the Goddess?"

The shaman just nodded, having no intention of explaining the intricacies of communication with the Earth Goddess, even if he was being asked about it by Dannu's man.

"Fair play." said Parrish, not prepared or even really interested in pressing the point. His words made those around him frown. He chuckled at their confusion. "So, let us get some food inside us, pack up and be away." There were more acknowledging nods. "And then," he turned again to the holy man. "Now we are all in this together and well north of the great temple, you can take the lead, Luke. Show us the way to go."

Luke nodded again, this time a full-blown grin on his face.

"It would be my honour."

As one they dropped to their haunches before the fire for maximum warmth and started in on the very welcome hot food.

7

At that same moment, other Chieftains were ‘getting the nod’ about the impending bad weather beyond the horizon.

Gant hissed through his teeth at the news. Only the day before he had sent a twelve man hunting team out to bring back fresh meat. His experience told him that it was only a matter of time before the real cold arrived and he wanted the village ready and well provisioned against it, but the news had come too late. He now seriously doubted that his hunting party, whether successful or not, would beat the snow back to Dane-bre. The timing could not have been worse.

On the opposite side of the east river, Chieftain Shimon received the news with unbridled glee. For him the timing was perfect.

His envious eyes were as ever locked on the village across the river. Always there, successful, prosperous and well run. A good place to be, and could be even better with him in control. Despite the severe lack of manpower in his own village, Shimon insisted that a lookout be always kept on Dane-bre. Thus, he knew that Parrish and his loyal friends had recently left the village. The little troupe had set off towards the north so his best guess was that they were off to the great temple for some reason. That meant they would be gone for many days. Good. There was a real resentment now tempering his envy at being within sight of Dannu’s man yet outside, even deliberately excluded, from being in his circle.

He was also aware that a large hunting party, more than two hands of men strong, had left Dane-bre not two days earlier. Even Shimon’s basic maths now told him that somewhere near to a third of all the warriors of Dane-bre, including their

Chieftain, were now missing from the village. Everything it seemed was falling into place for him.

A burst of oncoming bad weather with snow, the deeper the better for his purpose, would keep the missing men away, or at the very least hinder their return. Now was his chance to finally take what he had always wanted and felt he deserved. A satisfied grin settled on Shimon's face, and he squatted down by his fire and with delicious deliberation began to draw up a plan of action. A simple, and what he envisaged would be a successful scheme, soon began to fall into place in his mind.

His first objective would be to gain entry into Dane-bre.

It was accepted that the villagers there would be unsuspecting of an attack, especially if the horizon were clear. And knowing that the coast was clear, dawn would signal the opening of the main gate for early risers, nearly always women, to get out and go for water, empty night buckets and check the flocks. If Shimon allowed at least a full day of snow to cover the ground then under the cover of the following night he would lead his men in silence right up to the gate. Their footprints would be lost among all the others in the well-trodden slush along the entrance path. He would have his men flattened against the wall of the hillfort. They would be unsighted by any observer looking out across the landscape, and the moment some lonely female opened the gate he would pounce. He and his warriors would rush in, spread out and quickly take the village. He commanded more than enough men to have at least one per village hut and they would secure the Dane-bre warriors in their beds. He himself would find whoever was in charge, he would not deign to call him a Chieftain, kill him and demand loyalty from the rest of the Dane-bre warriors. Bow to him or face a swift death without honour. He would threaten them saying he could easily kill them all and simply move in. Then be the benevolent Chieftain and suggest surely it was better to live to serve him and Dannu. Not to mention it would help the chances of survival for their families. They need not know that Shimon really needed the extra manpower to make Dane-bre continue to function properly, but he was quite prepared, and truth be told more than happy to execute a few men to make his point.

Then Dane-bre would be his. Parrish was far away and would not be able to travel because of the snow, and the Dane-bre hunting party, when it returned, would be trapped outside the village walls. He would not allow them in, then they must surely surrender to him or die out in the cold of Dannu's land.

Hah! It was a great plan. A foolproof plan, planned by a great leader. A leader of men. A leader of two villages that, once merged into one, would be the biggest and most powerful village in all Dannu's lands.

*

Many, many kilometres to the north the little four-man patrol were pushing steadily on. If he was being honest, Parrish was having the time of his life. Doing something he loved doing, with no outside pressure barring the business to hand. Whatever might be happening elsewhere, he could neither change nor act upon. Even leaders of men must accept there were things beyond their control. They will run their course no matter what, so right now Parrish was taking the time to enjoy a simple pleasure. Good, old fashioned, footslogging soldiering. His team had bonded by now and he had enjoyed watching them become efficient and competent as a unit. The holy man had finally 'embedded', as was the military term. After his first attempts at mollifying Parrish, he had unbidden taken on the post of camp cook. In fairness, Klud and Tomps had completed many hunting trips before so had a good grasp on basic camp food. Parrish had his own training to fall back on, but he was surprised at how adept Luke was at rustling up hot morsels from scratch at the end of the day. He had always assumed that holy ones were constantly waited on hand and foot and would have no knowledge of hands-on work.

But it was as a team that Parrish was most pleased. Tomps, and after a fashion Klud, had gradually come round to speaking to the little holy man more as an equal although the older warrior, being more set in his ways, could not stop from showing some deference. Klud spoke boldly but could not help giving a small nod at the end of each conversation. Luke duly noticed but feigned ignorance of it for fear of Parrish, but he certainly appreciated it and it warmed the little man. It seemed the two men were slowly becoming friends.

The group now really began to gel, evident in the small, useful things they did without bidding. As each day end drew nearer the men would start to pick up the odd dry stick or twig as they walked. When Parrish finally called a halt they had to hand a ready pile of fuel when Luke set to starting a fire. The others would spread out to find some standing dead wood and, on their return, would find welcome warmth already available. They all proved their worth by the way they pooled their resources. Everyone had, packed in their supplies, a bag of ground flour, courtesy of their wives. Or in Luke’s case someone's wife! He would also pull out of his own bag a small wooden platter and with a handful of flour and some water make a small dough patty on it. One for each of them would be set on a stone at the edge of the fire and baked by the embers to make a sort of dense, chewy dough bun. Without yeast the things didn't swell much and each one was not much more than a mouthful, but it was hot. With some jerky under it, it wasn't too bad.

Parrish chuckled the first time he did it. On the next night he offered the man the larger of his two mess tins.

“Make one big one.” He suggested. “You can set this down right in the embers and when it's done, we will each have a bigger portion.”

Luke fingered the foreign metal object in total amazement before finally nodding.

The really basic bannock bread he produced was a personal triumph and when Tomps pulled a small clay pot a fruit preserve from his bag, courtesy of Karin, everyone scooped out a finger full and smeared it on the bread. Smiles all round then.

And so, on they went. Mostly they travelled in silence, only speaking to draw attention or point out some object or other.

The rolling countryside was for the most part heavily wooded but was interspersed with open areas. Sometimes, if these openings were on a down slope, it revealed great vistas across the bare trees and their leafless trunks that stretched away to the near horizon. Yet here and there splashed dark green puddles of great yews, holly groves and sometimes swathes of pine and spruce slashed across the landscape. Under the leaden grey skies the air was crisp and clear. Occasional animal sounds floated up out of the wilderness but although Parrish knew the land teemed with wildlife, now winter was upon it he wondered where they had all gone. He mentioned this to Klud, who just smiled and said that they were still there, if you knew where to look. Parrish simply nodded. He was no hunter. He knew it and so did his friend.

Parrish also spent some of this silent time pondering on how the holy man knew where he was going. He had to be checking the stars and the positions of the sun where possible, but that was so vague as to be almost useless when aiming at a hillfort over one hundred miles away. Also, the ground was undulating as they travelled. Parrish discreetly checked his little compass now and then, and they were definitely going north. But there were no modern landmarks for him to reference. He knew there were no huge hills or mountains in southern England so he could not know that he was crossing the eastern Cotswolds area and then moving on up into central England where one day that huge conurbation, the second biggest city in the UK, Birmingham, would one day sit. What was now laid out before him was a vast, undiscovered country, for the most part completely unsullied by the hand of man. There were no tracks, pathways or animal migration routes to follow, and yet, up over the rolling hills and down into the stream crossed valleys, Luke stuck to his course. Parrish could only conclude that the holy man must have walked this route before at least several times. But he never asked. Just let the little guy do his thing, he thought.

And still they marched on.

It was in the afternoon of the second day after the prediction, that snow started to float down, initially in small, delicate flakes from the heavy, grey looking sky. Parrish knew they had been travelling for five days now and his estimate was, at roughly fifteen to twenty miles a day he calculated that they had travelled perhaps eighty five miles, or about one hundred and thirty five kilometres. They must be drawing close now. He eyed the heavens. The total cloud cover above them had that soft 'illuminated from behind glow' that all heavy snow clouds had. The temperature was now a steady, crisp cold. Parrish looked at Luke and said ruefully.

"It does not look like it will be just a light flurry."

If Luke understood his last word or not it didn't matter.

"I think we are in for some fair measure of snow." he said plainly.

Parrish nodded. Just as he thought, but never said. “Early camp today then. Let us get a shelter up and plenty of fuel to burn.”

“Now?” ask Klud

“Why not?” Parrish replied looking about. “Be prepared! So, a good campfire, stock of fuel, warm food and some protection from what might fall out of the sky overnight. We will see how things are in the morning and go from there.”

No more words needed to be said. Everyone knew their tasks and set too.

8

The pair of wickiups constructed the evening before had done their jobs. The men had piled dead leaves up over the basic stick structures. Nowhere near thick enough to be waterproof but the constant snowfall had soon built up a layer that helped keep them dry and also provide some small amount of insulation.

The low, stacked log reflector walls, a few feet out from the open front of the wickiups had also done their jobs and reflected and partially protected the fire between them and the open fronted structures. Long logs had burned across the full width of the shelters and that combined with the pine boughs insulating them from the cold ground meant that the four had not slept too badly.

Now they were awoken by the chill. The fires had all but gone out and the men opened their eyes to find the land shrouded in a mantle of white.

Parrish’s first thought was that it looked beautiful. His second was that it looked about a foot deep in places. Not too deep to make further travel unfeasibly difficult, but it might slow them down a tad. So not really a problem then, and he allowed himself a small smile. He recalled there had been a Scotsman in his platoon way back, or was it forward, in the twentieth century, and when they had once been on a winter exercise on the Brecon Beacons, someone had complained about a few inches’ depth of snow. Jock had immediately piped up.

“Och. This is just wet. It is nay proper snow ‘till it's over the cat!”

It still made Parrish smile.

Breakfasts consumed, the men packed away. The three Neolithic men were all for dismantling their shelters to leave nothing behind, but Parrish decided against it.

“You never know.” He said when they looked quizzically at him. “We might need them again, maybe on the way back. Or it might save some passing stranger from a cold and miserable night.” The looks on his three companion’s faces said, so what? But they never spoke aloud. “Right then.” he continued. “Lead on, Luke. Still north?”

The holy man nodded.

“The snow may slow us a little, but I am sure that if we continue as we have, we will reach the first of the silent villages later today.” The casually dropped remark stopped everyone in their tracks. All eyes turned to Parrish.

“Oh, wow!” he blurted in surprise. “We are nearly there then?” The little man had wrong-footed him, but he wasn't angry about it. In fact, it was a bit ‘Army banter’’ and he grinned back at the shaman. “Cool... er, I mean, good. Let me know when we get close, and we will figure out some kind of approach. No point in just walking straight up to the front gate and getting an arrow in the ass for your troubles.” He nodded. “OK. Away we go.”

The men nodded at his words, instinctively kicked snow over the last of the fires embers and automatically fell into a line before trudging off, Indian file, between the white coated trunks. Luke leading Parrish, the two warriors bringing up the rear.

Pushing on through the snow, the men were each in their own way wondering what and how things would unfold when they reached the first of the ‘silent’ villages. Now they knew they were close, the tension and expectation began to mount.

But only a few kilometres further on, unknowingly only a short distance from the still invisible village ahead, a distraction arose. The group came to the edge of a fast flowing stream, wide enough to almost be called a river. Following it upstream, still heading towards their destination and keeping well away from the streams edge, made vague by the deepening snow, they saw footprints in the white crispness, leading out from the trees and across their path. They all momentarily stopped and looked hastily about, but could see no one. Carefully following the tracks they found themselves being led towards the edge of the stream. As they drew close it was clear someone had been there very recently, the depressions still crisp and fresh. The tracks that led out of the tree line reached the edge of the water, but then they showed there had been a disturbance at the river's edge where there was a broken cut-out in the edge of the snow. It had given way and dropped into the flowing water, revealing the presence of a previously hidden snowy overhang.

Keeping safely back, Parrish looked cautiously over the edge and down into the flow below. Through the crystal clear water he could see several fish traps beneath the surface but they lay higgledy-piggledy on the bottom, some even pointing in the wrong direction.

“Something went a bit wrong here.” he said, a lightness in his tone. “It looks like someone might have got an unexpected dunking.”

“And I know who.” said Tomps.

The other three looked to where the young warrior was pointing. Thirty or forty yards downstream from their position there was a fallen tree, its trunk angled down from the bank, stabbing down into the stream. Out in mid flow, half jammed, half submerged beneath it, was a man. Even as they watched he was struggling against the never ceasing flow, wedged as he was with his lower body beneath the log and only his head and arms above the surface of the water. He clutched desperately at the slippery, snow topped log, gasping as the water roiled against the back of his head, splashing icy coldness constantly over him. He began to slip bit by bit under the log, pushed down by the ever present flow.

The Danebury men and their holy partner walked quite casually down alongside the stream until they stood over him from the bank, being careful not to get too close though and suffer a similar fate.

"I think perhaps we should pull him out." said Parrish after a minute's thought. The other three looked at him, their obvious why? silent on their lips. "He might be of some use and there does not seem to be much fight in him. Go on, pull him out, and if he does not answer my questions, you can throw him back in."

The man in the water barely heard but his eyes pleaded for saving. Lips blue from cyanosis and shivering violently, he finally lost his grip and was pushed by the flow completely beneath the surface where he stuck between the underside of the log and the stream bed. Completely submerged beneath the glittering flow, his outstretched hands splashed frantically as he started to drown.

Klud and Tomps shrugged off their bags and jumped down into the stream with bright splashes. The water was almost mid-thigh deep and they took time for a sharp gasp of breath against the cold before plunging their hands beneath the surface and hauling the half drowned stranger back up into the life giving air.

The sodden, blue faced individual could not even cling to the Danebury men as they dragged him limply over to the bank. He just gasped for breath. Parrish and Luke leant forward over the banking to grip his outstretched arms and hauled him up onto the land. Luke had to lean further in than Parrish and he cried out in dismay as his religious hat tipped from his head, landed with a plop in the stream and was carried away by the flow in moments. But he could not release the man and chase after his hat while Parrish continued with his grip alongside him. Together they jerked the man up out of the river and dropped him unceremoniously to the ground where he lay gasping in the snow. Klud and Tomps climbed out after him, shuddering against the cold air on their wet legs.

"Never mind about the hat, Luke. Get a fire going." Parrish addressed the shaman. "We will get everyone warm and dry while I will ask this fool where he is from and what he knows." The stranger just lay shivering in the snow, looking up at his saviours. “And if I do not like his answers, we will throw this tiddler back. No fear of drowning without his head though.” The man’s eyes widened in fear.

Parrish managed to smother the smile on his face as he turned away, although the fierce looks on the rest of the prostrate man’s rescuers did nothing to quell the chill in his bones that suddenly wasn't entirely caused by the icy water.

Back among the trees Luke started clearing a patch of ground of snow before beginning to gather dry sticks, snapped off from the surrounding trees, to start a fire. Klud and Tomps helped even though their wet legs were now starting to make them shiver too. Parrish turned to the exhausted, cold and sodden stranger who was barely able to stand unaided. He pointed to the ground at the man’s feet.

“Stand there. Do not move from that spot. And take all your clothes off.” The stranger just stared. “Now!” Parrish barked.

As fast as his numbed hands could manage, the man began to undress.

Luke, Klud and Tomps returned with armfuls of twigs and small branches, most pulled off a standing dead tree discovered not too far into the forest. They began to make a wigwam of them on the ground. Luke fished in his pack and produced a fist sized bundle of tinder. And all the while Parrish could hear several sets of teeth chattering.

“Not fast enough.” he said. Turning to the now naked, quaking stranger he unhooked his cape from around his throat and handed it to the man with the blue tinge. “Here wrap this around yourself.” Then he reached into the front left pouch of his webbing and pulled out a blank 7.62 rifle cartridge, one of the several dozen in there that had travelled back with him from the future. The other men eyed the shining brass cylinder with unbridled curiosity. Un-noticing, Parrish quickly pried open the crimped end with the tip of his combat knife.

“Just shove your tinder in there.” he said to Luke, nodding at the unlit fire. The shaman complied without a word. Parrish slowly poured dark grey powder from inside the blank cartridge all over the tinder ball. Klud nodded in realisation. He had seen this once before. "Spark away. And I suggest you lean back as you do it." Parrish said to Luke, who was already clutching his chunk of iron pyrite and a large piece of flint.

The holy man started striking the two together with firm, glancing blows, making sharp, loud clicks. On the third strike a small spray of faint, cold looking pale blue sparks landed on the gunpowder dusted tinder ball. There was a pop, fizz and then the loose powder ignited, flaring into life. The sudden burst of flame made Luke jerk back in surprise while the timber mound of twigs immediately around it burst into flame too with a bright, morale warming sparkle.

All the Neolithic men stepped back in amazement. Parrish nonchalantly pocketed the now empty brass cartridge case and simply said. "Well, do not let it go out."

Eager hands reached to stoke the small, cheery flames.

*

Snow began to drift lightly down again as the men sat around the campfire. The mystery man still shivered gently. The cape gave him some warmth but not much, although being chilled was the least of his problems. Practically naked and barefoot, making a sudden dash for freedom wasn't really on the cards, and besides, the two warriors sat either side of him were more than deterrent enough. He had always held his own in a fight, in fact he had two skulls to his credit, but these two looked way out of his league. But even they did not scare him as much as the tall man who sat opposite him. This giant occasionally smiled in a gentle, disarming way but you did not have to look too hard to see that death was always there on his shoulder. It was fair to say he frightened the life out of him, just with a look.

That look turned in his direction.

"Right then. If we are all comfortable, let us begin." Parrish smiled at his Watch with Mother phrase. No one else did. He looked sternly at the prisoner.

"First things first. What is your name?"

Silence.

Parrish sighed in feigned exasperation. "You can die here and now if you choose, but it is a simple question."

The man held out for a few moments, one small act of defiance, but he had no wish to end here.

"Breen. My name is Breen."

"And where do you come from?"

The briefest glance to the north gave away the answer before Breen returned his stare to the fire, ignoring Parrish.

Klud thought this showed great disrespect to his Chieftain and grabbed the man roughly by the shoulder and raised his fist.

"It is OK." Parrish stopped his friend. "I can guess."

"He is from Foinyah-Tullock." interjected Luke, making Breen's head snap round to him as the shaman pointed northwards, away through the trees. "Over the next ridge, then across the valley you will see the village there up on the hill."

Breen looked even more scared now. How could he know? Who were these people? He of course had no idea that Luke was in fact a holy man.

Parrish just nodded. He was now fully conversant with the language of the people and in their Gaelic/Celtic tongue *fainne*, pronounced foinyah meant ring, and *tulach* or tullock, meaning mound. This place of Breen's would through the ages transform into Ring Hill, a fairly prominent hillfort just to the north of Birmingham, overlooking the densely wooded expanse of Cannock Chase. But that was away in the distant future.

Klud growled. "So, does that mean we do not need this fool anymore?"

Breen's eyes widened even more.

“Not so fast, my friend.” laughed Parrish. “I still have a use for him.”

He stood up and went to Breen’s bundle of sodden clothes lying in the snow and threw the boots at their owner. “Put those on. I will keep the rest though.” He added as he gathered them up. Almost as an afterthought he tossed Breen's hat to Luke. It was a fine black and white striped badger skin effort. A bit Davy Crockett, thought Parrish. “There you go. He caused you to lose yours so you can have his.”

Luke pulled it on over his damp hair. It was a surprisingly good fit.

Parrish laughed again. “Now you are starting to look like a warrior.” Klud and Tomps smiled and the young man plucked up Breen’s flint axe and thrust it into Luke’s hand. The holy man stared at it for a moment, not quite sure what to do with it, then tucked it into his belt.

“Perfect.” Parrish grinned before turning serious again. “Right. Everyone on their feet. We are going visiting and Breen here is our ticket into his village.”

9

Just as Luke described, when the little troop and their all but naked prisoner reached the crest of the next ridge, the man's village could clearly be seen across the shallow valley that separated them.

With snow covered pines, bare, deciduous trees and scrub sweeping down the near side slope into the valley bottom all encrusted in white, Parrish thought it looked quite festive. This was totally lost on the other men. Snow just meant cold, more hardship and sometimes death. From the valley bottom all the way up to the rampart of the hillfort the land had been completely cleared to allow clear line of sight. At Parrish's signal they moved down into the valley bottom, everyone in no doubt that they were being observed from the parapet on the near horizon above them.

Moving down through the wooded half to the valley floor, the group stopped perhaps half a mile from the pathway up to the hillfort gate, just stepping out into the open. Parrish turned to his prisoner, handed him his wet bundle of clothes and said with a smile.

"Off you go then." The others stared at him but he continued. "Tell your Chieftain I would speak with him. We will wait here for his reply, a good distance from any unnecessary trouble."

"No arrow in the ass then." muttered Klud under his breath, making Parrish briefly laugh out loud.

"True words, old friend."

That brought grins from the others.

"You... you mean I am free to go?" said the unbelieving warrior.

"Yes. We will wait here for your Chieftain's answer. I only want to talk. So, away you go."

The man genuinely thought he would be killed at this point and could not believe his good fortune at surviving this strange encounter. He turned to leave.

"Oh, just one more thing." said Parrish, stopping the man in his tracks. He turned slowly back, still fearing the worst. "My cape, if you would be so good."

"But..."

Parrish held out his hand and his voice hardened. "My cape!" It was very final sounding.

The man looked from face to face but there was no mirth there. Just menace.

He understood he would now have to walk back up to his home village naked and knew he had no choice. Reluctantly he unclasped the toggle at his throat, shrugged out of the cape and slung the long garment round until it fell, draping across Parrish's outstretched forearm. Without another word he spun on his heel and trudged away through the ankle deep virgin snow with his wet bundle under one arm as his skin erupted in goose pimples against the cold air.

Klud, Tomps and Luke couldn't help it. They all sniggered at the humiliation.

"Well," said Parrish, not looking at anyone. "No one gets to walk away without something to remember us by."

"Yes." said Luke. "He will never forget returning home while under the charge of other warriors. No honourable death. No saving face. No clothes. And not even any fish."

The men's laughter stung the departing naked man even more than the icy snowflakes on his bare skin.

*

The four men withdrew slightly into the forest tree line and settled beneath the outstretched boughs of a big yew tree, its evergreen limbs offering some protection from the silently drifting fall of the snowflakes. More importantly, it made them difficult to observe as they sat in its deep shadow, but still offered them an unobstructed view of the open valley slope, the half mile or so up to the close gated entrance of Foinyah-Tullock.

All four understood the significance. They were few and knew that behind that curving palisade wall on the near horizon were a large number of men. Parrish was hoping for, if not the welcome mat, at least some sort of measured response. A delegation to his request for a parley, perhaps? But he made damn sure that if there was a sudden massed charge towards them out from the hillfort, they would have plenty of warning and could make good their escape. So he ensured at least one set of eyes was always fixed on Foinyah-Tullock. Yet time passed and nothing happened.

Klud, Tomps and Luke began shooting the odd questioning look at their leader.

Parrish felt their glances. "We wait." was all he said. And more time passed.

The remainder of the day drew on and while Parrish patiently waited, the Neolithic men began to wonder if they should make preparations for a fire before nightfall.

*

It was late, not long until dusk, when a lone figure finally slipped through the hillfort gates up on the hill. The man walked in measured strides down towards them, his footprints in the snow a dotted line behind him.

As he drew closer the Danebury men stepped out from under their shaded camp and spread out in a line, Luke stood one pace behind.

They recognised the man, now fully clothed, from earlier in the day. He approached slowly until he was about ten paces short of the trio. In one hand he gripped his war club, the knuckles of his fist white with the pressure.

Parrish wasn't the only one to notice. It was clear the lone stranger expected to fight and die here now. After a moment he braced up, sucked in a deep, cold breath and said loudly.

"My Chieftain says to go away. He has no wish to speak with you. He has no wish to let strangers into Foinyah-Tullock and is not going to open his gates for anyone!"

There was a pregnant pause before Parrish stepped forward, an angry look on his face. The lone man took a pace back and came to readiness with his war club raised.

Parrish just scoffed.

"I am not interested in you, fisher man. But I am *very* unhappy at your Chieftain's words, and his cowardice. You can keep your head and go back and tell him that." The Foinyah-Tullock man stood, stunned by the response. He could not believe what was happening. Twice now he had been at the mercy of these men and twice they had not just let him live, but sent him away.

Parrish turned his back on the warrior, another insult to add to the rest, signalled to his men and as one they all turned away and moved off back into the wooded landscape behind them.

Totally baffled, the solo warrior stood silently in the snow for several long moments before letting the hand holding the war club fall limply to his side. Then he turned and once again started to trudge slowly back to Foinyah-Tullock to deliver the short and damning message to his Chieftain.

*

Once out of sight beyond the wooded ridge Parrish led his men off to the left, heading east, keeping below the level of the high ground. His companions said nothing but he could feel their questioning eyes on his back. Finally turning to face them, they all stopped in their tracks and just looked up at him. He smiled.

"Alright. I know what you are thinking. We are all equal, so I will tell you my plan. We shall swing around to the east of the hillfort. My idea is to then get as far round to the north of it as we can before nightfall. Once there we need to find a spot where we can light a small fire without it being seen from Foinyah-Tullock. No point in freezing to death in the middle of the night after coming this far."

"Er... then what?" It was Tomps who spoke their one thought.

"I want the people up there to get nice and comfy in their beds, and then I intend to pay their Chieftain a visit. With no one else getting in my way."

"Alone?" again it was Tomps who asked first.

"Well, I will need a little help from Klud to get in but after that, yes. You and Luke are to wait at the camp until we return." Parrish did think that his plan was a little vague but his men never questioned it. "So, as we walk gather what dry wood you can because if we do not hurry I think it will be dusk before we find our spot."

No one questioned him further and they all set off once more, beginning to circle around the eastern side of Foinyah-Tullock, all of them suddenly more stealthy in their movements, even though they were well out of sight and sound of its inhabitants.

*

Snapping off any reachable dead limbs from trees that they passed, the men gathered enough to get some welcome warmth going very soon after they settled in their chosen spot. Just as the light began to fade, at the bottom of a shallow valley they came across a sunken stream bed. The water was barely a trickle but in a former life it had been powerful enough to cut a swathe through the ground five or six feet deep. The little rivulet meandered inside its own water course and the men settled on a snow covered semi circular gravel/sand bar to one side of the flow, just large enough to accommodate the four. The high bank either side hid the firelight from direct view and as Parrish estimated them to be a good mile almost directly north of Foinyah-Tullock, he doubted any ambient light going straight up would be noticeable, as long as they kept the fire small.

Having a small water source alongside was a bonus and the men quickly cleared the snow on their spit, collected pine boughs as insulation and settled down in their woollen capes to see out the night.

"At least it has stopped snowing." said Luke, "And as long as the clouds stay it should not get too cold."

"Yes." agreed Parrish. "*And* stay dark enough to hide me from prying eyes."

"When do we leave?" asked Klud, keen to see some action and also to see his good friend in action. He was to be disappointed on both counts.

"No rush mate." said Parrish with a smile. "I only need you to help me get into the hillfort. From there I will go on alone. But you need to be ready when I return. I do not know if it will be a quiet trip back or we will be running for our lives."

Klud was disappointed but did not show it. He already knew some things Dannu's man did were not for the eyes of mere mortals.

"I understand." was all he said.

"Right." He started to brief his men. "Now, we will do it in shifts, but try to get some sleep. I will stand first watch... er, keep guard for a while, then I will wake one of you to be the next guard. And so on. When we get to the middle of the night, if I am not awake someone wake me and Klud and I will get cracking." He knew he kept dropping military and just plain English words into the conversation but he couldn't help it. He really was enjoying himself. All his companions just nodded, even if they did not fully understand his words.

And suddenly Klud was gently shaking him by the shoulder. He was instantly awake and sat up to find Tomps and Luke also awake, watching silently.

"Time?"

Klud just nodded as Parrish realised he had simply stated the obvious. He stood, shook himself and looked about. Overhead the cloud cover was total, the bare trees were crowding in around them and in their little ravine the low glow of the fire illuminated his friends faces, but not enough to really read their expressions.

"Right." Parrish checked himself, patted the haft of his knife with one palm then handed his long bow and quiver of arrows out to Tomps. "Look after this for me. I will be back in a while." Tomps stood, took the great bow and looked his Chieftain in the eye.

"Take care." he said quietly.

"Always." came the reply. He nodded to Luke, turned back to Klud and simply said "Let us go." And with that they turned away, scrambled up the lip of the riverbank and were lost amongst the inky black shadows in moments.

Moving silently between the bare trees, the only sound was the soft crunch of snow beneath their feet. It took them a while before the open land and the hillfort beyond came into view. Both men studied its silhouette from the tree line for a while before Klud whispered.

"It all looks very quiet."

"OK. Then this is what we will do. As quietly as we can we need to get to the base of the timber wall. There is nowhere to hide once we go out into the open but I think no one will be awake, and even if they are they should not be looking in this direction. So, we go quietly up to the wall. Then you cup your hands together like this." Parrish interlocked his fingers with the palms facing up. "I will put my foot in that and with your back to the wall, you can boost me up to the lip of it. Yeah?" Klud just nodded. "Once I am inside, retreat to this spot and wait for me."

"But..."

“I will be as quick as I can. Be ready to cover me..., I mean, to protect me if I return with people chasing after me.”

Klud nodded, unslung his unstrung bow and quiver and propped them up against the thick trunk of the tree beside them. He grasped the idea now.

“Right.” He emulated his Chieftain.

“OK. Let us go.”

The pair broke cover and made their way in a fast crouch across the open snowfield, slid down into the ditch, scrambled up the other side and flattened themselves against the palisade wall. They stood there in the shadow of the wooden construction, silent for several long moments but there was no shout or raising of the alarm. Looking up, Parrish estimated the wall to be twelve to fourteen feet. Do-able, he thought.

Without a word Klud put his back against the wall and cupped his hands before him.

Parrish took a step back, there was just enough room without falling backwards into the ditch, then planted his boot in Klud’s stirrup and lunged for the lip above them as Klud heaved him up. The twentieth century man's weight made it hard for his Neolithic friend, but Klud had the measure of it and hoisted his Chieftain as high as he could. With a wet slap Parrish’s hands clasped the top lip of the palisade through its capping of snow. He momentarily hung there before swinging one leg up and secured his heel on it too. With one huge grunt he pulled himself up and over, dropping slightly breathless into a silent crouch onto the walkway behind the parapet.

And in a strange moment of terrible symmetry, as one man was breaking into Foinyah-Tullock, another man was starting his break into Dane-bre.

10

Earlier that same day, Shimon had led his warriors across the east river at the rope strung crossing some six kilometres north of a totally unsuspecting Danebury. They had all waded naked through the chill waters, their weapons and bundled clothing held high above their heads.

Once massed on the other side, they quietly dressed, got fires going and set too warming themselves back up. And so they passed the afternoon. Shimon wanted his men rested, warm and well fed for he knew the coming night would be a trial. But the potential reward for such an endeavour was a new village, trophies, wives, prosperity and, for him, power.

His men had earlier been instructed on their roles but now they waited, seated around good fires and eating everything that they had brought with them. They would need lots of energy for the task ahead and there was no need to carry any excess weight. Low talk passed around the fires as the night closed in. Then they slept, saving their strength for the night time task ahead.

It was in the small hours when Shimon roused them all. The cloud cover was total but at least the snow had stopped. With a commanding wave he led his well-armed and well rested men off through the trees, crunching softly across the snow-covered ground, and in a time the dark silhouette of the ringed mound of Danebury came into view.

There were still a few hours till the dawn. Shimon of course had no modern concept of time, but he knew the next crucial step of his stealth attack on Dane-bre was still a while off. And he knew this would be a difficult time for him and his men.

They all skirted the open ground just inside the tree line, keeping themselves and their snowy footprints out of sight, and edged round till they were as close as possible to the well-trodden main path that led to and from the great gate of the hillfort.

"Single line." Shimon whispered to his men. The threat of dire consequences to anyone who disobeyed him was clear in his tone. "Get to the footpath and then we walk straight up to the gate. No noise now. No sound at all!"

Acknowledging nods were all but lost in the darkness but Shimon knew.

He led out across the snowfield and made for the well-trodden footpath that stretched away to the watering place in one direction and up to the object of his desire in the other. His thinking was correct in that the slushy pathway hid the additional footprints of his advancing men as they all crept up the approach path and the men reached the main gate of Dane-bre undetected. Shimon waved a raised arm first one way then the other and, to their credit, the warriors of Olann-bre fanned silently out left and right and lined up against the outside of the palisade wall, either side of the main gate. All flattened their backs against the timber and with a satisfied nod from Shimon at the head of the group, everyone tried to slow their breathing. Now was the hard bit. To stand silent, still and hidden beneath the parapet of the hillfort, weapons at the ready, while the cold started to creep inexorably in. Each man was locked in his own personal battle with the plummeting temperature, which they now had to endure till first light.

*

Although he would never say, Shimon was quite proud of his men. Other than the occasional shuffle of cold feet, everyone had stood their ground. The night dragged on and the cold was biting but his men's resolve was firm.

At its coldest moment, the false dawn began to softly back light the trees away out before them in the distance, and then the landscape began, indistinctly at first, to make itself known. It was in no way warming but a palpable sense of relief could be felt amongst the Olann-bre warriors. The light slowly strengthened and then, even before a watery sun started to appear, one side of Dane-bre's great gate abruptly swung inwards. It almost caught the waiting men by surprise and they struggled briefly to activate their cold and reluctant limbs.

In the opening entrance, by a terrible stroke of misfortune, the first person there was a young warrior. He had drawn the short straw that morning to be the one whose task it was to check the flock come first light. To check for any disruption, disturbance, wolf activity, injured or somehow stranded sheep. Behind him stood his wife Anna, clutching a night bucket and an empty water bag. Behind her were four or five other women, also clutching bark buckets with odorous contents.

Before the young Dane-bre man could even register surprise, let alone attempt to raise the alarm, those outside began charging in. Shimon led the way and was upon his lone, vastly outnumbered opponent in an instant. With a wide, full powered sideways swing he drove his war club straight into the Dane-bre man's face. With a sickening crunch the youngsters nose crushed and ruptured. Both eyeballs burst with the power of the impact and the front of his skull shattered. Anna gasped in horror but her unfortunate husband never heard. He was dead before he hit the ground.

All the other women just gaped at the sight, dropping their buckets with wet, dark splashes and stood, frozen to the spot. Being just mere women, the Olann-bre warriors naturally ignored them.

Shimon pointed into the centre of the village with his bloodied club.

"Spread out" he hissed. "At least one man to each hut. Hold the head man of each hut firmly in his bed. Kill him if you have to." He added coldly. The men set off at the jog. "And bring me the man who says he is Chieftain." Shimon raised his voice now. "I want his head." Then he too moved off after his men, ignoring the now fleeing and scattering women, including the only one that did not flee.

Anna took a moment more to gather her wits. Having clearly recognised Shimon, she cast a forlorn, final glance down at her dead husband then turned her back on the corpse and dashed off into the village as fast as she could. Not up to Parrish's cabin, nor to the Chieftains official hut, the places where Shimon and his men were heading, but to Gants family hut.

There were a few shouts now as the invading warriors set about their Chieftains orders, bursting into huts and jumping onto the men still asleep inside, who were roughly awoken to find daggers at their throats. Over enthusiasm by several of Olann-bre warriors resulted in the murder of three Dane-bre men before some semblance of order could eventually be made.

Anna knew nothing of this. She barely stopped to make her presence known before slipping into Gant's hut and found his wife Teri standing to one side while the man himself was still struggling out of his bed.

Anna averted her eyes from his bare stump as the man looked up.

"What? What is happening?" he snapped at her, seemingly unperturbed by her sudden entrance.

"Shimon!" she panted. "Shimon. He has gained entry into the village. And he wants the head of the Chieftain!"

Gant was still struggling into his clothes but through gritted teeth said.

"If he wants a fight, he will get one."

"But..." Teri blurted before stopping herself from interrupting. As Gant spun on his wife, about to shout at her for speaking out, the door blanket flew back and Juli stumbled in.

"They... They are looking for you." she blurted at Gant.

"Let them come. I am not afraid." He said evenly.

"But..." said Teri again.

"What!?" barked Gant. There was growing anger in his voice but no one knew if it was at the blatant disobedience of a woman, or at the growing realisation that as Parrish's de-facto Chieftain, he had failed in his duty. Knowing that even as they were speaking, the village that he had been charged to look after was being wrested from him.

"You will die." She stated the obvious.

"With honour." Retorted her husband, not an ounce of fear in his voice.

The three women just stared at him before Juli said slowly.

"But... If you die..."

"Yes?" Gant would not normally ask a woman's opinion, but this was the Chieftains wife. He knew Parrish sometimes conferred with her on some village subjects, so she must have at least some sense.

Juli bowed to him and continued.

"If you die, as Chieftain, then Dane-bre dies too. And, if Parrish returns not knowing what has happened here, he will also die."

Anna and Teri clapped their hands to their mouths at such boldness. Juli did not care. She simply did not want to lose the love of her life.

Gant grew red in the face with anger but then his fury died as quickly as it had lived. He was first and foremost a thinker and organiser. In the distance outside muted shouts could now be heard. He ignored them as his thinking clarified.

"Yes." A pause. "I see." He bit his lip in thought for a few silent seconds then added, almost as if explaining to himself. "I am Chieftain, but my honour must come second now. Dane-bre is my responsibility. It must be saved. And Parrish is the man to do it." He looked around at the three women. "I must get out of here. I must deny Shimon the head of Dane-bre and I must get a warning to Parrish."

He began to look about in desperation, his eyes falling on the pile of clothing beside his bed.

“I wonder. Tell me, do you think you women will be allowed to collect water, as is usual this early in the day?”

“The other women and me were ignored at the gate,” volunteered Anna. “And they killed my husband.” she added softly, dropping her eyes.

“No time for that now.” Gants reply was callous but he was determined to do the right thing now. “I must act quickly. So, if we all wear cloaks and hoods or scarves, I think we could all just walk out of the gate, with the good will of Dannu. I will hunch low, and we will need more women.”

Juli nodded and without another word darted from the hut.

“While I dress,” Gant nodded to Teri and Anna. “Make a hole in the back of the hut wall. We will go that way and they will see that I have escaped to avoid them. I will be dishonoured but it may save lives if Shimon is only angry with me.”

The two women snatched up some nearby weapons and attacked the wattle and daub wall as Gant continued to dress.

Surprisingly, it only took a few moments. The dried mud and hazel wand construction splintered quite readily under the attack of flint headed clubs and in very little time Gant, Teri and Anna had stepped through and were standing outside in the half light, the bulk of the hut between them and the village invasion.

Juli suddenly appeared around the side of the hut with several more frightened looking women in tow.

“I peeked in and saw the empty hut and the hole.” She looked suitably impressed.

Gant just nodded. “Everyone grab at least one bucket or water bag, huddle around me and walk, do not run, to the main gate.”

The women obeyed the order of a warrior and Chieftain instinctively and in seconds the little, to the casual eye, female group, like a small Roman *testudo* or protective tortoise formation, shuffled away through the snow and around the inside perimeter of the hillfort towards the main gate.

The whole operation went smoother than they could have hoped. At the gate was only a single Olann-bre guard and he could care less about some silly women, still going about their dutiful chores even when there was bloody chaos going on around them.

In fact, the last thing the dead Dane-bre man at the gate did for his village was to distract the guard as the female cluster hiding Gant passed through. The guard dismissed the group with a patronising wave, his attention fixed on the corpse. Having searched the body and helped himself to its warm looking cape, he was considering removing the smashed head to present to his Chieftain as a trophy when all the fuss had died down. Gant and his protective shield of females were through the gaping gateway and off down the slushy approach path almost before they knew it and what had worked earlier for Shimon also worked for Gant. His distinctive peg leg footprints were lost amongst all the others.

When the group at last reached the edge of the wood that held the watering stream, they all stopped. Gant stood tall and handed his 'disguise' bucket to one of the ladies.

"Fill your bags and return to the village. What happens there today will happen, but know this. However long it takes, Parrish will return. I am going to the great temple to warn him and will be with him when he comes back." He nodded briefly as a farewell to Teri, then stepped back so he could address the whole group.

"What you all just did... That was a brave thing. I..." He could not bring himself to say more but nodded briefly to them all, stood tall once more and growled. "Now go."

And without another word he gathered his cape about him and stumped with purposeful determination off through the snowy undergrowth.

Shimon was indeed angry that he had missed the chance to kill a Chieftain, have his head as a trophy and the mark of a

Chieftain killer on his neck. He did however make much of the fact that the head man, the leader of the great village of Dane-bre, had declined a battle and actually broken his own home in order to escape and had slunk away in the dark. He was a coward.

This he proclaimed loudly as he stood before the gathered mass of warriors before him. Only half the men who faced him were there voluntarily. The other men were each closely accompanied by an Olann-bre warrior who continued to hold a knife to his charge's throat.

On the freshly churned ground between the male throng and the posturing Shimon lay the three bodies of those who had been killed in their beds. They were still complete for even though they were technically killed under the orders of their Chieftain, those Olann-bre men who did the deeds did not feel it right to claim a trophy off a man who was not killed in combat. The men had in truth been barely awake.

Shimon ignored this small defiance and addressed the crowd in loud, menace laced words, ensuring that his threats carried also to the big group of sullen women stood almost unseen behind the immediate throng.

"Your Chieftain, this man Gant, has fled. Slithered off like a serpent rather than face me. You were all being led by a coward!"

The Dane-bre men eyed each other briefly then returned their steady gaze to Shimon. All of them knew and respected Gant. Knew the type of man he was. And knew he would not have done what he did without a good reason.

Shimon saw his words have little or no effect on those he was trying to intimidate. He changed tack.

"I now claim this village. I have won it by clever planning and through my skill and the skills of my men." He paused. Still there was no discernible reaction. "I now want, no, I expect you all to be loyal to me as your new Chieftain!"

This time there were several scoffs and many of the Dane-bre men deliberately looked away. They still all had a deep-seated belief of respect for a Chieftain, any Chieftain, but one who spoke false or foolish words did not impress them.

Shimon began to get angry.

"I want you all to give me your word of honour to be loyal to me, your new Chieftain." No one spoke. Shimon held himself back from physically attacking the man nearest him in his anger and instead said in slow, measured tones. "Because if you do not, I will have you all put to death! Now, I know you might consider this an honourable end, but I will add this. I can run the village with just my own men." His own men knew this was not strictly true. "But things will be easier for everyone if you help too. Also, if I do have to 'remove' you from the village because I cannot trust you, I will have to remove your families as well! They will be too much of a burden on a village with many more women and children than there are warriors to look after them."

The full callousness of the remark stunned the Dane-bre men. Gasps could be heard too from the female crowd at the rear.

The eyes of the captured and helpless warriors blazed back at Shimon but the Olann-bre leader shrugged off their unspoken threats. Unlike the bodies on the ground before him, he did not fear being killed in his bed. Not once he had the word of honour from each and every man he now faced.

He let the men stew on their dilemma for several long, chilling moments, then simply said.

"Well?"

Low murmurs of defeat floated up from the crowd and a few heads began reluctantly nodding.

A smug smile settled on Shimon's face.

He had won.

He finally had his village.

11

Parrish stayed motionless in his low crouch on the parapet walkway inside Foinyah-Tullock, one palm pressed into the cold snow, the silence complete as he turned his head slowly, looking for any signs of movement. All was still. After a few moments he rose slowly to his full height, gave the dark and shadowed hillfort laid out before him a second scan then turned and looked over the lip of the palisade wall and down at Klud.

The Neolithic warrior was looking expectantly up out of the gloom. Parrish thrust out his arm and gave a thumbs up. Klud simply nodded in reply and turned away, moving silently back away through the snow en route to his watch point at the edge of the forest. He was careful to walk in their previous footprints so as not to disturb anymore of the lying snow than necessary. Even so, Parrish still saw that their approach was broadcast by the indentations and he actually wished for more snowfall to cover them. Satisfied that his friend was well away, Parrish turned back, returning his attention to the village before him.

He could not make out too much in the dark night and, for the place he wanted to find, was banking on the fact that the villages of Neolithic Britain were all generally of the same layout, dependent to some extent on the particular lie of the land.

In fact, Foinyah-Tullock was like Dane-bre in not being a completely flat hilltop. Inside Dane-bre's circular wall its topography was really a gentle, conical shaped hill with Parrish's cabin at its peak. Foinyah-Tullock was an easy, mostly smooth slope, angling down from the higher northern side to the southern face of its own wall which was bisected there by the main gate.

Yet although Parrish found himself standing on the highest part of the north rampart and thus the highest part of the village, the sloping ground didn't give him a particularly good overall view of it. All he could see was a stagger of conical thatched roofs dropping gently away into the darkness.

Right, he thought, we will have to do this the hard way. He dug his heels into the wet ground as he slowly descended the inner slope into the village proper, reached level ground and moved swiftly away to the cover of the nearest hut. Circling noiselessly around to the entrance, he checked it but the building was just a standard Neolithic roundhouse with no additional or distinguishing features. He moved on to the next hut, silent, stalking and systematic. From hut to hut he crept, half expecting at any moment to be discovered and the alarm to be raised, but all was silent. It was tense and quite nerve-wracking, but Parrish couldn't help the grin that flowed onto his face at the rush of adrenalin he felt. He was the lone wolf on the prowl. The cold was his friend, keeping everyone else in their warm huts, and he felt the whole village was his for the taking as he examined the outside of each hut, looking for the one that he hoped would somehow show itself to be the Chieftain's dwelling.

Parrish had visited more than two thirds of the huts in Foinyah-Tullock and wondered if he would have to check out every single one, before he crept round to the front of the very next hut to be suddenly confronted by two huge timber pillars sunk into the ground, one either side of its entrance. Each easily as tall as himself, these wooden obelisks, stabbing up into the dark, sported various hanging skulls, including several human ones.

Well, he thought, someone likes to show off their trophies, but I reckon this must be the place. It has 'Chieftain' written all over it.

A few moments listening at the tied down door blanket revealed nothing and no light back-lit through its rough weave, but very subtle flickering light around its edges where there were chinks or folds told him that at the very least a central fire still burned low inside.

He carefully cut the tie thongs down one side of the blanket, his carbon steel blade making short work of them, pulled the blanket aside and slipped in.

All was still silent. The low burning fire in the central hearth softly illuminated the interior of the hut with a reddish-yellow glow throwing irregular, dark shadows against the curving inside wall.

The man he wanted to question was fast asleep on his back to the left side of the hut with only a single blanket over him for it was surprisingly warm and comfortable inside. Parrish took a moment to savour the pleasing temperature change. At the rear of the hut, opposite the entrance and curled up close together slept two women and a very young child. To the right was a jumbled pile of the day-to-day items every family needed to hand while going about their business.

Parrish padded softly across to the sleeping Chieftain, knelt quietly beside his bed and paused briefly, hovering his clawed left hand over the man, before in a flash it clamped down hard on the unsuspecting man's throat.

He jerked awake and instantly goggled as his body realised it could not draw a breath. He began to kick and squirm and his hands grabbed at the painful restriction around his windpipe. Parrish just leaned more of his weight down through his arm onto his victim's throat.

"I want a word with you." He hissed down at the man, whose face was now starting to go bright red. "I will let you breathe a little now, but if you so much a shout or make any loud noise, I will tear your throat right out of your neck. Yes?"

The man was now just starting to go a faint tinge of blue, his eyes bulged, and his strength was fading, but he had just enough reason left to manage a very restricted nod. Parrish kept hold but loosened his grip a little and the whoosh of air being sucked down into starved lungs was loud in the silence.

Allowing his prisoner a few moments, Parrish glanced up at the two women who were now sitting bolt upright, their eyes also bulging, but this time in fright. He put the index finger of his right hand to his lips and simply said.

"Shhh!"

And got definite, emphatic nods in reply. He returned his gaze to the prone, gasping man.

"Now my friend, we will have words." He eyed the man sternly. "It is not my plan to kill you in your bed, but make no mistake, I will do just that if you provoke me. So, no loud noises or sudden moves, and I will release you. You can sit up, but no standing. Yes?"

Another restricted nod.

"OK." Parrish removed his hand and rocked back onto his heels but was ready to pounce at the first sign of rebellion. This did not go un-noticed.

The man gasped several more times. Tenderly fingering his sore neck, bright with the imprint of Parrish's vicelike grip, he came slowly up to a sitting position.

"Now, am I right in thinking that you are Chieftain of Foinyah-Tullock?" Parrish quizzed.

The man just nodded, still getting his breath and reluctant at that moment to test his recently strangled vocal chords or say something that might upset or antagonise his attacker.

"Good." There was a pause. Parrish squinted at him and then in a soft, but menace filled voice added. "First, I want you to know, I am NOT happy at the way me and my men were treated yesterday. Trust me, you do not want to see me anymore unhappy, so just answer my questions, and perhaps we will both finish this talk still alive." The village Chieftain's eyes widened again. It was almost comical but Parrish was in no mood to laugh and pushed on. "You are Chieftain…?" He raised his eyebrows.

"Ray... Raif." the man croaked.

“Good to meet you, Chieftain Raif.” Parrish’s tone mocked him, but he still condescended to give the man a nod and a totally humourless smile. “So, tell me, what was that all about, eh? Turning us away without even finding out who we were?”

“We...” Chieftain Raif coughed several times and rubbed his throat again.

Parrish turned again to the women. He’d used the stick, now just a little bit of carrot. “Can we have some water here for the Chieftain? And a bit more light.” he added almost as an afterthought.

The women had never moved so fast. They let the sleeping babe lay and one dashed to grab the nearest water bag while the other went to the fire and lit a stick taper with the intention of going around the hut to light as many of the tallow lamps as she could. Parrish assumed the woman with the water bag was the first wife but either way, she was at their side in moments. Parrish nodded again as the woman held out the softly yielding leather bag to her man but he was still looking to the big kneeling stranger.

“Fill your boots.” said Parrish in English.

Chieftain Raif did not understand the strange sounds but got the gist. He snatched the water bag and gulped back several big draughts of the cooling fluid as the increasing number of newly lit lamps began to throw everything into sharper relief.

Sore throat soothed, he returned his attention to his interrogator, who just sat there in quiet expectation, yet looked very much like a man it did not do to keep waiting. As a Chieftain, Raif wanted to baulk at being dictated too, but as a warrior also he knew he could not lie and strangely he felt a little relief at being able to unburden his worries, even to a total and aggressive stranger. For his woes had been long and difficult. This huge invader before him was both terrifying and yet at the same time almost benevolent. He braced up in his sitting position, hoping to look as Chieftain-like as possible.

"We... we have not let anyone in for several seasons." Raif tried his voice again then found himself almost readily explaining to the big man with the piercing eyes. "And we only send out warriors for food in very small numbers. I keep my men here, ready. There could be an attack at any time."

Ah, thought Parrish, that would explain the lone fisherman we stumbled across and also why this whole village was not seen at the last solstice gathering. But he was much more intrigued by the man's last words.

"Attack? By who?"

"The pack." he said bluntly.

"Eh? Pack? What pack?"

Chieftain Raif looked at his assailant as if he was talking to a small child. How could this big man not know?

"The Wolf Pack."

Parrish's silence got him a second patronising look and he did not like it. He felt his control was slipping. Time to re-assert himself.

"I do not know of this wolf pack." He barked. Chieftain Raif's eyebrows started to go up and Parrish growled. "If you give me another 'who is this idiot' look, I will beat you to a pulp. Just explain yourself, and be quick about it!"

Chieftain Raif gulped and nodded quickly. He rapidly gathered his thoughts.

"There are a group of men. They all wear wolf pelts and call themselves the Pack. They are led by a strong leader who wears the pelt of a great white wolf. They control the villages to the north and want my village too. But I will not give it up without a fight."

"Good man." said Parrish softly before he could stop himself. "Er... Where can this Wolf Pack be found?"

"All I know is that they dwell in one of the villages they control."

Parrish wanted to ask how many men constituted a 'pack' and how far away these other villages were, but he knew the questions were too specific for the man before him. It was obvious however that the villages he referred to were the Avebury holy men's missing ones.

As the silence drew out, Parrish's gaze became unfocused as he pondered, while Chieftain Raif's face began to show more fear. The Neolithic man coughed and said in a quiet voice.

"That is all I know. The Pack, or at least some of them, pass by Foinyah-Tullock often, making threats and promising punishments and death if we do not open our gates to them." His expression suddenly turned fierce. "But I tell you, I will never give up this village to these wolf men. I will protect my people till my last breath!" He looked defiantly into Parrish's eyes, and was surprised to see a smile flow onto the big man's face.

"Well said." came the reply. "Now I know that you locked the village shut rather than bow down to these wolf pack people, I can see you are a good Chieftain."

"I... I thought you were one of them." Chieftain Raif stuttered.

"And so you did the right thing." Parrish moved back to give his fellow Chieftain some breathing space and nodded to him. "Your actions make sense now and I honour you for them. But know this. I am not a "wolf man". In fact, I am looking for this pack, now I know about them. I want to understand what is going on here."

Chieftain Raif nodded back, relief slowly filling him as he felt his immediate danger receding.

"Er... so, what then is your aim?" he asked gingerly. "If you are not a wolf..."

Parrish gave the Neolithic Chieftain a smile that chilled the man's blood, then pointed to the slightly fading tattoo on his cheek just below his right eye. Raif had not noticed it before in the previous half light and his heightened state of fear. Now, as he examined it more closely he could see it was a cross hatching tattoo very much like a hash mark, with five big dots beneath it.

"... I am the wolf *killer*." Parrish finished quietly. There was a sudden and complete silence.

"Just who are you?" whispered Raif, finally asking the question he was desperate to know.

Parrish reached out his hand. Raif reluctantly gripped it with his own. Parrish rose effortlessly to his feet pulling the smaller man up with him. Now standing together the Neolithic man found himself looking up into the face of a towering giant.

"I am Parrish, Chieftain of Dane-bre." came the proud answer.

Chieftain Raif finally gasped in recognition. Every Chieftain knew about the tall man seen around at the annual solstice gathering.

Dannu's Man!

"I... I am honoured!" Was all he could say. Parrish waved the accolade aside.

"Fair play. I honour you for your actions too, and for what you have told me." He bowed lightly. "I will leave you now and wish you well." Parrish reached into his pocket and pulled out the empty brass bullet casing that nestled there. The completely unknown, shining cylindrical piece of metal caught Chieftain Raif's eyes as it glinted in the lamplight. Parrish pushed it into the man's hand and said with a half smile. "Here. Perhaps next time we meet, we will be a little more friendly, eh?"

Raif nodded then looked down at the casing in his palm and examined it more closely. It looked and felt like nothing he had ever seen before. He fingered it briefly then looked back up to thank Dannu's man but all he saw was the door blanket falling back into place. Looking around to his two wives who were still stood motionless and spellbound, all he could do was shrug in amazement.

And Chieftain Raif's totally unexpected and astounding brush with Dannu's man was not quite concluded. He did not know it at the time, but later that coming day he would have to explain all to his people, after the stressed and siege weary folk of Foinyah-Tullock had emerged from their roundhouses in the cold light of dawn to find mysterious footprints in the virgin snow throughout the village. It was totally unnerving to them all to realise that a lone man had passed throughout the village, all around their homes and right up to their very doors in the dead of night. And all the time unknown, unheard, unseen and unchallenged.

*

Under that same dawning light Parrish and his men were breaking camp in their sheltered gully. He had told them what he had learned during his mysterious 'meeting' with the Chieftain of Foinyah-Tullock. No one dared ask how the meeting had come about but they were all intrigued by his news. Luke nodded in understanding at the mention of the other villages.

"There are two more villages this far north, at least this side of the great divide." he revealed. No one pressed the holy one on just what 'the great divide' was, although Parrish was aware of the high moors areas that straddled central England, known in the modern era as the Peak District, North York Moors and the Dales. They were harsh, inhospitable places of windswept, open moorland, particularly so in the winter. He briefly wondered if perhaps they were all part of some barren, natural divide that split what was in the south from whatever might be in the north? He kept these thoughts to himself.

"Only two villages?" quizzed Klud, something he would not dreamed of doing to a holy man only a week or so earlier.

"Yes. From here, one is away towards the setting sun. The other village is the opposite way, towards where the sun rises."

Parrish turned to face due north and thrust his arms out, each at forty five degrees to his front. He looked very much like he was boasting about the size of a big fish he had caught.

"OK." He pondered briefly. Partly through natural instinct but mostly through routine through his life in the twentieth century, he withdrew his right arm. "We go left."

Everyone else of course agreed.

"That way lies the village of Cournan-Tullock." Luke informed him, his secret holy knowledge coming to the fore again.

"How far?"

"Less than two days travel."

12

It took almost three full days for Gant to reach the holy village beyond the great stone temple of Avebury. And it had been a tough journey.

The ground, even where the snow had not laid, was wet and soft. It would have been a tiring trek for an able bodied man, but Gant's peg leg stuck at every step. He could not feel hidden objects under the several inches of snow with his wooden prosthetic and stumbling had become a regular occurrence.

He did not chill too much at night, making a fire could take some time and effort but was second nature to a seasoned warrior. But as he travelled the cold, while not so bitter as to be life threatening, was relentless and without mercy. Water was no problem either with fresh snow everywhere to quench a thirst, but he had left Dane-bre in great haste and carried no food. By the evening of the third day when he stumped slowly up to the holy village gate he had gained a long stave-cum-quarter staff to aid his walking, but had lost a little weight, fallen countless times in the mud and slush and was now gripped by a fierce hunger. Gant looked just how he felt. Muddy, bedraggled, hungry and rather the worse for wear.

He stopped short of the village gate, very much aware that there was a large village before him and with a holy shrine village attached behind that, but he had never actually being this close before.

Unsurprisingly, the raggedy man limping up towards the entrance had drawn some attention and was challenged.

"What do you want?" came a firm shout from the entrance. The gate was open, after all no one expected an attack on the home of the holy ones, but a slew of warriors blocked its access.

"I am here to see Parrish of Dane-bre." Gant called back. "And some food would be good too." he added.

“There is no Parrish here.” The reply made his heart sink. “And we do not let rough, unknown strangers into the village. Be on your way.”

Gant opened his mouth to reply but the figures before him retreated before he could do so and the village gates swung firmly shut to emphasise the point.

Close to exhaustion, a long, disheartened breath sighed out of him and he sunk slowly to the ground to rest his sore stump, aching body and troubled mind. He did not care or even notice the wetness of the ground beginning to soak into his dirty trousers.

As he pondered what to do next, feeling eyes on him from the parapet but not caring, he knew he was stuck. He could not go forward and going back to Dane-bre, even if he had the strength within him, was not an option. He felt bad for those he had left behind and bitter that he could not find or do anything for his Chieftain.

Just as he began to look to the near future and see his own death, the village gate opened and a lone figure ran out towards him. He did not have the strength or the will at that moment to get up but simply gazed up at the approaching warrior.

“My friend!” was the unexpected shout and it took Gant a moment to recognise the young man who approached. “Gant. I came as soon as I heard that a man with only one foot was outside. It could only be you.”

Gant squinted up. “Hew?”

“Yes. Come on, my friend.” The youngster helped him to stand. “Come on in. What in Dannu’s name brings you here all alone?”

Hew pushed his shoulder into Gant’s armpit and with an arm wrapped around the older man's back, helped him towards the entrance of the village.

They got no further than the village threshold before being stopped by a line of warriors.

“Who is this?” One asked sternly. “And what does he want here?”

“As I said, I have come to seek Parrish of Dane-bre.” answered Gant as firmly as he could. “I have news of his village and I know that he was headed here.”

“He has moved on.” was the curt answer. “No one knows to where or for how long.”

“Then I will wait for him.” Gant was starting to become desperate. He had much to say and had come here under difficult circumstances to see his tall friend, and hopefully to save his life and that of his villagers.

“It is winter.” The warrior spokesman was in no mood to be benevolent. “We do not have food just to give away or the time and resources to look after every wandering scruff who turns up hoping for free lodging. Be on your way.”

“But...”

“Then he will stay with me.” Hew stood up to the warrior. “He will be no burden to the village. I and my family will welcome this man in. He is my friend.”

The warrior spokesman eyed the youngster for several long moments before saying gruffly.

“So be it. But remember your words here and now. The burden is yours.” And with that all the men turned their backs and simply strode off.

“Come with me, Gant.” said Hugh in a more friendly voice, ignoring the guarded threat and potential insult. “We have food, warmth and shelter.” He gave a small laugh. “And you look like you could use some.”

Gant finally grinned back.

“You are in the right of it, my fine friend.”

The pair entered Hew’s modest hut. As he had described, it was warm and a familiar sight. The central fire burned brightly, beds lay ready beyond it and the usual paraphernalia of home life was scattered about. Seated together one side of the fire was a woman about the same age as Gant's wife and a young girl of perhaps nine years. They promptly jumped up and bowed to both men.

"Sit, sit." Gant said automatically before he remembered where he was. He would not apologise but gave the smallest of bows. "Besides." He offered a small grin. "I am about to fall down myself."

The joke fell flat and the females just looked on as Gant dropped with a thud to the well insulated, mat covered floor and gratefully held his hands out to the heat of the fire. Mother and daughter immediately sat too so as not to cause insult.

"This is Gant." explained Hew to his mother and little sister. "He will be our guest for a while."

"And I thank you for it." Gant added sincerely.

"Then you will want something to eat." said the woman and rose to start to prepare something.

"Your mother?" Gant quizzed Hew.

"Yes. Mara." The woman nodded. "And my little sister Mimi."

The small girl just continued to stare.

"And you are the man of the house?"

Hew nodded. "My father died several seasons ago." There was no need for further explanation.

"Here. Eat this while I prepare some hot food." interrupted Mara and handed Gant some jerky. He accepted it gratefully and took a huge bite, chewing with relish. He was much less surprised or offended at the bold actions of some women now. Especially after several Dane-bre women had saved him with their own bold actions. This Mara had obviously held sway over Hew as a boy until the death of her husband. So even though he was now the man of the house, the youngster would still defer to his mother while inside it. Gant found it somehow comforting.

“Er... Thank you.” he said, surprised at his own ease of acceptance.

“You are welcome. While the food heats, I will prepare you a bed and there is water in that bucket if you wish to clean off some mud.”

Gant simply nodded. Hew grinned and Gant looked at him sideways before saying flatly, “It is a strange house here.”

“Agreed.” Hew replied, “But it is a good arrangement. We survive and what goes on in a warrior’s home is his own affair.” He thought the man from Dane-bre might be angry or even try and take charge as oldest male, but he did not know of Gant’s recent experiences.

“I am a man who understands when something works.” The older man said. “I am honoured to accept you offering me the comfort of your home.” And to prove his point he broke the habit of a lifetime and bowed deeply to Mara, who grinned in realisation of their sudden agreement and bowed warmly back.

Later that evening they were visited by a holy man. He briefed Gant in broad terms about how Parrish had gone off to the north, but in truth the whole religious community beyond the main village knew little more than he already did. The holy man left with everyone as much in the dark as ever.

“It is my wish to stay here until Parrish returns.” Gant addressed Hew and his family. “Is that permitted?”

The question was of course aimed at Hew.

“Of course. I am Parrish's friend too and I would be honoured if you would tell me what brings you, with much difficulty I can see, all the way here in the grip of winter.”

Now comfortable, fed, watered, cleaned up and happy in the knowledge that he could sleep safe and sound this night, he leant back and looked at Hugh, Mara and little Mimi. In clipped tones he briefly ran through the events of the Dane-bre takeover only three days earlier.

Eyes were wide and there was a long silence when he had finished.

"So you see." Gant concluded. "Parrish must be told if anything is to be done to regain Dane-bre from the clutches of Chieftain Shimon."

"Of course. I must say, I am at a loss as to what the great man can do, but if any man can, it is he." Hew shook his head.

"Agreed." said Gant and there was another long silence as they both racked their brains for some miracle solution. Nothing came to mind.

*

The evening drew on and finally it was time for bed. As Gant detached his wooden prosthetic from his leg he caught Mimi staring at his red, slightly sore stump. He looked at the girl and simply raised his eyebrows.

"Does... does it still hurt?" she asked in awe.

"The stump does sometimes but you know, sometimes also I am sure I can still feel my foot. Sometimes it itches and sometimes it is cold. And I look down but of course it is not there." The girl's mouth hung open. "And I am thinking that you are wondering where my foot has gone?"

Mimi nodded. At that her mother interrupted.

"It is not the done thing to question a warrior." she scolded.

"No." Gant waved away the words. "I am happy to tell the tale. It is the least I can do in return for your hospitality."

A grin split the little girls face. After all, who did not love a good tale?

In fact, Gant had never considered himself to be a storyteller. He was a man of logic. He saw things in a straight forward and reasoned way. Secretly, he had always admired those who could paint vivid, exciting pictures with their words. He would never say but he was in great awe and admiration of the old Dane-bre flint knapper, whose story telling prowess was unmatched.

But now, he actually had a tale to tell, and an enthralled audience to tell it to. He reflected Mimi's grin with one of his own, and leaned back on one elbow.

"Well...."

13

The village of Cournan-Tullock stood atop a gently sloping isolated hill on the western edge of what would one day be called Cannock Chase. It was not a large village, with a mere six and a half acres of ground within its ringed and walled embankment.

It had once been an area exceptionally rich in berries and fruit bearing trees, although these had long since been cut down to clear the sight lines for the settlement.

Caornan, pronounced cournan, was the Gaelic for a small berry and with *tulac* the word for mound, the name of Cournan-Tullock would over the millennia evolve through 'small berry mound' to the modern name of Bury hill.

All of this was completely lost to the small band who now eyed the village defences from the safety of the tree line a good half mile short of its approach road to the firmly closed entrance gate.

Cournan-Tullock looked quiet and untroubled from the outside, but the hidden observers wondered what was going on within.

They all knew there was no handy messenger to send in this time, so first order of the day was to attract someone's attention.

"How do we go about this?" Klud asked no one in particular, but the question was clearly aimed at Parrish.

The Chieftain gave a humourless grin.

"I guess we shall just have to ask someone out."

"Ah."

"So, keep well back and I will see if I can attract someone's attention."

With that Parrish stepped out into plain view and advanced across the ankle-deep snow field towards the approach ramp. He was sure to stay well out of arrow reach, even the reach of *his* arrows, and stopped a good two hundred plus yards short of the small hillfort. Heads could be seen bobbing about just above the palisade wall, but no one seemed keen to make any sort of move.

"Hello the village!" shouted Parrish through the sharp, chill air.

"We see you." Came a return shout.

"I would speak with your Chieftain." Parrish replied.

"He does not lead this village anymore. We killed him," came the brutal boast. "This place is now under the charge of the Great Wolf."

"I see. Then I would speak with this great wolf person."

"He is not here." The distant fool gave away vital information without realising. "We are not interested in talk so you and your pitiful band should leave this place."

Parrish turned at the crisp sound of crunching snow underfoot behind him, surprised to see that Klud, Tomps and Luke had followed him out of the trees and now stood just a few paces behind. Before he could speak Luke said.

"Ask to speak with their holy man."

Good idea, thought Parrish, there is universal respect for Dannu's servants.

"Then I would speak with your holy man." he called.

"He is also dead. We killed him too," came the second boast. "We are all under the leadership of the Great Wolf."

Luke gasped in horror at the revelation. Klud and Tomps gaped in shocked amazement. Parrish just became angry. Over the past few years, he had had dealings with many holy men and knew the servants of Dannu were benign, non-combatants and always have the welfare of the people at heart. There was never any need to kill, no murder, a defenceless holy one. His voice hardened.

"That was very brave of you, you coward! Come out and talk to me. Let us see just how brave you are!"

"You are a few. We are many. If you wish to die today, I can do that for you!"

Klud and Tomps immediately took up aggressive stances, both gripping their battle clubs. Parrish carefully nocked an arrow to his longbow, not having a flint weapon at his side.

"Keep back, my friend" he heard Tomps hiss to Luke.

There was a flurry of movement along the hilltop parapet then a few moments later the main gate was flung wide.

The first five men to step out were all wearing wolf pelts across their shoulders, the eyeless heads of the dead wolves as headwear, with the fanged snouts projecting like the peak of a cap. They formed a line abreast and marched steadily down the snow and slush covered approach path. Perhaps a dozen or so paces behind them a gaggle of more than two dozen warriors then appeared, although Parrish got the distinct impression from their body language they were not so keen to engage in a fight.

Five against three was still daunting enough for Parrish and his men. The 'wolf' men steadily advanced towards them with cruel grins on their faces. They knew the balance was in their favour. This was a good chance for easy trophies.

"Let's see if we can't even the odds a bit." Parrish said quietly in English and drew his bow. He didn't like to use it in very cold conditions and hoped it would not break at the crucial moment. But there was no need to fear. His friend Mars had been a master bow maker. Parrish had no compunction about shooting and killing any of these men. In his military mind the assessment was simple. The approaching force intended to kill him. To survive, the imminent lethal threat needed to be neutralised.

The wolf men thought they were still well clear of the odd arrow, even when they saw the taller man of the little troop taking aim.

The arrow flew through the crisp, cold air in a blur and to everyone's shock it thudded into the second man on the right of the line. It struck high in the left side of the unfortunate's chest, just above the heart, a palms width below his collar bone.

A look of complete surprise swept over the man's face before the pain struck. His damaged lung and main ventricles instantly poured blood into his chest cavity. He staggered a step, then fell to his knees, clutched at the wooden shaft with clawed hands and coughed up a great volume of blood as he collapsed onto his back.

The wolf spokesman looked furiously down at his suddenly dead companion, realizing that this might not be a straightforward massacre. He waved his war club over his head at the warrior crowd behind him.

"Come on." he urged. "We will rush them before they can shoot more arrows." He turned back to face Parrish and his men and broke into a run towards them. His fellow wolf men kept pace.

This lead man clearly thought that the crowd of warriors to his rear would blindly follow his orders. Some immediately grasped that he was encouraging them to basically become cannon fodder. To absorb or at least deflect some of any additional fire from himself and his wolf companions. Yet the bigger warrior group did in fact start to run but as the first of them made to pass the dead man on the ground, the man abruptly stopped. He quickly knelt beside the corpse and inspected the arrow. An arrow with jet-black fletching.

"It is a sky spirit arrow!" he gasped in recognition.

"Yes." said another, also making the connection. "And the only man who shoots those is Parrish, the Chieftain of Danebre!"

All the men stopped now and stared past the still running wolf men who were closing rapidly on their target. The very tall target.

"Dannu's man!" several of the watching warriors gasped in unison.

"Sent by the Great Goddess." said the still kneeling lead man. He rose slowly to his feet. "Strange forces are at work here. I want no part in this."

Murmurs of agreement came from those gathered about him and suddenly all their eyes were on the impending fight before them, the wolf men not realising they were on their own.

They would not have cared at that moment, even if they had known. Their blood was up. It was still four against three and this was fine with them.

The Danebury trio spread out as the wolf men simultaneously attacked.

The lead man went straight at Parrish, his belief in his combat skills making him supremely confident. There were nine circles above the line on his neck after all. And no one he knew had a bigger trophy tally.

Parrish threw his longbow aside and stood wide footed, his right leg leading his left, hands raised before him at chest level. He locked onto his opponent's eyes. The wolf man's cry turned into a triumphant shout as he saw the tall man now did not even have a weapon. This would be easy. He wanted another trophy.

Parrish wanted answers.

Closing fast, the wolf man swung his battle axe in a vicious overhead chop, aiming for the cleft where the tall man's neck joined the shoulder.

Parrish used the basic bayonet attack counter. To his opponent's surprise, rather than back away or attempt to retreat to avoid the intended blow, Parrish lunged forward at the last moment, stepping inside the man's attack. He parried the downward strike with his left forearm against the Neolithic man's wrist, simultaneously thrusting his right arm up past his opponents left ear. He drove his right armpit into the man's left shoulder while hooking his raised right arm around his opponent's neck. With a savage twist he pulled the man off his feet, clamping his right forearm across his attacker's throat and continued his turn to put the man between him and the ground. Off balance, they both crashed together onto the snowy earth, the Neolithic man landing flat on his back. His arms flailed about but his axe was ineffective as Parrish squeezed, choking the man of air, and he began to kick and struggle. Parrish locked his legs around the man's lower body and clamped down with everything he had, squeezing the man to near unconsciousness, only then taking a moment to look to his friends to see how they fared, or in case he needed to be aware of any second attack.

At that same moment the two middle wolf men both launched at Tomps. Individual greed for the easy trophy of a young and inexperienced looking lad actually worked against them. They got in each other's way and as they charged in the pair jostled, shoulder to shoulder, axes in their right hands raised.

Tomps stood ready. If the attacking men had been more observant, they might have noticed that his stance was much like the tall man off to their left. Then they might have been more wary.

Tomps gripped his war hammer at the very end of its shaft and to his attackers surprise he swung it in a wide, sideways arc coming in from his right. The long length of the weapon gave it massive impetus and it crashed into the side of the first man at chest height, striking him hard across the left arm midway between the elbow and shoulder. The man cried out in pain and was driven into his companion close by on his right, knocking this man off balance, before the first man with the now useless, broken left arm fell to the ground.

As the second man staggered to his right Tomps dropped his war hammer and leapt for him and they clashed together. Both men went full length into the snow with a loud wet splash, the wolf man keeping hold of his axe. It was a fatal mistake, the formidable weapon being useless as long as his opponent clung to him. The pair rolled in the snow, locked together. Even so Parrish's sideways glance was in time to see when, as Tomps became topmost during their roll, the youngster's right hand, snake-strike fast, whipped the flint dagger from his belt where it lay tucked in, snug against the small of his back. The roll continued and the boy disappeared from sight. Although Parrish never saw it, the sudden, involuntary arching of the wolf man's body on top of his young friend told him the dagger had struck home. The rolling stopped, Tomps now holding his opponent in a lethal embrace, until the body stopped thrashing.

And while all this was happening Klud clashed with his own opponent in the more traditional form of Neolithic combat. He found it difficult to resist running to meet his man but understood that his opponents speed would be to his disadvantage. Klud leant forward to try and absorb some of the wolf man's impact and concentrated on blocking the man’s strike. With a loud, wooden ‘clack’ the two club shafts locked together and the men thudded hard together, also face to face. The wolf man sneered into Klud’s face and pushed hard while Klud tried to counter by pushing back, retreating as he did so. The sneering man sensed victory and pressed harder. But Klud had picked up a few tips himself from his fighting friends over the years. As his opponent felt his target lose ground, he leant on in, at which point Klud brought his knee hard up into the man's groin. Pained surprise flashed onto the previously sneering features and with an agonised gasp the man leaned over his white agony of pain, which enabled Klud to simply step aside and let the man’s momentum carry him past in a groaning, groin clutching stoop. The Danebury man brought his war club down and smashed it into the man's spine right at the nape of the neck. It was a perfectly timed blow, and the wolf man was dead before he hit the ground.

Klud just stood there, looking down in satisfaction before turning his head to the left to see how his friends were faring. Tomps was just squirming out from underneath the dead man. Parrish still had his own man in a chokehold, but both were looking back at Klud in horror.

Before anyone could do or say anything, there was an unmistakable sound that closely resembled the bite of an axe chopping into a log. Klud turned around to see the man whose arm Tomps had moments earlier broken, standing right behind him, axe raised to strike. But the blow never came. The wolf man's eyes glazed over and he just dropped to his knees, before slumping forward. Klud had to step smartly aside as the body face planted in the snow beside him. He immediately saw the gaping slash of the axe wound in the back of the head before he looked back up to see a wide eyed, terrified looking Luke standing there. The bloody flint headed axe was still clutched in his outstretched hand.

Instantly realising what had happened, Klud just nodded to Luke who nodded hesitantly back while still continuing to hold the bloody weapon in his fist out before him, seemingly not quite sure what to do with it.

The sound of many approaching feet broke their gaze and everyone, now all on their feet, spun back towards the hillfort, instantly on guard, Parrish still keeping the arm lock around his prisoner's throat.

The warriors of Cornan-Tullock had gathered just out of harm's way before the scene of the fighting and were staring at the Danebury men in silence, stunned at the astounding, deadly efficiency of these strangers.

"No one else has to die here!" hissed Parrish, breaking the sudden hush. "I just want some answers."

The lead man of the warrior group simply raised his hands.

"We will not fight with you." he said quietly. "We are all happy to follow the word of Dannu."

Parrish was the only man who didn't fully understand what that meant but he did not dwell on it.

"Then just stay where you are while I talk to this..." he hauled the half conscious wolf man around to face him. Tomps and Klud closed up to their Chieftain. Luke was being helped by the older man. The holy one was still in shock at what he had done. A keen eye would have seen his hands shaking at his sides. Klud pulled him close with one arm, protective of his friend now.

Everyone was now watching in silence as Parrish's attention turned back to the limp wolf man. He callously slapped him back to consciousness.

"Wha... what?" the man blurted.

"Quiet!" barked Parrish. "Listen to me. Listen to me." The wolf man took a deep breath that seemed to revive him and he became suddenly alert. Alert to the rough hands gripping his shirt front. Alert to the tall man's frightening gaze blazing at him. And alert to the eyes of everyone else on him. "Tell me what I need to know." continued Parrish, apparently prepared to bargain with the cold hearted killer. "Tell me what I want to know, and I give you my word of honour that I will not kill you."

The wolf man could feel the hate of everyone radiating out towards him. He turned to look away from the tall man's gaze but Parrish held him firm.

"Where can I find the leader of this wolf clan?" The words came out hard and even.

"And... and if I do tell you?"

"Then you have my word. I will not kill you."

There was a stony silence. Which dragged on. Parrish quickly lost patience. This man had just tried to kill him. This man had just tried to kill his friends and one of them had been quite prepared to strike down Klud while his back was turned. He angrily shook the wolf man by his jacket front and shouted into his face.

"WELL!"

"They... The wolf den" which he pronounced as *Faol-Sid*, "is off towards the sunrise. Three days travel. The village on the edge of the cliff." He added as if that explained everything.

Parrish just looked on baffled, but the words sparked something in Luke's mind and he jerked out of his daze, eager to help the Chieftain.

"I... I know this place. It is called *Baile oir Creige*." Which basically meant, 'village on the cliff'.

"*Faol-Sid.*" corrected Parrish's prisoner, some of his cocky arrogance returning. "The wolf den. And they will come for me here and for this village of theirs. Then you will all feel their anger."

Parrish just scoffed and looked the man in the eye.

"This village is no longer under their control. It is back in the hands of its villagers." He looked up at the warrior crowd before him. They all looked suddenly grateful at the declaration. He eyed them all coldly.

"Is this the man who killed your Chieftain and your holy man?" he asked them all.

"Yes." Was the brief, flat reply from the lead warrior.

"I have what I need now. He is all yours." said Parrish grimly and with one arm extended he thrust the wolf man out towards the crowd.

"You... you gave your word that you would not kill me." bleated the man, only now truly realising that he was fighting for his life.

"True enough." said Parrish. "And I am a man of honour, I cannot kill you. But, I do not have to save you either. Take him." Again he offered the man to the crowd.

The wolf man flung up his arms to shield his face as many arms from the crowd reached out to grab him. As he was pulled squirming into the throng of warriors several more arms were raised, each clutching a flint dagger.

The last wolf man let out a terrified squeal, which turned into a cry as the weapons plunged down and Parrish turned away as he began screaming. And continued screaming, for Parrish was pretty sure the man was still alive as they started to cut him up.

A few moments later there was silence. Parrish turned again to face the crowd. Klud was now at his right, still with a supporting arm around Luke's shoulder. Tomps was at his left, the front of his shirt glistening with fresh blood. He had already retrieved his war hammer and was leaning on it as if nothing untoward had just happened.

The lead warrior from Cournan-Tullock stepped forward and held out the dripping head of the wolf man.

"We killed him but the trophy is surely yours."

"I do not want it." Parrish shook his head. "Do what you will with it."

"But we are in your debt."

"Well." There was a pause. "You can repay that debt by offering us hot food and a warm bed for the night."

"It would be our honour." The man opened his arms to indicate the crowd behind him. This was greeted with a sea of nods.

Parrish finally allowed a small grin to cross his features. He looked to his companions, who all nodded too.

"Then we accept your kind offer." he said magnanimously.

There were grins from the crowd then and they parted to make a clear pathway for Dannu's man up to the open hillfort gate behind them.

14

That afternoon the four Danebury men found themselves asked into the Cournan-Tullock shrine hut.

They had earlier been given a standard hut in which to recuperate, clean up and warm up after their combat outside the village gate. But now they were asked to a meeting in the great hut. They were not intimidated or concerned about entering another village's most holy place. It was an invitation after all and besides, they had shown their worth in battle. No one wanted to mess with them and there was an overriding feeling of gratitude from the local occupants over the immediate freeing of their village from this mysterious 'cult of the wolf'.

They walked in undaunted and were led to the double stall that was the seat of their dead Chieftain, immediately to the left of the large Dannu shrine. The four all gleaned the same information about the village as they crossed the floor and passed around the bright central hearth, scanning left and right as they went.

Cournan-Tullock was not a large village. It seemed comparable in size to Olann-bre judging by the number of people they spied. About seventy or so souls, Parrish guessed. Perhaps forty odd warriors, half that again of adult women and the rest made up of children of different ages. But unlike Olann-bre, this place at least seemed to be a solid, functioning village. No one looked particularly starved. The warriors were well turned out and had a steady, not desperate eye. And yet he could see that a handful of hard, ruthless men could rule over these people by fear easily enough. After all, he thought, it had worked for the Normans after 1066. Then, twenty thousand organised men from Normandy under William the conqueror controlled around three million English Saxons by fear and ruthless retribution for any indiscretions.

It might make the question Parrish wanted to ask a bit difficult, but that wasn't going to stop him from asking it. Later though, he conceded, let's see what they want first.

Once the group reached the Chieftains stall they stepped just inside, turned and looked back out at the small sea of faces gazing back. Faces that were a bit puzzled, a bit scared but it seemed mostly relieved. As far as they were concerned, they had a lot to thank these strangers for. Something of a new experience for them all.

The man who had been the lead warrior earlier stepped up, arms open.

“We have asked you here because we are in your debt. We are happy to offer you warmth and shelter but also have a bit of a surprise for you.”

Parrish's eyebrows went up, but no one spoke.

“The wolf men killed our Chieftain as a show of force.” the lead man continued. “They also killed our holy man *and* another holy man who appeared later, asking about what was going on.” There was a gasp of realisation from Luke and shaking of heads from Klud and Tomps. “And yet the youngster our Holy man had been training before the pair intended to set off to the great temple, well, we kept the lad hidden from the wolf man’s axe.”

Parrish nodded at that with an understanding smile. Small victories. During escape and evasion training, it was drilled into the men that if you were captured and the situation seemed hopeless, take heart from any small victories you can create. No matter how small they might seem it was resistance and defiance, even if the oppressors weren't aware of it.

The spokesman flung back an arm and a young boy, very possibly in his early teens, stepped out from the crowd and moved up besides the spokesman, hands apparently clasped behind his back, and eyed them in silence.

"Well, this is indeed good news, but I'm not sure what this has to do with us?" Parrish tried to keep too much curiosity out of his voice.

"He... he already has many holy skills." The man saw that he would have to elaborate on their surprise gift. "All of you had a great victory this day and have taken new trophies. This holy boy is here to mark those honours for you." And with that the lad produced from behind his back a peculiarly napped but not unknown looking flint cutting tool and a round, clay pot with unusual markings imprinted around the sides. Parrish knew without having to look that inside that pot was tattooing ink.

Klud and Tomps eyes lit up. Parrish's mouth set in a grim line. Luke just shook his head.

It wasn't completely the reaction the lead man or the silent boy was expecting. Surely any warrior who took a head and survived wanted, almost demanded that his triumph be marked on his neck for all to see?

There was a moment of stony silence before the youngster stepped forward, holding out the objects in his hands.

"Oh, great Chieftain. You would be first?"

Parrish's first thought was that the boy was the ideal candidate for induction into the religious order of the Great Goddess. He was already showing the first signs of the self-important confidence that seemed a pre-requisite attitude for a Holy man. His second thought as he eyed the sharp flint blade was, I don't think so!

"No." he said bluntly.

Confusion showed on every Cornan-Tullock face.

Tomps looked sideways at his tall friend.

"With your permission?" Parrish gave a tight nod. Tomps continued in a proud tone. "My Chieftain already has many marks to show his skill and honour. So many in fact that he chooses whether or not to add another trophy to his neck. The man killed must be deemed worthy by him."

After initially being cross at having another man speak for him, Parrish silently applauded Tomps' creative thinking. His was a good excuse not to be cut and also a deft way of saying how great he was. Parrish struggled to prevent the smile springing onto his face.

The people of the village all stared up at the tall man, the more intelligent of them making the connection that, although this tall stranger had many marks on his neck, including the signs of a *two times* Chieftain killer, there were other trophy kills that were not deemed worthy to be included. Just how many warriors had died at this huge man's hands?

The holy boy coughed, stopped from what he thought was his duty, bowed in respect to Parrish then without a word turned to Tomps. The younger warrior stepped forward with Klud one pace behind and together they took their turns to suffer the cutting flint for their personal glory and the honour of the Earth Goddess.

Finally, the boy turned to Luke, once more holding out the tattooing tools..

"I say no also." the small man said quietly.

"But, my friend." Klud turned to him in sudden dismay. "You saved my life. I would take it as a great honour and a sign of respect if you took the mark." There were nods from everyone, especially those who had witnessed the deed earlier.

"But... it is not known for one such as I..."

"Luke." Parrish interrupted, drawing everyone's attention. "Tell me, did you strike that man down to save your friends life?" There was a nod of reply. "Did you also save the life of a great warrior of Dannu?" Another nod. "And in so doing, did you also kill an enemy of the Earth Goddess?" Luke could not deny it. "Then I... no, *we* all say, take the mark and wear it with great honour."

Luke bowed to Dannu's man, turned, stepped up to the boy and slowly shrugged out of his winter jacket to expose his bare neck.

A chorus of gasps came from the crowd as they all caught sight of the necklace about Luke's throat. The series of drilled stones that hung there, all miniatures of the stones in the circle of the great temple of Avebury.

"A Holy one!" came a breathless gasp of realisation from somewhere in the watching throng.

Everyone there then bowed to Luke, including the apprentice Holy boy. When the lad straightened up Luke just said softly.

"Do what you must."

And everyone there felt privileged to watch as the deed was done.

A rather timid woman stepped bravely up from the front of the watching people and after a swift application of the healing poultice was applied to the necks of the three bleeding men, retreated back into the throng.

There was another stony silence.

Parrish returned his gaze to the lead man, still standing at the head of the crowd. The young tattooist appeared to automatically take up his position just behind and to one side of him in a very familiar looking formation.

"Just what is your name?" Parrish asked the warrior.

"Er... Barron." the man answered in surprise.

"Well, Barron. It is clear that the people of Cournan-Tullock will now need to choose a new Chieftain, and I am thinking that you are the most likely man!" Parrish nodded and raised his eyebrows to indicate the people at the man's back.

"What?!... Why..." Barron turned to face the gathered villagers behind him and there were lots of nods. "It is not agreed, but you certainly seem to be the best man at this moment." Parrish's voice spun him back. "And I think that you are about to find out that being a Chieftain is not always an easy thing."

"Eh"

"I would like to borrow some of your warriors."

It was suddenly all going a bit fast for Barron and he just gaped in reply before stuttering.

"They... they are not *my* men..."

"But they could be." And Parrish could see more nods, specifically from the men in the crowd. "This village, your village, is now back in the hands of its people. But only while you all remain shut in behind your gate. And you are not alone in this. We have already visited another village that lives in fear of the wolf men too, hiding behind their own closed gate. I do not believe this is how the people of Dannu should live. Keeping their homes safe but not being able to roam Dannu's land, free to hunt, to travel and to meet and worship without fear.

This 'cult of the wolf' is against all of that. Against allowing the freedom of men, against allowing travel to the solstice gathering and against the respecting and worship of Dannu."

There was total silence in the shine hut as everyone there hung on each word Parrish spoke. The words were clear and true, reaching to the furthest corners of the round hut. Even the children were silent, not fully understanding the words but grasping the power of the voice and the great significance of the moment.

Parrish took a deep breath.

"I now know where the den of these wolf men is, in this so named 'village on the cliff'. So, I intend to go there and put an end to this cult of the wolf. To hunt down these wolf men in their lair and rid this land of their danger and disruption and to put an end to all the deaths they are causing on Dannu's land. So, I want some of the warriors of Cournan-Tullock to follow me. No, to join me, in this task for Dannu. Not just for the future safety of this village, but for all other villages too. To return this land back to the way it was. The way it should be. The way of the brave and honest warrior. Back to the way of the Earth Goddess!"

The stunned silence that followed was complete. The sound of the flames crackling in the central hearth was suddenly loud, almost like distant thunder. Almost as if the Goddess herself were applauding his speech.

Unbidden, Klud stepped up to Parrish's right while Tomps simultaneously took position on his left. Luke joined Klud, and these partners to Parrish of Dane-bre stood shoulder to shoulder with him, solid and magnificent, their chests almost bursting with pride at being associated with this great man.

Barron bowed deeply to Parrish and also took a deep breath himself before answering.

"But I am not their Chieftain. I..."

Parrish gave him another knowing nod and Barron turned to face the people of Cournan-Tullock once more and found them all staring back at him.

Then came the first bow from a warrior, follow almost immediately by more, all directed at him. Then even more and before anyone realised it, everyone there was bowing deeply to Barron.

"It looks like the people here have decided." came Parrish's voice behind him. The chosen one spun back to face the tall man again and just shrugged, astounded, and his hands splayed open in a 'how did this happen?' gesture.

"I know." Parrish laughed. "That is sort of how it happened for me too. So, come and sit with me, *Chieftain* Barron, and I will explain how many men I would like, and why. Then you can decide if you will permit me to take some of *your* men to come with me and mine."

15

The Danebury men were back in their ‘recuperating’ hut, waiting.

Parrish had asked his question and the newly crowned Chieftain of Cournan-Tullock, still unsure of his new position, had in turn asked Parrish to wait while he put the request to his men. Parrish didn't blame him for being cautious and uncertain, and if truth were known, when it came to leading fighting men, he would rather have volunteers at his back then men ordered to do so against their will. And there was also the point to consider that Cournan-Tullock was not a large village. If Chieftain Barron did give his men permission to deploy with Parrish, just how many could be spared while still retaining enough warriors to protect their village and families?

Parrish was considering his own options, especially if the four of them had to carry on alone, and just how he could achieve what he had earlier announced to everyone that he would do. He sat, pensive and silent, staring into the central fire.

The others picked up on the mood within the hut, while snowflakes drifted gently down outside. Not heavy enough snow to build up anything resembling a layer on the ground, but a light dusting was slowly accumulating across the landscape.

Tomps looked across at his Chieftain, coughed then said quietly, just to break the silence.

“As Klud would say, interesting times lay ahead, my Chieftain.”

Parrish gave a short laugh at the youngster's crudely diplomatic attempt to see his leader’s thoughts. These men had put their lives on the line, stood shoulder to shoulder with him and he suddenly felt it unfair to keep anything back. Especially as whatever happened next, he knew they would still be by his side. To the bitter end if necessary.

“I was just wondering what the new Chieftain will do.” he explained. “I cannot now say what that might be.”

“He will do what is right.” chimed in Luke, absently fingering his tender neck.

“Yes.” agreed Parrish. “But right for who? Us, himself or Cournan-Tullock?”

That stopped everyone dead.

“But we go on anyway.” said Klud with quiet determination. “We will also do what is right.”

There were nods from the other men, although Luke added.

“If we live through it.”

“If we live?” repeated Klud a slightly incredulous tone to his voice. He rose to his feet. “There is no *if*. Look at us.” He pointed to each man as he spoke their names. “We have ‘two men at a time’ Tomps.” He pointed at Parrish. “We have the great Chieftain of Dane-bre.” He did not add Dannu’s man, although he wanted to. He next pointed at Luke. “We walk with Dannu! There can be no doubt. There is no *if* we live. We *will* live!” He finished proudly. Standing before them, feet well-spaced, balled fists on his hips and chin jutting out, to Parrish he looked a perfect copy of the pose in that famous Hogarth picture of Henry the eighth.

Parrish couldn't help it. He burst out laughing, and everyone joined in, Klud at the centre of it, glowing with pride for himself, his companions and their brave achievements.

At that moment a call came from outside.

“Enter.” barked Parrish, the smile still on his face as the door blanket swept back and Chieftain Barron stepped in.

“It is good to see you all in good spirits.” The man said, although his facial expression was deadly serious.

The smiles dropped from the faces of the others. Klud dropped back into a sit so as not to be seen standing over his Chieftain while others were present. Chieftain Barron moved to join them and also sat, between Luke and Tomps, facing Parrish.

They were all expecting bad news while Chieftain Barron stared momentarily into the flame as he gathered his thoughts.

"I will tell you all straight." He said, then looked up. "I put it to my men." Parrish gave a small nod at that which Barron accepted before continuing. "And I tell you I had to deny some of them when they all wanted to go with you." Grins broke out on all the faces then. "I can say to you all here, it makes me greatly proud to be the leader of such warriors. That they would all be ready to follow men they had only met shortly before, into a possible battle, somewhere they have never been. All for the honour of Dannu and Cournan-Tullock."

Tomps, Klud and Luke all nodded firmly in agreement. Parrish caught Barron's eye and the two of them understood that part of the reasons for the men's willingness to go was perhaps to try and claim back some lost pride. But that did not take away from the fact that every warrior in the village was prepared to back Parrish and his men.

"You have become leader of a fine village." was Parrish's acknowledgement. "But I see your problem."

"Yes. I must keep enough men back to ensure the village's survival. If, Dannu forbid, no warriors return, I must still be able to maintain the village." There were sudden, understanding nods from the men who were not Chieftains. "So I have decided to give you two hands of my men."

It wasn't as many men as he would have liked, but it was more than Parrish had hoped for. He knew he was being given one quarter of Cournan-Tullock's fighting men. The more he considered it the more it seemed about the right number. Add on Klud and Tomps and he had just about all the men he could comfortably control. Mind you, he also had no idea how big a pack of wolf men were and whether or not any of the warriors of this 'village on the cliff' would back them up. Still, if the numbers weren't so big that they got immediately massacred, they were at least in with a shout.

"Ten men... er, two hands of men will do. And I must say that I understand and agree with your thinking. The people of Cournan-Tullock picked the right man for Chieftain."

"Agreed." chorused the others beside him.

Barron smiled and held up one hand.

"I thank you all for that, and I must say, I too agree with your earlier words, Parrish." Parrish smiled at the sudden Chieftain to Chieftain familiarity. "You are right. Being Chieftain is no easy thing. My first decision has been difficult."

"Welcome to the club." Parrish laughed, then laughed again at the men's puzzlement over his odd word. "Thus it is for a leader of a village, and I think that it will always be so."

Barron nodded and rose to his feet.

"Thank you for accepting my decision without argument." he said, although as Chieftain he did not have to say it would have made no difference. It was purely an acknowledgement to Chieftain Parrish. "I will ensure you have what you need, and I will make sure my men will be provisioned and ready to go at first light tomorrow."

His words were strong, firm and most Chieftain like. The other men rose to their feet and bowed to Chieftain Barron, even Parrish.

The Chieftain of Cournan-Tullock nodded in reply then spun and left the hut without another word.

The men eyed each other for several long moments before Luke said quietly.

"Well. He grew into his Chieftain's boots very quickly."

"You are not wrong there." agreed Parrish, and as one they all laughed before the hut fell silent as everyone began to consider what tomorrow might bring.

*

Late that night the sky had cleared and the dawn, on what Parrish if he had known, would have celebrated as New Year's Day, broke crisp with a bright sky. He and his men emerged from their hut into a Christmas card image of chilled white ground and frosting everywhere. The low early morning sun made everything glitter, but the natural beauty of it all was lost to everyone gathered outside the tall man's hut.

Chieftain Barron stood at the head of a silent and patient gaggle of well armed men, their eyes all locked onto Parrish as he emerged from behind the frost encrusted door blanket. Klud, Tomps and Luke were but a pace behind and as they also appeared, took in the full picture before them.

Behind Chieftain Barron and his selected men was a second, larger group. It seemed everyone had turned out to witness this unprecedented event. The rest of Cournan-Tullock's warriors were looking on and behind them stood the gathered women of the village, some clutching babes in their arms. Older children stood at their parents sides and the crisp, sharp air seemed somehow to magnify the silence as every soul there looked to Parrish.

The man at the centre of it all took a moment to scan all the faces. His three companions used that moment to soak in the astounding sight and their hearts lifted with pride at their closeness to the great man who had brought this unusual event to be.

Parrish bowed, ostensibly to Chieftain Barron, but the whole village bowed back. If he was expecting this or was surprised by it, his face never betrayed any emotion. He simply stepped up and said to Chieftain Barron.

"These are the men you are loaning to me?"

The ten straightened proudly up as their Chieftain nodded and stepped aside, offering the group to him with a sweep of his arm. The men's faces showed surprise as, instead of speaking a greeting, the tall man simply said.

"Form a line before me, so I can look at you all."

In silence the men shuffled into a raggedy, unevenly spaced line abreast. Parrish went to the left end of the line and, aware of everybody looking on in puzzlement, began to walk slowly along the line. As he passed each man he looked briefly into his face, speaking as he went.

"I know you have all stepped up of your own choice, and I am grateful. Your Chieftain has chosen you for your fighting skills and we all hope that you will return, bringing great honour to your village. But I want you all to know also that some, maybe all of you, maybe all of us," he indicated to himself and his own men. "May not return. Know this now. Know this so if any man does not want to face this, now is the time to let me know. Step aside and your Chieftain will find another to take your place."

In immediate response to this the line of men before him, to a man, bristled with indignation and thrust their chests out.

To everyone's surprise Parrish laughed out loud and turned to Chieftain Barron.

"You have chosen well, my friend. They are all fine men." There was a murmur of approval from the crowd. "We will set off now for this *Baile-oir-Creige*, 'village on the Cliff', this wolf den." He stepped back up to the men and said quietly. "I will do my best for you all, but if there is a battle, there will be deaths. This might be the last time you men will see your families and homes."

"We all understand." Chieftain Barron spoke for everyone. Parrish turned again and reached out his right hand to the man. Barron hesitated, a frown on his face, then hesitantly reached out his own hand. Parrish grasped his opposites forearm and Barron did likewise.

"Be well, Chieftain Barron."

"You also, my friend. Go with Dannu."

There was a solemn moment before they released and Parrish turned to his friends.

Well, he thought to himself. I could be leading all these men to their deaths. You should be careful what you wish for, Parrish. Looks like you finally get to be the squad leader you always wanted to be, and it's not quite what you expected now, is it, eh?

"Let us go."

The three picked up their food and water bags. The ten warriors took their lead and did the same. Parrish simply watched in silence until everyone's kit was strapped across their bodies and they all held their weapons before them. Parrish was interested to suddenly note that the ten men of Cournan-Tullock each held a long, flint headed spear as well as the usual personal weapons. Not something the people of Dane-bre relied on much, but he made a mental note of it for possible future reference.

He nodded again as everyone became still once more, then he gave an over the shoulder wave like a cavalry commander in an old western movie, and in silence, watched by the whole village of Cournan-Tullock he led his squad away across the crisp ground towards the main gate.

16

As it turned out, to travel from Cournan-Tullock, virtually due east, to the Wolf den of Baile-oir-Creige was approximately thirty miles or fifty kilometres, as the sky spirit flies.

Across unknown ground, the British Army expects progress to be no less than two miles per hour. Parrish and his squad adhered to this, unknown to the Neolithic men, military gauge. The chill weather actually helped in this respect. It was brisk but the winds were very light and the open woodland landscape made cross country travel in the local area fairly obstacle free. Comfortably managing the fifteen miles a day by using Parrish's 'new' yomping method, the fourteen men arrived within sight, but were careful not to be seen by, the 'village on the cliff' almost at last light on the second day.

In silence, Parrish led his men back away from the hillfort a couple of miles until he was absolutely sure they were well out of sight and sound of their target. Only then did he permit the troop to set up camp and even then only with very small cooking fires, hidden in dug out pits in the ground. These mystery 'wolf men' did not know anyone was near, but Parrish was taking no chances. He did not want to risk giving up his crucial element of surprise.

Parrish waited till they had set up the camp, arranged their bedding and were consuming hot food against the chill air before he gathered his men and told them what he wanted to happen next.

Firstly, he arranged a roughly staggered system of changing camp guards through the night. He had enough men to achieve this and still ensure everyone had a good amount of sleep. The men of Cornan-Tullock suddenly saw the advantage of this system and there were several nods of approval and agreement. The next part of his plan was to send pairs of men covertly out towards the hillfort the next day. To watch, unobserved, designated sections of the hillfort to assess how steep the villages approaches were, what the encampments battlements were like and, if any 'wolf men' were seen, how many?

In truth Parrish didn't really care how many of these wolf men were seen at this time. Random sightings by his men of men in wolf skins and wolf skull caps would be a hazy count at best and unless they were all seen the same time, as intelligence gathering this headcount would be useless. But he felt it would help or inspire his men if they might at least get a distant sight of their intended quarry. Parrish also planned to circumnavigate the entire encampment himself and look for any potential chinks in the fort's defensive armour.

So it was agreed that everyone would set out at first light and regroup back at this camp site before night the next evening and then Parrish would hear all the gathered information and hopefully figure out what to do next.

*

The following morning Parrish briefed his men. The frost had gone although he doubted it was more than a few degrees above freezing. The air was crisp, with intermittent cloud cover and it promised to be at least a dry day.

Parrish drew a rough circle in the hard earth with a stick and pointed around it to roughly where he expected each pair would go to overlook their 'section' of the hillfort. His diagram, with its centre circle ringed with dots to mark the rough positions of the observation posts, or OP's, reminded him of a clock face with no hands.

"Now, know this. We are just watching today, to see what we might see. There might be areas that are used more by the people, and some may be used less which could help us with some sort of attack. There could even be some sort of smaller back gate we do not yet know about. Who can say, but we will watch for this day to see. It might be that nothing at all will be revealed but it is important you all understand one thing. No one here must be seen by the people of the village. We stand a better chance of success if they do not know we are coming and so do not get the chance to be ready for our arrival.

These wolf men do not know it, but we are hunting them now. So, just as if you were on any hunt, my friends, quiet, hidden and watchful is the way of things this day. I will be doing a full circle around the hillfort myself, and I have my own ideas too. So, we all meet back here before nightfall, yes?" There were universal nods. "Good. Then we can plan what to do next." All the warriors appreciated the 'we' in his words. It was an honour to be included in the thoughts of a Chieftain. And an even greater honour to be closely involved in an adventure with Dannu's man. What a tale they would have to tell around the campfire. If they survived, of course.

"I trust you have already chosen partners?" Parrish continued. There were more nods. "OK. Off we go then. And remember, stalking, as in a hunt. Silent and unseen."

"We will not fail you." came Klud's voice from the group, followed by murmurs of agreement.

"Good men." Parrish finally offered them all a smile. "One step at a time is the way. Slowly, slowly, catchy monkey."

And to a small sea of suddenly confused faces, he turned and led them off through the trees.

As they drew nearer, pairs of men silently broke off and headed away to their designated areas of observation, Parrish taking a few moments to realise they knew which way to go because they were approaching, as they all had on their initial arrival, from due west towards the village. The men's actions were silent, deadly efficient and if one wasn't paying attention, another pair could easily leave this shrinking group unnoticed. It impressed Parrish and reminded him that he must practise what he preached. He must be sure to encircle the camp and see what he could with his military eye, without himself being seen. Time to switch to full combat mode, he decided, and went tactical to the extent of applying some of the remaining camouflage cream kept in one of his webbing pouches to his face and the backs of his hands. Finally, he too crept silently away through the woodland, well back from the tree line that marked the open approaches to the 'village on the cliff'. Which, after several careful hidden approaches to the edge of the tree line, where he had viewed several sections of the hillfort, he realised was well named as he came upon an arresting sight.

Early in the afternoon, although it was difficult to judge through the cloudy sky, Parrish bellied up between the last of the leafless trees to be confronted by the eastern aspect of the hillfort. Or more exactly, the vertical approximately eighty foot high sheer cliff face of the 'village on the cliff'.

He couldn't tell if this side of the hill that was topped by Baile-oir-Creige had long ago somehow weathered away, or maybe the hill had been a normal dome shaped feature in the landscape which has suffered some sort of ground fissure and a huge landslip sometime in its past. Either way, Parrish found himself examining open mouthed this almost perpendicular rock face of a rich red colour as best he could from his mid-distant viewpoint. Darker streaks and numerous black blotches on the rock face looked like possible hand and foot holds but even during the day it looked like a very challenging climb.

On the plus side, at the top of this imposing cliff which took up the whole eastern face of the hillside, there was clearly no palisade defence wall. It made sense. There was no way anyone was going to gain access to the village from there, so why go to the time and effort to build something that was completely unnecessary.

Parrish spent more time studying that facet of the hillfort defences than any other aspect of the village perimeter, before finally returning to the covert camp off to the west.

The hidden sun was low behind the clouds and the light was beginning to fade when he got back and found himself to be last man in. Hot food was ready for him. As he squatted down to eat and soak up some heat from the fire, he smiled.

"I did not see a single man as I went around the hillfort." There were grins at the compliment. "But I suppose most of you saw me, eh?"

There were murmurs and a few uncomfortable looking faces when the men suddenly weren't sure if they should admit that the Chieftain wasn't as stealthy as themselves. Even if they had the advantage of being stationary while he was on the move. But Parrish helped them out. He laughed as he saw their expressions.

"OK. It is clear that I need a few hints and tips from the more skilful men around me."

Everyone laughed then, before his face fell serious once more..

"Now, to business." He ignored the brief puzzlement over the English word. "Let us see if we noticed the same things today."

Everyone huddled together but it soon became obvious as each pair made their report that no one had a breakthrough piece of information, or potential point of observation that could possibly be exploited to some advantage. In fact, the only thing everyone agreed on was that the village behind the palisade wall was almost *too* quiet. There was very little movement along the battlement's walkway inside this 'wolf den' wall, and not a single person had ventured outside during the whole day. Several warriors did mention the fact that the actual palisade wall was high. Very high in fact. Much higher than their own village. Parrish had to agree. He had noticed it too. By his estimation it was a good ten feet higher than Dane-bre's defences, definitely higher than the more hastily erected wall of Olann-bre and easily three times the height of the admittedly low walls of the holy village of Avebury.

"Yes. I too saw that." He confirmed. "I wonder if it is really big to keep attackers out, or perhaps to keep the villagers inside, inside?"

“That would make sense if you add it to the lack of people movement.” said Tomps, a suddenly pensive look on his face. “Like the people of Cournan-Tullock, perhaps the people of Baile-oir-Creige may not be so happy for their village to be a wolf den.”

“Well thought out.” Parrish praised his young friend. “So we all agree the wall is very high, but it still does not help us find a way to somehow deal with the wolf men.”

“Yes.” said Klud slowly. He looked to his tall friend. “Too high for a boost up then?”

None of the Cournan-Tullock men grasped the man with a badly broken nose’s meaning but the solemn look on the Chieftains face as he nodded in agreement was enough.

“So we have nothing to show for our day's work.” said Tomps quietly.

“No... not quite.” said Parrish. “The way I see it now is that we have two options.” Three if you count just walking away, he thought but did not say. “We have to somehow draw all the wolf men out into the open, or we must tackle them inside the village.”

“But no one came out today.” said one man.

“And how would we draw out *all* the wolf men in one go?” added Tomps.

Parrish gave the lad a dry, humourless smile.

“Quite... er, agreed.”

“So...?” Klud left the question hanging.

“So, I guess we are going to have to go in after them.” said Parrish in a blunt, final sounding voice.

17

It was after midnight, perhaps three or four hours before the dawn. The total cloud cover kept the temperature slightly up. If Parrish had taken the time to check the little Survival Aids thermometer attached to his combat jacket zip, he would have seen it was a comfortable five degrees.

But he did not. There was a much bigger issue to deal with now.

He had a plan. It wasn't a good plan and he didn't like it. If the warriors facing him across the flickering glow of the little campfire were not happy either, their faces did not show it. He was a Chieftain. He had greatly feared and respected warriors at his side and walked with a holy man. His words were more than enough.

This was a basic plan. It was so basic Parrish couldn't believe it was being accepted without question. He wanted his warriors to sneak up to the main gate of the wolf den of Baile-oir-Creige, hide in the shadowed darkness at the foot of the gates and be ready at first light when Parrish would open the gates from the inside and let them in. Then they would all sweep through the village, catching the wolf men either in their huts or as they were emerging, and eliminate them all in the name of Dannu. Parrish bit his lip but otherwise hid his feelings.

Unknown to anyone, it was a moment of cosmic irony that his scheme was all but identical to that of the Chieftain of Olann-bre, which unknown to Parrish had already proved successful against his own home.

The main difference was that Parrish's plan decreed him to be the one to unlock the main gate. And how was he going to get inside? He intended to climb the eastern cliff face! In the dark!!

There were dubious looks when he announced this but no one else was in a hurry to volunteer to go in his place... apart from...

“I will go with you.” said Tomps firmly, the moment Parrish had outlined that part.

“There is no need.” Parrish waved the offer away. He did not want to have his brave young friend die uselessly too. “I am quite strong enough to open a village gate on my own.” He fudged a reason to deny the lad.

“You will need someone to watch out for you while you do that.” countered Tomps. “And if we are discovered in the village before we reach the gate, I will keep those others busy long enough for you to complete the task.”

Damn the rise of the thinking man, thought Parrish, but could not refute the logic.

“And I will come to.” Klud joined in, once he realised what might be involved once his friends gained access into the village.

“No, no.” Parrish was more blunt this time. “I need you, my right hand, to lead these brave men.” He swept his arm to indicate the ten Cournan-Tullock men, who sat up straighter in honour. “And to be ready the instant the gate opens. I would trust no one else to lead them through.” He did not know how much longer that would keep his friend in the land of the living, but he wanted to give him every moment he could.

There was a long moment of silence. Everyone looked to their leader, waiting for the Chieftain to give the word that would signal the start of the whole operation.

Parrish looked back at all the expectant faces, lit bright, reflecting the light of the little fire they were all gathered around. At that moment unable to hold their eyes, he glanced down at his hands, still dark striped with cammo cream. He suddenly remembered his face was still cammoed up too, and yet no one had said a word. Classic Army, he grinned, to let him sit there looking silly. He looked back up and said with a smile.

"If you want to get to the main gate unseen, you will all be needing to mask those glowing white faces of yours."

The men looked at each other, eyes widening as for the first time they looked into their fellows faces and did not see the man, but the white flag in the dark night of a pale skinned face.

"Rub up some mud in your hands then smear dark stripes across your foreheads, nose, cheeks and neck."

There were several grins as distant memories of making mud pies and daubing as children were recalled, then the men dug into the soft wet earth with their bare hands and in moments were busy blacking up.

In very short order, to a man they were dark, muddy faced and Parrish nodded in satisfaction.

"That will work well on such a night." There were shaded nods, split into white toothy grins. "As of now, my friends, you are all dark warriors of the night. *My* dark warriors and I will always remember you this way. We go now to do our best for Dannu and each other." He stood up and the rest followed. Almost unseen the whole time, he caught sight of Luke at the back, blacked up like the rest. He wanted to tell his holy friend he had nothing to contribute. This was a combat mission and he should remain behind and stay safe. But he did not. He respected the little man too much.

"Tomps, with me." He barked in a suddenly cold and military manner. "Klud, lead off the rest and, Dannu willing, we will win the day." He hoped those final words didn't sound too hollow. Stretching out a hand to Klud, who grasped his tall friends forearm in response, he said softly. "See you when it is over."

"And you." said Klud, who then bowed, broke his grip and turned and led off without another word.

Parrish turned to see Tomps kicking wet loamy soil over the hissing fire. Suddenly it was very dark and the Chieftain of Dane-bre's voice just said into the night.

"Let us away then."

*

The two Danebury men were standing at the base of the cliff and the silence was palpable. Roughly a couple of hours before dawn, the cloud cover was still complete, making it warm enough but so dark you could hardly see your hand in front of your face.

Parrish looked up to where their destination lay, the summit, somewhere up there in the blackness above them.

"How on earth are we supposed to climb that?" Parrish wasn't really asking Tomps, just speaking out loud almost in desperation. "This whole idea is completely stupid."

"We must try." said Tomps quietly. It was the right answer but Parrish could sense the futility of their task in his tone.

Perhaps we will be lucky and get high enough up the cliff before we fall, thought Parrish, which he knew would be the inevitable result. At least then we would die quickly once we've plummeted to the ground. He grimaced, reached tentatively out and placed his palms on the cold rock face. At arm's length he could just about see the limestone directly in front of him and there were actually a couple of handholds visible. But no one would climb a cliff just by feel.

The sinking feeling in his chest increased. A resigned tone weighted his voice also as he repeated quietly.

"How can this be done?"

The words had barely passed his lips when a soft light bloomed from behind the pair and the rugged, craggy nature of the rock surface before him became illuminated in a pale blue glow.

Both men spun to look and their jaws hung open as they saw the bright three quarter moon low in the sky, not a hands breadth above the dark horizon, shining through a sudden opening in the cloud cover.

"With Dannu's help!" gasped Tomps in realisation and turned to smile at his tall friend.

Parrish just nodded back.

"I'll take any help I can get at this point." he said in English "Up and away then!" He added in the language of the people.

And as quickly but carefully as they could, the two began to scale the rock face, silently praying for the life saving glow of moonlight to continue.

In truth the two men found that the sheer face of the cliff was anything but. Cracks, lateral shelves, small fissures and lumpy nodules always seemed to be just in reach for the pair and although they were climbing almost side by side, progress was always in the right direction. There seemed no need to move very far laterally to pursue hand or footholds that might help them in their progress. The purchase points on the rock face were either highlighted as they bulged out, or marked as inky black pockets of shadowy recesses. A tentative probe with the fingers or foot and if it was good, a firm grip gave a secure point from which to search out the next hold. The men naturally fell into the three point climbing technique. Have three good points of contact before reaching for the next foot or hand hold.

Tomps had his war hammer slung diagonally across his back like a rifle, a leather thong looped under the mace head and tied off at the base of the long shaft. Parrish found the front pouches of his webbing did not hinder him too much as he climbed, but they did occasionally rub loudly against the rock before him. Now both men thought they had a genuine chance of making the cliff top alive, as long as they had the moonlight to see by, the pair had returned to more tactical thoughts and were trying to be as stealthy as they could.

There was no way to measure the time but no more than perhaps an hour later Tomps heaved himself over the top lip first. Only taking a moment to recover his breath, he then reached back, grasped Parrish's outstretched hand and hauled him to safety too. They both sat grinning then turned to look out and away across the chasm below them. Out past the softly illuminated countryside and sprawling canopy of the great forest. Out to the far horizon and the glowing orb of the moon, now just starting to disappear beneath the horizon.

Parrish gave the moon a salute and nodded to it. The far clouds swirled lazily about and the glow hazed, dimmed then was gone as the celestial satellite became fully obscured by them, leaving just a light glow along the horizon as the first glimmer of the false dawn began to push back the night.

The two shared another grin.

The Goddess is looking after her man, thought Tomps and as he looked at Parrish, Dannu's man, he had the first inkling that perhaps this foolhardy endeavour might somehow actually work. His brief reverie was broken by Parrish's quiet whisper.

"No time now to enjoy the view. Not long till dawn. To the gates then my friend, and no noise."

Tomps nodded, unslung his weapon and the pair glided silently off through the last of the darkness towards the cover of the nearest village hut.

Moving slowly and cautiously, they were careful not to make any sound and be especially wary of the constant threat of stumbling over some unseen trip hazard. A random piece of equipment, drying rack, log pile or even a loose hearth stone might lay in their path, left abandoned outside a hut. They began to cross the village towards the main gate. Most village layouts followed the same basic pattern, but it was still more than a little unnerving to pass unchallenged through a strange encampment in the dark.

The sky continued to slowly lighten and as the pair drew closer to the main gate and the universal, well trodden open 'courtyard' area in front of it, things were becoming clearer. Their timing was perfect and things were going smoothly.

And then they were not.

18

Parrish was just passing the entrance to a roundhouse. It was the last hut before approaching the open area which lay between it and the main gate some forty yards away, the clear space becoming ever more visible in the growing clarity of the dawn light.

Tomps was a few paces behind his Chieftain. He stopped, turned and checked behind them for the umpteenth time. Turning back he was just in time to see a warrior suddenly emerge from the roundhouse door.

Catching unexpected movement out of the corner of his eye, the man looked to his right and momentarily stared at the tall stranger's back as he silently passed by, knowing instantly that the unknown man was an intruder. In a flash the warrior's hand went to the flint dagger tucked into his belt. But he had not looked back to his left.

"ATTACK!" the mystery man shouted loudly into the still air. "Attack... oof!"

Before he could fully raise his weapon, with the obvious intention of plunging it into Parrish's back, Tomps had rushed the man from behind and dropping one shoulder barged him squarely in the middle of his back. Parrish spun at the shout and saw Tomps knocking the unknown man face first to the ground. Before the prostrate warrior could even turn to face his unknown attacker, let alone try to regain his feet, the young Danebury warrior followed up his barge and in one flowing movement brought his war hammer up over his head and down onto the prone man as if he were driving a large stake into the ground. Parrish gritted his teeth as he saw the deadly weapon smash with a wet crunch into the back of the man's skull. Tomps just looked up, saw his Chieftain standing in shocked amazement, and shouted.

"The gate! Go to the gate!"

Parrish just nodded and, with any hope of stealth now gone, turned and sprinted across the courtyard towards the gate and its glaringly obvious horizontal locking bar.

Tomps turned his back to his running Chieftain and moving as quickly as he could, walked backwards across the open ground, eyes scanning left and right looking for new threats, his war hammer at the ready.

Parrish almost slammed into the gate, barely slowing as he approached at speed and arrested his run with the slapping of his palms on the woodwork. He grunted with the effort to push up the slightly sticking and unwieldy crossbar, but it finally lifted free and with a heave he threw it to one side. Pushing the big gate open he was pleased to see Klud and the dark warriors poised right there but said nothing. Turning to find Tomps now standing only a few paces away, his back to the gate and facing the village across the courtyard, a lot of things started to happen at once.

Men were beginning to gather at the far side of the courtyard, quickly increasing in number and stringing out into a line. Some were barely dressed. A couple held bows. All of them held a weapon of some sort. And all of them had wolf pelts across their shoulders and wolf skull skullcaps on their heads.

The dark, muddy faced warriors of Cornan-Tullock seemed compelled to emulate those men opposite and as they rushed in through the gate they also fanned out into a line either side of Parrish and Klud. Parrish called Tomps back and the youngster duly walked backwards to join his friends, always looking forward, his eyes daring the first man to come at him.

There was a silent standoff. The warriors at Parrish's back just stood in the line, like sentries, the spears in their fists pointing skyward, staring in silence at the gathering wolf men, who stared back. It seemed that no one wanted to make the first move. As the last of the wolf men fell into line, Parrish counted fourteen men. Plus the five killed at Cournan-Tullock, he reasoned that these must be all of the remainder. After all, he thought, how many fur clad men does it take to make up a cult? So at least they were evenly matched and if it came to a fight, which it definitely would, they were in with a shout.

Then a tall man, at least for a Neolithic male at perhaps five foot six inches in height, pushed through the middle of the wolf men line and stood at the head of the pack.

"The White Wolf!" someone behind Parrish gasped, and at least half the words were true.

The man held a bow down by his side, an arrow already nocked to its string, but all eyes were drawn to the snow white pelt that draped across his shoulders, and the skull cap he wore of the same colour. Parrish looked at the man's face and was shocked. It was brutally scarred. Ragged, fairly recently healed wounds rippled across both cheeks and down along one side of the jaw line. One pinched scar ran from his hairline down through his left eye and onto his cheek. The eye itself was opaque, clouded and stared blankly.

There were gasps from more of the dark warriors which made this obvious pack leader grin wickedly, while Parrish felt his men's morale beginning to sink at the sight of this striking individual who oozed menace. But it was still almost man to man and so he still thought they were in with a chance.

Then more shuffling could be heard and additional warriors began to gather behind the line of wolf men. It was the warriors of Baile-oir-Creige. And the wolf pack leader, this brutally intimidating alpha male, grinned some more as he glanced back to see these 'back up' men gathering. It took mere moments before just about every man of fighting age stood behind the wolf line. There were easily forty plus men and it was at that moment Parrish, and everyone at his side, suddenly knew they were all going to die here.

Then a small man pushed between Parrish and Tomps and took several steps out into the open. Before Parrish could call him back, Luke stood proudly erect and shrugged off his heavy coat.

"See my totem of loyalty and honour." he said loudly and held the drilled stone necklace around his neck out for all to see. There were a few gasps from the far side of the clearing now. "I am a proud servant of Dannu." He stretched out an arm and pointed his finger at the crowd opposite and Parrish realised his words were not aimed at the wolf pack, but at the village warriors behind them. "I am here to save you. To save you all. I have come from the holy village of the stones, with these warriors. This," he pointed without looking back towards Parrish. "This man is the Chieftain of Dane-bre. Dannu's man. And he has come to save you too. If you are all still sons of the Earth Goddess, then I say stay your hands. Let us rid Dannu's land of these wolf men and their false leader, and she will welcome you back into her arms. Stay your hands and let us save you."

Parrish thought the gesture was nothing short of magnificent. The wolf pack on the other hand began to laugh but the laughter died as a sudden shuffling of feet could be heard behind them. Several of the Baile-oir-Creige warriors started backing up. More men began to follow and everyone there, good and bad, began to witness and appreciate the power of the servants of Dannu.

The scarred alpha male suddenly saw his support troops starting to fade away and the grin fell from his face, to be replaced with fury. He would put a stop to this. In a blur of motion he raised his bow, drawing it at the same time and all in one movement loosed off the arrow. It might have been because of his speed, or perhaps his blind eye that hindered his judgement of distance, but the arrow did not strike quite where he intended. It punched low left side into Luke, just above the hip and almost a palms width in from the edge of his body.

The brave shaman gasped, clutched at the embedded arrow and staggered back. Tripping over his previously discarded coat he fell back onto the ground, a look of pained disbelief on his face.

The shot was counter-productive to the wolf pack. The village warriors that were still undecided, on seeing the pack leader strike down another revered holy man made them even more convinced they were right to get away from these wolf men and their false prophet.

Parrish did not see any of this though. He glanced down at the now panting Luke, flat on his back on the cold ground, hands tenderly grasping the shaft of the arrow where it stuck out from his body. Looking back up at the White Wolf Parrish's eyes blazed as he hissed.

"I will have your head for that, you bastard!"

He turned to signal the dark warriors beside him only to see them all still standing like statues, as rigid as the spears they clutched.

A sudden thought popped into his military brain. Artillery!

"Spears!" he shouted. "Throw!" and he pointed at the wolf pack.

The men under his command jumped at his shout, then every man there, on both sides of the confrontation, understood what the commanding tall man wanted to happen.

As the wolf men with bows raised their weapons, to a man the dark warriors stepped forward and launched their spears across the gap and they flew with graceful, deadly trajectories into the wall of wolf pelted men.

None of the wolf pack made any real attempts to avoid the missiles hurled at their line. In truth, they would have needed to be extremely athletic and very quick witted to have successfully done so. But the four of them who were armed with bows managed to draw, aim and loose before the spears struck.

One arrow flew just wide of its target, one struck low into the meaty part of a Cournan-Tullock warrior's thigh. The first man to die was a dark warrior who was unfortunate in that two of the bowmen unintentionally drew on the same man. He simultaneously took two arrows in the chest and fell on his face, gasping for a breath that never came.

Moments later the spears struck home. Like the much faster arrows, some missed, some injured but four of the wolf pack were killed outright as the heavy weapons with their fist sized, leaf shaped flint heads punched into the chest and abdomens of the their throwers intended targets.

Parrish seized the opportunity of his men's slightly greater number now and the spear men, now standing and watching the results of their effort, jumped again at Parrish's next shout.

"GO!" he yelled. "Attack!" And they were galvanised into action as he led off at the run towards the wolf line up. The line up that now had several gaps in it.

Klud and Tomps were right with their Chieftain, Klud leaping over the fallen Luke in his eagerness to get to the opposition. The dark warriors were only a pace or two behind and battle yells came from their throats as they surged forward.

The wolf pack were not shy in coming forward themselves though, something Parrish half admired and half hated. He had hoped they would be more intimidated by his men and their actions. But this was the Neolithic and here a warrior's word and deeds were his bond. His actions spoke loudly and prowess in battle was greatly respected. Fear was not big in a Stone Age warriors make up.

The two groups clashed together.

Parrish only had eyes for the wild eye and scarred face of the white wolf. Klud and Tomps were either side of their Chieftain. They both wanted their own trophies but in a huge act of loyalty, there first concerns were that no fur clad wolf man would get anywhere near Parrish from the sides. They were intent on taking down the men either side of the pack leader and allowing their Chieftain to deal unhindered with the man in the white wolf pelt.

The two leaders clashed head on. Quite literally! Parrish had his size advantage but the one-eyed white wolf reached full speed as they met. The insane look on the man's scarred face, mad was the fleeting thought in Parrish's mind, warned the tall man his opponent was more than a little unhinged and not to be underestimated, but too late to avoid. With no intention of slowing even a little for the impact, the white wolf crashed headlong into his tall opponent. As well as waving his war club high over his head with the attention of smashing in the top of Parrish's skull, he leapt up and head-butted him, bursting the eyebrow scar Parrish acquired several years and several millennia ago.

Parrish in turn had his left arm up to block the impending club. This had the unintentional result of adding to the impetus of the man's head-butt, while his own intention was to drive his knife, held low in his right hand, in under the rib cage and up into his opponent's heart. But their clashing impact cancelled each other's attack out and they both staggered back and fell, the white wolfs intended club strike wildly off target. By the same token, the jarring impact offset Parrish's attack also and his metal blade, instead of stabbing fatally up through the soft tissue, hit the scarred man's lower rib, deflected outwards and wedged in the edge of the diaphragm muscle. Not a lethal blow and as both men flew back apart, driven by the others momentum to fall on their backs, a momentarily stunned Parrish lost his grip on his knife and it remained gruesomely embedded in the wolf man's side.

Unseen by either leader, to Parrish's left Klud crashed into his own opponent, this time both men at a more expected attack speed. Their battle axes locked together at the chunky flint heads and the two men almost bumped chests. The nameless wolf man actually snarled into Klud's face. Klud would have laughed back if it were not a life or death situation but his intention and concentration was absolute. He had learned from his good friends about the effectiveness of more than one attack point at a time and the wolf man's snarl was cut short as Klud brought his knee hard up into the man's groin. The snarl turned into a great explosion of breath and pain as the warrior lost his attention. Klud quickly shouldered his opponent in the chest to force the man off balance, and brutally finished him with a vicious strike to the base of the neck even as he fell to the ground. Knowing the strike was good he turned to his left looking for his next opponent.

Tomps attack on *his* opponent was more elegant but nonetheless effective. The wolf man he came up against looked at the youngster as he approached and began to smile at what he assumed was inexperience, before he saw the look in the Danebury man's eye. He hesitated and Tomps, seizing on this indecision, brought his long handled weapon round in a low, lateral swing parallel with the ground, striking the man with perfect accuracy on the outside of his knee. The limb kinked sideways at a completely unnatural angle with a horrendous popping noise. The man's cry was very high pitched and as he fell away to one side Tomps spun and brought his war hammer right around, helping his victim on his way to the cold ground with another powerful sideways blow which crushed in the side of the man's head. Blood burst from the man's nose, mouth and pulped ear canal. Like Klud, Tomps knew without needing to check that his strike was lethal and also turned away to search out another victim.

Right across the line men were engaged in mortal combat. The wolf men were giving a decent account of themselves but the dark faced warriors of Cournan-Tullock quickly gained the upper hand. True, they had slightly superior numbers but also, Chieftain Barron was a man of his word. He had indeed given Parrish his best warriors, and they were very proficient. On top of that these fine, simple and honest men knew they were fighting alongside a holy man, Dannu's man, and his two heroic friends. In short, they believed the Earth Goddess was with them.

But initially the battle was not one sided. Everyone clashed with their opponents at more or less the same time. Most of the life or death fights were settled in only one or two blows. Those who struck down their victims and dispatched them were then freed up to seek out another enemy.

Klud and Tomps were two such men and searched out secondary targets, gleeful bloodlust pounding inside them as they scanned the thrashing, blood splashed mêlée around them for additional trophies.

Two Cournan-Tullock men were killed outright in the first moments of contact by extremely aggressive wolf men attacks but the remaining seven were holding their own against the fur clad wolf pack. Klud only took two paces to his left to step in and help a dark warrior who was being hard pressed. His black faced comrade had received a painful, arm numbing blow to the right shoulder and as his war club fell from his lifeless fingers, his left arm came up in a futile attempt to stop the killing blow that he knew would come next. It never arrived. Klud lashed out with his own weapon and landed a rib cracking blow just beneath the pressing wolf man's armpit. The man yelped and his club also clattered to the ground. Klud kicked the attacker's legs out from under him and as the man joined his club on the ground Klud barked at the dark warrior.

"He is all yours."

And in a flash the man pulled his dagger free, left handed, and fell upon the gasping wolf man, stabbing and slashing his way to the trophy he had been gifted.

The wolf man to Tomp's right killed his opponent with brutal efficiency and turned on the Danebury warrior expecting to do the same again. Tomps was steely eyed as the man attacked and he skilfully blocked then rode his opponent's club strike down the shaft of his war hammer, twisting the long handled weapon using his extra leverage to spin the club from the man's grip. He jabbed the man in the midriff with the handle end of the unique weapon before clubbing him down with the business end, knocking him to the ground, then pulverising his sternum and ribs with a pile driver blow.

Each wolf man killed while a dark warrior kept his feet increased the pressure on the remaining wolf pack and sensing victory the more numerous Cornan-Tullock men fell upon the enemies of Dannu and the remainder of the pack were slaughtered in a only few more blood splashed moments.

While all this went on around Parrish and the wolf pack leader, the two men at the centre of it all were locked in their own life and death struggle.

Parrish was slower to recover than the white wolf, and the madman, still clutching his war club and with the apparently unnoticed haft of Parrish's twentieth century knife still protruding from his side, was first to regain his feet. He leapt again to the attack and rushed forward to overwhelm Parrish, who was still on the ground, keen to close and pound the tall man into the earth with his club.

Parrish remembered his basic hand to hand combat training, particularly the part about the crucial moment of getting inside the opponents attack to deny him the strength and power to kill. The wolf leader expected Parrish to backpedal as fast as he could along the ground in fear of his life. In complete contrast Parrish did not even attempt to rise, but rolled as fast as he could towards the man. For a second time they both closed too quickly. In an instant, surprising the white wolf as he rushed forward, Parrish clattered into the man's feet and shins. The one eyed man fell forward on his face again, measuring his length on the hard earth and this time losing his club as he sprawled flat.

Parrish executed a couple more quick rolls than sprang to his feet. The white wolf also leapt back up and turned to face his frustrating opponent, the pair no more than five or six paces apart. There was a moment's pause as both men realised there was no chance for a rushing attack now.

Their attention on each other was complete, neither of them seeing the carnage around about, with corpses littering the ground. All the wolf pack men were now dead or dying and the dark warriors of Cournan-Tullock stood transfixed amongst the dead. Forgotten at that moment were any thoughts of collecting their grisly trophies. All eyes were on the remaining two combatants.

It did not seem to matter one jot to the white wolf that all his men were dead and his wolf cult destroyed. What had remained of his sanity was gone. Blind rage and madness was all consuming. Nothing else mattered now. He just needed to kill Parrish.

The Dane-bre Chieftain simply stood his ground, feet planted a shoulders width apart, hands raised out before him in readiness. Blood still trickled unnoticed down the side of his face from his ruptured eyebrow. His eyes bored into the eye of his opponent. Somewhere in the background he thought he heard Klud's voice cut through the deafening silence around them.

"Now you will see something." His friend said quietly to the watching crowd.

Parrish's senses were heightened by the fear laced adrenaline coursing through him and he clearly heard the wolf pack leader snort in fury through gritted teeth, then suck in a great lungful of air. With a berserker look in his one wide eye, the last wolf standing lunged forward for Parrish's throat, arms extended and clawed hands reaching for the soft tissue to rip and tear.

Parrish let the man come. At the last moment he windmilled his left arm over in front of him, slapping away the other man's the lunging arms. The white wolf completely missed his target, momentum carrying him past to Parrish's right.

As Parrish's left arm dropped, he swayed away to his left and brought his fully extended right arm round horizontally. The hand was flat, palm facing down, fingers extended and with the thumb tucked in underneath it. He leant forward, putting all his weight into the blow and drove the knuckle of his thumb as hard as he could in underneath the man's hair covered chin to smash into his throat. The Adams apple was instantly crushed, the larynx destroyed and the windpipe ruptured.

The white wolf staggered, choked several times and fell to his knees, his eye now wide in pain and panic, hands clutching at his ruined throat.

Parrish didn't even hesitate. Spinning back, his kick drove squarely in between the now kneeling man's shoulder blades, knocking the man flat to the ground. The last wolf man was already dying but Parrish was in his fighting frenzy. Controlled in his actions, but driven on by his blood fuelled fight or flight response, unable to stop himself from ending the man's life. As the white wolf lay there before him, he stepped up close and aggressively stamped down so hard on the back of the dying man's neck the sound of crunching bones could be heard by everyone.

Parrish did not notice this. At that moment he did not care. He held his boot on the neck of the corpse until it stopped moving. Then he slowly bent down and pulled his knife out of the body.

Standing back up and stepping away from the result of his murderous work, he eyed all the warriors, still standing motionless amongst the bloody bodies on the bare earth. They all gazed back, astounded looks on their faces. No one dared speak. Then Parrish turned to face the massed spectators of the battle that were all the gathered warriors of Baile-oir-Creige.

With a terrible, grim look on his face, blood dripping from his chin and eyes like chipped flint, he put a boot back on the white wolf's corpse, pointed his bloodied knife at the crowd and said in a harsh, rasping tone.

"Does anyone else want to be a wolf man? Eh? Speak up! Step forward and we will settle it here and now!" No one made a move. "No?" Parrish waited several long, silent moments.

Finally, some of the tension seemed to leave him, his shoulders relaxed and he just nodded at the crowd.

"Good. Then I say, go with Dannu!"

19

Parrish stood very still, closed his eyes and took several deep, calming breaths. He began to come back to his normal self, starting to feel more centred again. And then also felt the rising self-loathing as his reasoning mind understood that he had once again succumbed to his baser instincts and with unrestrained determination, killed a man. The first wave of bitter disgust was just beginning to rise when he felt them.

Opening his eyes he found everyone around the field of conflict still motionless, silently looking at him. They were looking to him for guidance and instruction. They needed him. In their eyes he also saw the gratitude in their thinking that he had saved them all. But as he saw them all silently looking to him for leadership, he knew that because they had all turned to him for that need, they had actually saved him.

Scanning the full scene with a renewed sense of purpose, he braced up. He was the Chieftain of Dane-bre and he should bloody well act like it. Klud and Tomps had seen the brief conflict and turmoil in their tall friend's eyes. They had seen it before. But then he stood tall, viewed everything with a steady gaze and his eyes cleared. They knew that look too. Their great leader was once again standing before them.

Parrish wiped his bloody blade on a sleeve then sheathed the weapon.

"Right!" He barked in a decisive tone, looking back at Luke, still flat on his back, the arrow shaft sticking up, an unnatural and unwanted protrusion out of his body. "Take Luke somewhere warm. Do not try to pull out the arrow. I will see him shortly." Turning back to the still waiting warriors, he waved an arm wide. "Men, collect your trophies then take all the wolf pack bodies a good way outside the village and burn them." There were a few gasps. Parrish just raised one palm and condescended to give then all an explanation. "Those who denied Dannu, then went against her, tried to make people worship a false god and caused many of her honest and loyal followers to die, do not get to go to the great shrine house of the Earth Goddess."

No one was about to argue with Dannu's man. As he was speaking Klud and Tomps had calmly walked up and once again stood beside him. He turned to the pair and offered a small smile.

"Well done you two. Still here. That makes me happy. Now, let us see what can be done for the wounded and get this mess cleared up." The pair smiled and nodded back. "Well?" he continued. "Chop, chop!" and clapped his hands together before striding off towards his injured friend. There was a moment when everyone else stood in confusion before grasping that the speech was finished.

Everyone jumped gladly to their tasks.

Some Baile-oir-Creige warriors rushed past the three Danebury men and made to pick up Luke but Klud and Tomps caught them up and stood between them and their fallen friend.

"No." Tomps put up a hand. "We honour you for your offer but we will carry him. Just show us where to take him."

Parrish joined them and knelt beside Luke who still lay flat and motionless to prevent any extra pain by unnecessary movement. His hands were clasped carefully around the base of the arrow shaft where it protruded from his clothing, just above the point of his left hip. Parrish briefly inspected the wound site. There was very little blood. Luke was breathing quite quickly as shock took hold.

"Is it mortal?" He gasped quietly to his tall friend. "Am I dead?"

Parrish gave him as friendly a grin as he could muster under the circumstances.

"You are speaking to me, so you must still be alive. We will see what can be done once we get you somewhere nice and warm, OK?" He laid a gentle hand on the holy man's shoulder.

"I am sorry, my Chieftain." Came Luke's soft reply. "I thought I could help and all I have done is to get killed!"

Parrish knew that in these hard times wounds were deemed either minor or fatal, but he was not prepared to give up on his friend.

"You think you did not help?" He asked incredulously. "My friend, your actions saved us all. And," he added in English. "I'm ashamed to say I thought you had nothing to contribute!"

All those around him bar Klud and Tomps frowned in confusion. What were these mumbo-jumbo noises the tall man now spoke? The two Danebury men did not understand the words either, but they knew without a doubt that they were words of power. Klud and Tomps exchanged slight, knowing nods. Their little holy man friend was not done for yet. Not if Dannu's man had anything to do with it.

Parrish patted his injured friend gently on the shoulder, nodded and the two Danebury warriors gently lifted Luke up between them and were led off somewhere into the village between the huts. Parrish turned back to the site of the battle, and witnessed the victorious warriors begin collecting their grisly trophies. Gritting his teeth against the awful sight he turned away and spotted some keen Baile-oir-Creige warriors already heading out of the hillfort gate, some of them carrying armfuls of kindling. That would no doubt be to aid the start of the mass funeral pyre. His mouth set in a grim line of satisfaction as a sudden thought struck him.

The wisest of the wise ones would be happy. The Cult of the Wolf was about to go up in smoke.

*

Parrish found Luke being attended to in one of the stalls of the village shrine hut. It was warm enough, with a small central fire burning and was draught free. Klud and Tomps were with him and there were several women around the trio. They hovered in the background in complete silence. Everyone was just looking down at the poor soul with the arrow in his side. Luke lay on a bed of straw, head propped up by a roll of animal skins and with a water bag handy. He was almost tenderly cuddling the spot where the arrow projected from. To Parrish, it looked like some horrendous, bastardised version of the nativity scene, but a shrine to pain instead of hope and glory. Everyone appeared to be waiting for him.

The look of pain and terror on Luke's face gripped Parrish but he moved into the stall with an air of confidence.

"OK my friend. Let us see what can be done."

Klud and Tomps nodded agreement but as much as he tried, Luke could not muster even the smallest smile.

"If... If I am dead, you will not let me suffer?" The small man stuttered.

"Don't get ahead of yourself." Parrish said in English then reverted to the language of the people. "I promise. But let us see what-is-what first."

Explaining no further he knelt beside the little holy man. Drawing his knife, he deftly cut away Luke's leather shirt and pulled the remnants clear to fully exposed the injury. The arrow was deeply embedded in Luke's torso, only two or three inches in from his side and about the same above the point of his hip..

"A hands width to the right and he would have missed you." Parrish smiled. The rather poor joke fell flat and the grin fell from his face as he added, "A hands width the other way and you would indeed be dead." He really hoped that the flint headed missile had missed any vital organs. If it had cut through the little man's colon or large intestine, then he was surely doomed.

Parrish rolled Luke gently onto his right side, bringing his left hip uppermost enabling him to properly assess the problem. Carefully probing with his fingers allowed him to feel the four or five inches of the hard wooden shaft inside his body and the flint head that tipped it.

Luke gasped as Parrish felt his injury until he was satisfied as to what needed to be done. He recalled that the arrow had a barbed head fitted so there was no way to pull it back out without causing serious additional or possibly fatal damage.

"Right." He rolled Luke carefully back and when he was laying flat again Parrish took his knife and scored a cut right around the exposed shaft about eight inches above Luke's body. Parrish looked back up, past his two friends to the women behind them and said curtly. "I want some sort of soft pads, some strips of cloth or leather for bandages and a good helping of that healing poultice, if you have any."

Three of the women nodded and darted out past the men, needing no second bidding.

Returning his attention to the arrow, Parrish gripped it, one hand above the scoring, one below. With a sharp twist he snapped the shaft in two. As much as he tried to hold the lower part still, Luke still gasped in pain.

"Sorry, old friend." He said, tossing the fletched end of the arrow away into the straw at the back of the stall. "Could not be helped. Chin up." No one else understood the phrasing but everybody nodded, even Luke.

It seemed no more than a few moments later that the women returned holding the requested items.

Like the three wise men, thought Parrish, unable to shake the nativity analogy from his mind. One women held several squares of loosely folded of cloth, flax most probably. The second had a football sized lump of the heady smelling poultice, wrapped in dry dock leaves, in her cupped hands. The third woman has several long soft leather straps hanging from her grip.

"Good. Pass me one of those straps." He held out a hand. No sooner was one passed to him than he wrapped it multiple times around his open hand, carefully ensuring several layers of leather ran across his open palm. “Tomps, Klud, sit Luke up.” The Danebury pair hooked their hands under the holy man armpits and gently lifted him into an upright sit. The shaman hissed with pain but did not resist.

Parrish knelt close and looked into his small friends eyes.

“It cannot pull out, my friend, so must be pushed through.” Luke’s eyes widened and sweat beaded his brow. Parrish placed his leather padded palm against the freshly cut end of the arrow shaft. “I will count one, two, three and then push. Ready?”

Luke’s fear was palpable now but to his credit he barely paused before nodding and gritting his teeth in readiness.

“OK.” Parrish paused. “One…”

With a firm thrust Parrish plunged his hand forward till it slapped against Luke’s bare skin. Pushed from the front, the bloody arrowhead burst out through the small man’s back with a wet tear that was masked by a great gasp from Luke.

“Well done” said Parrish, and reaching around steadily drew the remainder of the arrow out of the body with a slight sucking sound.

Dropping the bloody half of the arrow he held out his hands, palms up.

“Pads!” He demanded and one was placed in each of his open hands. He slapped one on each wound and leaned back so he could better look into Luke’s face.

“You… You said you would count to three.” The little shaman gasped in pain.

“Two, three. Happy now?” Parrish grinned.

The two Danebury warriors also grinned. Luke was hurting too much to laugh but managed a relieved sigh.

“We will give the blood a while to slow, then apply fresh pads with some poultice on.” Parrish instructed. “Strap the pads to him, not too tightly, and let us all hope the blood will clot naturally." The women nodded. Naturally assuming his instructions were for them. "Keep him warm and comfortable. Give him plenty of water and some food if he wants it. I will return regularly to see how he is doing." He looked down at Luke as his friends laid him gently back down. "You will not understand fully, but I think that if we can keep infection at bay," He was putting a lot of faith in the heady poultice but knew from personal experience how effective the muck could be. "And if the bleeding stops, I believe you will not die here."

"Thank ... Thank you..." Luke's eyes were full of gratitude even through his pain.

"No problem." Parrish smiled and rose to his feet. He looked to his friends. "Stay here or go as you please. I want the best of care for him and you will not be asked to do anything else if you choose to stay." He looked to the still silent women. "Thank you for your help." They all bowed deeply. "Do not leave him alone. Just do as I have said. If there is a problem, *any* problem, come and get me at once. OK?" More bows. "Good. Now," He looked down at his hands. "First I am going to wash my friend's blood off me, then I am off to get some food. You guys want anything?" Mouths gaped open at the sudden, unexpected question. Chieftains did not do such things.

"Fair enough." Shrugged Parrish, taking all their silences as a no. He threw Luke a brief salute. "Take it easy, my friend. I will be back in a while."

And with that he turned and left the stall with its full complement of stunned, gaping faces.

*

Early that same evening, after popping in occasionally during the day to check on Luke, Parrish returned to the shrine hut to bed down for the night. It had indeed been a long day, one of the longest and he felt bone tired. As a Chieftain he had been very respectfully looked after, well fed and had been offered the choice of warm and comfortable huts but chose to return to the big central shine hut, for several reasons. Firstly he wanted to keep an eye on his injured friend. Plus Klud and Tomps were also there, sharing the stall next to his, which just happened to be the currently unoccupied Chieftain stall, and also because the dark warriors that had fought alongside him had also taken stalls there. They were all quartered in the stalls on the opposite side of the large roundhouse to give their great leader the space respect demanded, but they wanted him to know that they were still with him.

The bodies of the four dead Cournan-Tullock men were tightly wrapped and lay in state in the stall to the right of the Earth Goddess statue.

Parrish walked across and looked in on the remaining six men, who made to jump to their feet on his approach, but he waved them back down.

"Are you all fed and comfortable?" he asked

"Yes, Chieftain." Came a rumbly chorus of replies.

Parrish's eye caught one man whose thigh was strapped up. He detected the now familiar whiff of poultice.

"Are you badly injured?" he asked the man.

"It is a small thing." The warrior replied but it was clearly paining him.

Parrish had been told of the arrow wound the man had received, and that it had been dealt with the same way as Luke's injury.

"Good man." Parrish nodded. "I am hoping we will make our way back to Cournan-Tullock before too long." He raised his eyebrows in an unspoken question.

"I am ready when you are, Chieftain." Said the warrior defiantly.

Parrish nodded then smiled.

"Chieftain Baron chose his men well, and I am grateful." This brought grins from all the men. "I do not know which one of you leads but I want whoever it is to pass this message onto Chieftain Baron if I forget." As if he ever would! "There is no holy one here, so when we get back to your village I am sure you will want to get your trophy tattoos done as soon as possible." They all nodded. “Even by that little half ready holy boy?” More nods but accompanied by grins at Parrish’s gently mocking disrespect of the lad. “Well, when you all have sore necks, I want you all to also have a wolf killer tattoo.” He tapped his index finger against his right cheek. The men looked pleasantly surprised. “You not only killed in battle, you also destroyed a wolf pack too. Your marks of honour should show this. Also, I will be able to recognise my dark warrior brothers at a glance should we meet again sometime later.”

“We are at your service.” Said one man, clearly speaking for them all by the looks on their faces.

“And I thank you again for that. Now, get some sleep. You have all earned it, and there will be no need for early rising in the morning. We will leave this place soon, but not for at least another day.”

To murmured thanks, Parrish turned away and crossed to the Chieftains stall, where Klud and Tomps stood, grinning.

“They are your men” said Klud. “For as long as you want. They will follow you anywhere, all the way back to Dane-bre if you so wish”

“Why would I want seven very good warriors when I have the two best men in the land at my side.” He said quietly, grinning.

His Danebury companions laughed out loud, nodded several times then looked into their tall friend’s eyes.

“Let’s not get all mushy here.” Parrish said quietly in English recognising the hero worship, then clapped both men on the shoulders. “Get some sleep, my friends. Tomorrow is another day and we will see how Luke is.”

The two Danebury men bowed deeply to Parrish, who nodded back, then all three retired to their stalls.

20

The next day, Parrish was standing just outside the entrance to the shrine hut, taking in the air after checking on Luke. The holy man's wound was thankfully infection free but he was fatigued and in some pain. The shock had not helped and also the fact that, as a holy man, he had very little experience of hard graft, carrying an injury or suffering a more prolonged period of pain. In short, thought Parrish, it's just what happens when a body is shot or otherwise injured.

He scanned the scene before him, an ingrained habit, and had to concede that this little Village on the Cliff really looked no different to the other small villages he had recently experienced. It made him appreciate Danebury all the more and he suddenly missed his home, family and his people deeply. It startled him to realise he had been struck by a bout of home sickness.

Someone appeared at his side, interrupting his suddenly dour reverie and he looked to see Tomps standing there, clutching a bulky leather bag down at his side.

"Yes?"

"I would like to show you something." said Tomps rather mysteriously.

"Of course. What?"

In answer Tomps fished briefly into the bag and pulled out a skull, all freshly cleaned, and held it out for Parrish to examine. He did not take the gruesome offering but looked at his young friend.

"What is this?"

"A trophy." Tomps replied in an even tone. "Your trophy. But look at it more closely."

Parrish reluctantly took the skull and made to give it no more than a brief glance. But then his repulsion was forgotten as he immediately noticed the oddness and now genuinely examined it.

"This... this is the skull of the White Wolf?" he asked.

"Yes. And do you see what I saw?"

"Yes. It is clearly damaged around the sides and there are also some holes in it."

An even closer inspection showed scratches and gouges on parts of the bone. Some of them grouped around the left eye orbit and also at either temple. And there were holes. Some were smaller but a couple looked almost big enough to insert a pencil in.

"What on earth happened to this man. I am amazed that after all that he was still standing!"

"Yes." Tomps nodded in agreement. "When I had de-fleshed it," Parrish couldn't help it, he made a face. Tomps smiled and continued. "When I de-fleshed it and saw this, I was curious and went out into the village and talked to some of the people here." Parrish's eyebrows went up. He thought it a bold thing for his young friend to do but he suspected the people of Baile-oir-Creige probably would not refuse to speak with Tomps because they had seen him in deadly action the day before.

"What did you learn?"

"Well. The White Wolf was quite proud of his injuries and boasted openly many times about how he got them. From what I learned, it seems that he once led a large hunting party out, tracked down and came upon a big wolf pack in their den. This pack was led by a great white wolf. Old, wise and the most powerful beast anyone had ever seen.

The pack and the hunting party fought. Some men died but the wolf pack was overcome. During the battle the old white wolf attacked this man." He nodded to the skull in Parrish's hands. "Your man, and those who saw it say it was a battle like no other. Both man and beast fought tooth and nail. The great white wolf had the man in his jaws, biting and savaging his head. That is when I think he received his scars and skull damage."

"I'm amazed he lived to tell the tale." said Parrish in a shocked tone.

"Yes. So were his hunting party warriors. But somehow he got free of the wolf's jaws and managed to kill the great wolf pack leader. It was said that he was in a bad way, but still in a rage and everyone there saw the person change before their eyes.

The man they all knew before was gone in that moment and someone, or something had taken his place. He ranted to the sky above that the great, wise and powerful wolf's spirit had passed from the now dead beast into him. *He* was now the great white wolf and the pack should follow him without question."

Parrish understood 'the pack' meant all the surviving men of the hunting party. Knowing how the minds of these Neolithic people worked, he understood the basic reasoning and their fervent belief in the spirits.

"After seeing him being almost eaten by a wolf, then surviving and claiming the wolf spirit as his own, I am not surprised they skinned their kills and followed the now two legged white wolf. With a totem like that, no one would dare defy him." Parrish nodded and looked again at the battered skull with a growing sense of amazement. "It is almost unbelievable that the man could survive such an attack." Forming his index and middle fingers into a vee and placing them on a pair of the puncture wounds, he saw that the spread was exactly right for a match to the fangs of a large wolf's jaw. Bite marks plain and simple. The skull had been completely punctured in several places, no doubt causing internal bleeding and most likely brain damage to some degree. The fact that the man lived was not in doubt, but after the attack and with such injuries, whether he knew what he was really doing half the time afterwards was unlikely.

Parrish slowly turned the skull in his hands and a small part of him felt pity for this brute who might not have been completely in control of his mind or actions. But he had still killed or ordered many people killed. And that included at least four holy men that he knew of. Not to mention trying very hard to kill Parrish too.

The Chieftain of Dane-bre handed the skull back and Tomps dropped it unceremoniously back into the bag.

“That explains something to me,” he said to Tomps by means of a vague explanation, “And I will pass my thoughts on this to the Wisest of the Wise Ones when I see him, but the deed is done and we have put an end to the cult of the wolf.” He sighed. “Now I would really like to go home.”

“Yes.” Tomps could not agree more. “Say the word and we will go, my Chieftain. I will not be sorry to be gone from this place, or the other villages we have been to. Dane-bre calls to me. It is where I belong. It is home and is a fine place to be, and to be proud of.”

Parrish laughed and rested his hand on his friend's shoulder.

“You speak wise words, Tomps. I was thinking the very same thing just before you approached. I need to speak again with Luke but I can tell you now, we will not stay too much longer in this place.”

*

Parrish took a leaf from Tomp’s book and started to stroll around the hillfort. He had no real interest in interfering in the villagers lives so decided to keep out of their way as best he could and just do a lap of the inside of the perimeter wall. He needed a little time to think. Even moving outside the central area where most of the roundhouses were, he still passed close enough to several people to receive acknowledging bows. He would nod back before those he nodded too scurried away. But this could not raise a smile from Parrish.

His circumnavigation clockwise around the boundary meant it was inevitable he would eventually come to the wall-less section atop the cliff. The lack of disturbance of the ground near the edge told him everyone here gave this aspect of Baile-oir-Creige a wide berth.

Parrish stopped and gazed out across the vast uninterrupted woodland, the great swathes of bare trees vying for position with clusters of evergreen pines, the whole, uninterrupted forest a sweeping vista all the way to the horizon. It had looked so different in the moonlight. Then he looked down over the lip of the sheer drop to the hard ground far below and shuddered to think of the foolishness of what he and Tomps had accomplished that night. It was definitely time to go home.

Parrish made his way back to the large shrine hut, swept in through the angled passageway and crossed the open central area to Luke's stall. The man was propped up, bandaged up and lay still, with eyes closed. A lone female stood vigil behind him and did not raise her eyes as the tall man approached.

"Luke..." Parrish began.

The holy man's eyes flicked open. The lines around them were deeper now but the spark was still there. He caught the different expression on Parrish's face and knew straight away that this was not just another health check.

"Ah… yes?"

"I have come to tell you that it is time for us to leave. Well, not all of us. You are clearly in no fit state to travel."

Luke just nodded. "I understand. You and your men must go. But do not consider me to be left behind. I know I need time to heal and this is the right place for me." Parrish's eyebrows shot up in question. "There is no holy one here. And until they choose a new Chieftain the people will need guidance. After that I will stay as village holy man till someone else is sent in the spring. Or perhaps I shall stay until the village takes the long walk and returns to the great temple at the next solstice gathering. It would be my honour to lead them. There is much to do here with these people."

Parrish was slightly taken aback at Luke's bold statement but of course, he was right. It was just a bit of a shock to realise that suddenly this really would be goodbye to his friend.

"You are wise and speak great words." Parrish bowed to the man at his feet. "But more than all that, I am honoured to call you my friend."

Luke waved away the accolade. It instantly reminded Parrish of how the Wisest of the Wise Ones sometimes gestured and a soft smile crossed his face. His little injured friend had come a long way from their first meeting when he had just stalked past in his big hat, with his nose in the air.

"The honour is mine." said the man Parrish was secretly admiring. "If I could bow..."

"No need for that." Parrish laughed. "These people will all be bowing to you when you are back on your feet. And so they should. They are very lucky to have you. After all, I do not think there is another holy man on all of Dannu's green earth who carries not only a battle wound but also has a head to display in his stall."

Luke did not have the actual skull of the man he had killed but he knew what Parrish meant. The tattoo on his neck said everything. Luke's hand went to the mark and he nodded slowly.

"Yes..." He didn't sound quite so enthusiastic.

"Wear your marks with pride, my friend." Parrish smiled. "You earned them. Now, I have some arranging to do but I will see you again before we leave. Look after yourself and I will see you at the next solstice gathering. If you are not there, I *will* come looking!" He gave the prone man a mock scowl and they both laughed.

"Of course. Do what you must do, Chieftain Parrish. I will hopefully be on my feet tomorrow to see you off." He raised one hand.

Parrish nodded in response and with a wry smile turned away.

He next approached the seven men who sat in silence in the stalls opposite. They had been watching and listening to the previous conversation in awed silence. As he drew close they all rose to their feet.

"My warriors." He saw how they still straightened with pride when he addressed them that way. "It is my intention to set off back to Cournan-Tullock tomorrow after sunrise." To their credit the first thing they all did was flick their eyes towards the stall that held the four tightly wrapped bodies of their compatriots. He tried to set their minds at ease straight away. "They have not been forgotten, and will be fully honoured." He too looked at the still, cloth shrouded cadavers. "We will carry them back to their homes and families on stretchers." The last word made the men frown in sudden confusion. Parrish expounded. "I will show you how to make stretchers. It is a way to carry a body but will need a warrior at each end to do the lifting." He did not need to say that that meant eight men needed, and one of the seven men before him everyone knew was nursing an ugly arrow wound to his thigh. Carrying half the weight of a man with such an injury was expecting too much. "I will get Klud and Tomps to help with one stretcher." He added.

The wounded man stepped forward, limping heavily as he did so.

"I am able to do my part." he said. The words did not come out as confidently as he had intended, or hoped.

"Well said," Parrish addressed him directly. "But I do not think so. You will find the three day journey hard enough on its own, but I do not want to lose one more of my dark warriors because I ask too much of him. We will manage as best we can.

Your task is to be sure to still be alive and with us at the end of the trip. That is what I ask of you."

The man bowed. A Chieftain's request was a warriors order.

Parrish scanned the men. "I want you all back home safely." He continued. "So, we will make four stretchers. Talk to the people of Baile-oir-Creige. Tell them you all need three days supplies, and we will leave early tomorrow. Any problems, you just come and see me, OK? Questions?"

No one spoke.

Parrish gave a final nod.

"Good. Then let us be about it."

21

Everything was ready. The new day was heralded by a low, watery sun casting a thin light through the dull, cloud scudded sky. It was a cool five degrees above freezing but everyone there accepted that it was just chilly. People were gathered on the open ground before the village gates. Ground that had only a few days earlier was blood splashed and littered with the dead.

All eyes were on Parrish and his men. Many were curious about these new things called stretchers. To Parrish they were just roughly six foot long tubes of cloth, skin or woven matting. With two long poles thrust through the middle and spread apart as far as they would go, now the double skinned centre was wide enough to lay a body on. And that body could be dead or alive the people realised, as emerging between the last two roundhouses came a pair of stretcher bearers carrying a person. Flanked on either side by two women, Luke lay stretched out on it, wrapped in a warm blanket. Parrish looked at his six dark warriors and Klud and Tomps, all standing by their more sombre stretcher cargos, and shrugged. Each as needs must. Luke's stretcher bearers stopped in front of Parrish and set their charge gently on the ground. They went to the holy man's aid, lifting him gently to his feet. Then they fell in alongside him as he paced gingerly and slowly up to the tall man.

"I could not let you leave without wishing you well, but I find even just a few steps are at the moment a struggle for me."

"And the new stretcher comes in handy?" Parrish smiled at his small friend.

"Yes." Luke chuckled, then hissed and clutched at his side. "Oww. I have never known laughter to be painful before." he said through gritted teeth.

“That will pass, my friend. But we must go now, the day is moving along.”

“Yes.” Luke repeated, moved closer and managed a careful bow of the head. “Go now, Chieftain Parrish. And I strongly urge that you waste no time. Trust me when I say there will be only a few more days like this.” He rolled his eyes skyward. “There is more cold weather on the way. Very cold. Not soon, but soon enough. And there will be plenty of it.”

“Ah.” Parrish assumed he meant snow. “The word of Dannu?” He just got another nod in reply. “And how long have I got then.” He accepted Luke's words as the truth. The holy men had never been wrong before in their predictions.

“A short while. Snow will begin to fall heavily by the end of the full moon.”

Parrish nodded, momentarily deep in thought. He recalled the three-quarter moon as he and Tomps had scaled the cliff face. With a quarter phase to go and the three days of the full moon, he reckoned he had roughly seven days before travelling would become difficult. He ran through it in his mind, thinking that if he was lucky, he could get to Cournan-Tullock in a couple of days. After that, five more days, perhaps four at a push if he could chivvy Klud and Tomps along, he should just make Avebury before the arrival of the really bad weather. From there he considered it just a hop, skip and a jump to Danebury. Home.

“Fair enough.” He finally said to Luke. “So, I will waste no more time.” He turned to his stretcher bearers, raising his voice. “Men...”

“Hold!” came a shout from the crowd.

Everyone looked as a group of men stepped from the gathered Baile-oir-Creige people. Parrish counted eight, each one with bandolier strapped bags at their sides. One man stepped forward and spoke slowly and loudly, as if he had been pressed into being the spokesperson.

"We would like to honour those who fought for the life of our village. Especially for those who gave their lives for ours. We will help carry these great men forwards on this part of their journey to the great shrine house of the Earth Goddess."

Everyone on Parrish's side of the group was stunned. Even Parrish was momentarily taken aback. What an unprecedented thing! Not just that warriors were volunteering to help strangers from another village, but to help take them *and* their dead back there also!

Parrish turned and looked questioningly at Luke, who shook his head.

"This is none of my doing." he said, clearly as astounded as everyone else.

Parrish looked back at the eight men, who had proud, expectant looks on their faces. He knew to refuse them would be to dishonour them in front of everyone and a great insult. Thinking on, he realised the eight would ease everyone's load, and they could get to Cournan-Tullock and back in, say five days. Safely home before the snow comes. He stood tall and nodded almost magnanimously to them.

"It would be our great honour if you would give us your time and strong arms to help get these brave warriors back to their families."

Grins broke out, not just on the faces of the eight, but on all the faces of the watching villagers.

The men moved smartly across to the four stretchers and waited while every dark warrior at the head and foot of a shrouded corpse looked to Parrish. He gave a curt nod and as one his men stepped aside, and the Baile-oir-Creige men step proudly up to the stretcher ends.

Parrish smiled at the looks of slight bafflement on his warriors faces then turned to the crowd. Klud and Tomps, also released from their duties, walked over and fell comfortably in beside their Chieftain, who finally spoke.

"Well." He drew a deep breath. "If there are no more surprises, we will be on our way."

As if his words were the signal, several people pushed the village gates wide. Parrish gave a final nod. "Farewell. I hope I will see you all at the next solstice gathering."

The entire population bowed to the great Chieftain of Danebre before them. Dannu's man. It stopped Parrish in his tracks for a long moment, but as all their heads came back up he recovered his composure, smiled broadly and gave a cavalry wave.

"Let us go."

The eight new men bent and lifted their charges, and Parrish's whole troop, now eighteen men strong, made their way out through the village gate.

*

The men and their sad cargo had not been travelling all that long, Parrish estimated less than two hours, when it became obvious that the warrior with the thigh injury was beginning to struggle. He began to drop back a little, and would then hurriedly limp in a painful way back up to the group, before starting to drop back again. The group's pace was good but not too rigid or fast, yet the wounded man was already struggling to keep up.

Parrish called Klud over, quietly told him to just keep the men going in the right direction, then dropped back to the injured warrior at the rear.

"Stop." Parrish ordered. "Stop!"

The man pulled up, trying to mask the combination of discomfort and relief on his face. He bowed to the Chieftain then looked up with a blank expression. He did not want to appear to be in any distress.

"I can see that you are doing your best to keep up," Parrish acknowledged his efforts, "but even now it is clear this is difficult for you, and we have still a long way to go."

The man said nothing, neither admitting nor denying the tall man's observations.

"What is your name?"

"Rob." came the blunt reply.

"Well, Rob. I want you to reach Cournan-Tullock and I think you want to reach Cournan-Tullock also, yes?"

"Yes."

"Well." he repeated. "This is not the way to go about it. Let us see if we can somehow make your trip a little less difficult."

"I cannot heal any faster." The warrior was almost apologetic in his reply.

"Of course not. And I am pretty sure you would not want to be carried by any of the others." The pair looked briefly off to the main group, which was now marching steadily away from them through the trees.

"It would look like I could not be my own man." scoffed Rob, but not so loudly that his words might be overheard. "I would lose face and the respect of my fellow warriors."

"I understand." As if Parrish needed it explained to him. "So, I will help as best I can and give you some advice too."

"I am always ready to listen." Rob stood as straight as his leg would allow.

"Good. Now, this is what *I* think you should do. I want you to go at your own pace from now on. Do not try to keep up with the rest of us. We are travelling directly into the setting sun, so you will not get lost. You can follow our tracks and when night falls, you will see our campfire. I believe there are no unknown warriors loose in the great forest looking for an easy trophy, so you should be safe enough. And I promise you this. No one gets left behind. No matter how long it takes for you to reach the night camp, someone will be awake and ready with hot food for you."

It was quite a speech and Rob could do no more than nod at the tall man, mouth open in surprise.

“OK.” Parrish continued. “Now, we will cut you a crutch. It will help take some of the weight from your bad leg as you walk.” The smaller man wasn't sure what a crutch was but just nodded again. “And from now on, as you walk, do not strain yourself anymore than needs be. When the tiredness or pain becomes strong, stop. Simply stop and take time to recover your breath and strength. Stop as many times as you need during the day. As I have said, no matter how late you arrive in camp, we will be there for you. Do you understand me?”

“I do.” said Rob finally and bowed deeply. “I will not let you down, Chieftain Parrish.”

“If you die on this trip, you will only have let yourself down.” He clapped a hand on Rob's shoulder and gave him a warm smile. “Come now and let us try to find a well shaped length of wood. We shall make a crutch to fit you and then you will see what a help it is.”

“I am yours to order.” Rob stood up straight and bowed again to Parrish. “And I am grateful for your concern.” He added.

“Ha!” Parrish barked in a half laugh. “So far I have done nothing but talk. And once you have the crutch to aid you, the rest is up to you.”

The pair nodded to each other in agreement then turned to the nearest stand of leafless trees, Parrish’s practised eye looking for a limb or two that might have the correct shaped cleft somewhere along its length.

*

At the end of the first day’s travel, the campsite was chosen, the dead men were laid respectfully down and everyone was well fed and bedding down for the night around the campfire before Rob came limping/hopping in with his crutch. He appeared out of the darkness and without even acknowledging those around him just flopped, totally fatigued, near enough to the fire to feel its reviving warmth. One of his fellow Cournan-Tullock warriors gave him some hot food and he saw the approving nod across the fire from Parrish, who said nothing.

Flexing his aching leg out before him, the sole of his foot aimed at the welcome heat of the fire, he barely managed to finish his food before falling fast asleep.

The next day was another long trial for him. The warriors carrying stretchers continued to work in shifts and kept up a steady, constant and almost relentless pace.

Parrish noticed a few words being passed among the men and those who were relieved at their positions stayed close to their opposite number who picked up where they had left off. He thought he also might have seen the first inklings of friendships sprouting up between the men of both villages, uniting in honouring the dead, and also starting to pass the patrol time with talk about their families, village and the deeds done by past and present warriors whenever there were short stops for rest or food. He even heard his own name mentioned once when those speaking thought he was out of earshot.

As dusk fell on the second night the group were drawing close to Cournan-Tullock. But not close enough to push on into the night over unknown ground so Parrish had everyone bed down for one more night in the open.

The fire was well stoked, food had been consumed and the quiet chatter died away as men began to fall asleep, yet Parrish was aware that Rob had not yet appeared. Quietly he rose to his feet. Klud flicked an eye open and started to rise also but Parrish signalled him to stay with a downward wave of his open hand.

"Just going back for the last man." he whispered.

Klud nodded in reply and turned over, although Parrish didn't doubt for one moment his friend would be sleeping with one ear cocked till his return.

*

Rob was limping on through the dark. It had been a very difficult day for him. He had stopped many times and was genuinely caught out by the sudden falling of dusk. He tried to up his pace more and his bandaged thigh really began to hurt. He put his palm down to the site of the wound and it came away feeling wet. He was bleeding again, the blood looking black and glistening in the darkness as he held his hand up close to his face to see.

He quietly cursed, then almost jumped out of his skin as he dropped his hand to see Parrish standing directly before him! He had not heard the man approach. How had he done it? There were mysterious forces at work here.

Parrish saw the man almost leap right off the ground in sudden fright and a huge grin split his features. He never got tired of sneaking up on these Neolithic men and making them jump. What fun.

"I... I..." Rob just blustered.

"Simply wondering where you had got to, so I came looking. Come on." Parrish urged. He stooped, thrusting his shoulder into Rob's armpit and slipping his arm around the man's back. "Let us get on to camp. We are almost at your village now. Not long after dawn and you will be home."

Rob's arm naturally hooked over the Chieftains opposite shoulder.

"I am sorry to have slowed you down..."

"You did not. Do not think you are the only man who is tired after two days carrying. Besides, I told you, no one gets left behind. Come on."

And together they finally limped into the camp, Parrish half carrying the smaller warrior into the glowing circle of firelight. To both men's surprise, most of the camp were awake, all watching in hushed amazement at the great Chieftain of Dane-bre, who had gone out of his way to help a lowly warrior. Chieftains did not do such things.

"Why?" asked one uncomprehending man.

From nearby came a quiet voice.

“It is just Parrish's way.” Tomps said as he bent to collect some hot food, still warming in the embers at the edge of the fire, for Parrish’s companion.

“Yes.” agreed Klud in the same quiet tone. “That is the way of Dannu’s man.”

22

Not too long into the new day Parrish led his band out of the tree line and stopped to gaze up at the hillfort on the high ground above them. It was very cool now, not much above freezing. The sky was again dull and the cleared ground between the forest edge and the hillfort somehow looked particularly barren in the flat light.

Obviously they were seen immediately. The occupants of Cournan-Tullock knew nothing of the events at Baile-oir-Creige and were still at the alert, constantly on the lookout for approaching wolf men in particular, but any strangers in general.

The men of Baile-oir-Creige in Parrish's troupe, who happened to be carrying the wrapped corpses as they emerged from the stark trees, set the stretchered bodies carefully on the ground and stepped away. Parrish could see the wariness in their eyes and felt their sudden heightened sense of alertness. He turned to face them.

"You men have been true to your word, and helped deliver the brave fallen of Cournan-Tullock back to their home and families." He knew what they were thinking now and tried to put them a little more at their ease. "There is no need for you to enter this village. We can take it from here and I am sure you wish to return to Baile-oir-Creige as soon as possible."

There was a silence before one of the dark warriors spoke up.

"It is as Chieftain Parrish says. We of Cournan-Tullock honour you greatly for your gift of care and effort."

"Well said." nodded Parrish in agreement.

The spokesman tentatively bowed to these warriors also, now clustering together for protection, just in case. But they were pleased to see all the other Cournan-Tullock men bow as well. The warrior Rob, who had received extra assistance during the journey stepped limping forward and offered even more of an olive branch to these warriors from another village. Warriors who they would normally consider a deadly enemy.

"You have all shown us that you are great men of honour. But Parrish is right. My village is still being careful. They do not know you like we do."

Parrish waved the compliment away and looked to the eight men.

"I suggest you leave now. By my reckoning, if you keep a good pace it will see you safely back in Baile-oir-Creige before the snows come."

The eight men nodded in agreement, some briefly wondering how he would know just when bad weather might strike. But then, he was Dannu's man.

"Have you enough food for a safe return journey?" the tall man added.

"I believe so." said one man, not sounding too sure.

The six Cournan-Tullock men unslung their now much lighter food bags and handed them over to the surprised eight. There were several wordless thanks, spoken by eye and nod to each other.

"Good stuff." said Parrish softly, pleased to see the unexpected extra *entente cordiale* pass between them, then spoke up. "There you are. It has been my great honour to travel with you all, but now, away back to your homes brave warriors, and may you go with Dannu."

The Beile-oir-Creige eight bowed deeply to Parrish, then to the six surviving Cournan-Tullock men, and without another word turned and moved off back into the trees, quickly lost from sight between the huge trunks.

"That was well done." Breathed a surprised Tomps.

"Yes. Who would have thought it." agreed Klud. "Men from different villages, banding together and helping each other."

“There is hope for us all then.” said Parrish to no one in particular and signalled the remaining men to take up their positions. Klud and Tomps moved to one of the laden stretchers and at Parrish’s wave, four pairs of men lifted and set off one last time with their sad cargos, on up towards the entrance path and the gate in the front of the hillfort wall.

Chieftain Barron and his men had witnessed the discussion away by the trees, but could not know what had been said and were greatly puzzled as they watched the group split in two and half of the men slip quietly away into the great forest. But he recognised Parrish and did not doubt that his tall friend had everything under control. Some of Barron’s men recognised the approaching warriors and there was an enthusiastic and slightly undignified dash to the gate. It was quickly unbarred and flung wide, and a crowd had gathered by the time the small procession walked in through it.

The village warriors began to gather round the little troupe. Once fully inside the stretcher bearers stopped and set their loads carefully on the cold ground. Chieftain Barron stepped forward to greet Parrish and the pair nodded formally to each other.

“I am so sorry.” Were Parrish’s first words, causing gasps and frowns of disbelief from the crowd. Chieftain's never apologised. Chieftain Parrish ignored the looks and just glanced sadly back at the still, tightly wrapped bodies on the earth behind him. “I could not bring all your men back alive.” Chieftain Barron bowed deeply. Klud and Tomps weren't sure if it was to their friend or to the corpses.

“It is as you said would happen. And they all knew this might come to pass. It is not your fault.”

Parrish couldn’t agree with the man’s words but kept that thought to himself.

“Know right now that they were all brave men and fought well for the honour of Dannu and for their village.” Parrish wasn't about to go into specifics either. “Now they need taking care of.”

Barron nodded again and waved someone forward. The holy boy of Cournan-Tullock stepped up, bowed to the two Chieftains then moved to the bodies. Kneeling, he laid a hand gently on each one, then waved an arm and some warriors leapt to his bidding, moving to his side, and at his signal gathered up the dead. The boy said nothing and just led the men and their dead charges away through the crowd.

Looks like it didn't take someone long to get their feet under the table, thought Parrish momentarily, but as the crowd parted for them it was then he saw the women, gathered at the rear. There were some smiling faces but what clutched at Parrish's heart were the four women with pained, downcast eyes who dutifully fell in behind the stretcher bearers. They knew who lay hidden beneath the swaddling.

Chieftain Barron and the other warriors paid the bodies and their mourners no more attention.

"Come." he said warmly. "Come and we will find you warmth and food, and then you can tell me…" He paused to look at the expectant faces of the men around him. "Tell us all, about what has happened and how things now are."

"I am happy to." Lied Parrish but he knew there was no way to avoid it. And it was the way of the people in this land of the young. Always ready to fight when they needed to, to die when they had to, and to celebrate whenever the opportunity arose. Chieftain Barron stepped up, a big grin on his face, reached up, put his arm around Parrish's shoulder and led the tall man off towards the shrine hut. Klud and Tomps fell in immediately behind their Chieftain, also grinning, followed by the six surviving dark warriors of Cournan-Tullock. The crowd flowed around the lead group then closed in on the little warrior band to the rear. Excited chatter and claps on the back followed as the whole group made off towards the shrine hut.

Unbidden, the women moved away to start preparing a feast for the evening. A great event was soon to take place, with food, friendship and a great tale to be told. And all in an atmosphere of true relaxation. The tensions that had gripped Cournan-Tullock for almost half a year were fading fast with the rising hope of the demise of the cult of the wolf.

*

Dusk had fallen, not that anyone had noticed. All the people were in their stalls inside the great shrine hut.

Parrish, Klud and Tomps were greatly honoured by being offered a place in the double stall with Chieftain Barron and his family.

The place was warm, well illuminated and comfortable, both environmentally and emotionally. It was now general knowledge that the threat of the cult of the wolf was no more. Food and drink had been liberally dispensed. The people were relaxed. The holy boy had briefly taken centre stage and given thanks to Dannu for Cournan-Tullock's good fortune. His ceremonial efforts were halting, his words were not too elegant and he stumbled through some parts.

Hmm. Not quite up to the usual standard of a holy man, thought Parrish with a smile, but at least he remembered to include the names of the fallen during his speech. He'll do, was the Chieftain of Dane-bre's silent approval.

Another part of the boy's religious duties had in contrast been carried out earlier with great aplomb.

The men who fought in the battle of Baile-oir-Creige had all received their tattoos of victory, and that meant *all* the men.

Parrish had been cajoled, almost shamed into having a head circle added to the collection on his neck, Klud and Tomps silent, reproachful looks the final decider for him. All the other warriors accepted their marks of honour with wincing gratitude and, true to his word, Parrish insisted the six men of Cournan-Tullock, his dark warriors, all received a wolf killer mark.

They now all proudly sported a rough hash mark on their right cheek just below the eye, with a single blue-black dot beneath it. Parrish had one more dot added, in solidarity with the men, the tally on his own cheek now stood at six.

Finally, with great expectations inside the shrine hut, Chieftain Barron stepped out into the open area of the roundhouse floor.

"Are you all well fed?" he asked the people loudly.

A cheer was the reply. Parrish could not help it and a smile crossed his face as he saw Barron's chest rise. He knew well the pride the new Chieftain felt.

"Good. Now," he turned to face the guest of honour. "Me and my people would dearly like to know what happened out there." He thrust his arm majestically and dramatically out, pointing somewhere off into the great beyond. "We here want to hear all about it."

"But, your brave warriors would have told all by now." Parrish protested.

"True, but only their part. Come, Chieftain Parrish, tell the whole tale. This must be a story to be told around the campfire for all time."

"I do not think so..." Parrish's voice trailed off as quiet groans came from many stalls around the great hut.

Tomps understood his great friend's reluctance to speak out. He knew his Chieftain did not boast of glories, or dwell on tragedies. It was not his way. But the Dane-bre warrior had spoken for his leader once before and thought to chance his arm again. He stepped up beside his tall friend and asked quietly.

"Would it offend you if I told the tale in your stead? Perhaps with Klud's help?"

Parrish scanned the disappointment on the sea of faces around him and he next looked into Barron's expectant face. There was a long pause before he finally nodded. He did not like to boast of his kills, but pleasing the people was always his aim, and not just his own people.

“As you wish.” He let out a resigned sigh. “But please do not make me look *too* good.” He managed a grin. Another cheer rang through the shrine hut and as Parrish sat back down Klud rose to his feet and joined Tomps at the centre of everyone’s attention.

“You lead, my young friend, and I will add words where I can.” The anticipated pleasure in the grin on the battered face of the Danebury man was clear to see.

Tomps took one more step out into the open and with Klud at his shoulder scanned the now silent, excitedly expectant faces of this strange yet oddly familiar village. He took a deep breath.

Parrish leaned in close to Chieftain Barron and said quietly.

“Make the most of this. Me and my two friends will need a few days supplies. We set off for the holy village in the morning.”

“Of course.” said Chieftain Barron then sat back and made himself comfortable, expecting now to hear possibly the greatest tale of his life.

“One day, not very long ago...” began Tomps in a loud, proud voice. “The great, Wisest of the Wise Ones from the holy house of Dannu sent word to the Chieftain of Dane-bre. *My* Chieftain.” he added proudly. “To come to the village beyond the great stones. Things are not right in Dannu’s land and the Earth Goddess has need of you...”

23

The three men from Danebury stood motionless in the gateway of Cournan-Tullock, facing the crowd braving the weather to see them off. It was cold. The sky had clouded over during the night and although it was now past dawn, the grey sky made any colour in the landscape look dull and flat. On a warmer day, what would have been drizzle now fell as very soft snow flurries. But the wind was light so had little effect on the ambient temperature.

It could be worse, thought Parrish as he looked at those, looking back at him. He was well wrapped up in his big, coarse coat. The water and food bags he carried slung either side were not overly heavy, and he actually found the cross straps over his chest and back pulled his clothes snug about him and he genuinely felt warmer because of it. In one hand he held his longbow, unstrung and well wrapped up in strips of cloth to protect it from the cold and any scratches or gouges it might pick up as he travelled. Klud and Tomps were similarly clothed, with their shorter bows unstrung and jammed in their quivers, and loaded with the same bags of supplies. They all had fresh applications of the healing poultice on their necks and Tomps also had an extra bag across his back outside of his cape. Somewhat bulky but apparently not very heavy, Parrish briefly thought it looked very much like his friend was carrying several footballs, but he knew the sack contained skulls.

Central in the front of the watching crowd was Chieftain Barron and beside him the six dark warriors, these men also smeared with poultice. The Chieftain stepped forward, eyes squinting against the swirling snowflakes, and gave a deep nod.

"We wish you safe journey my friends, and I hope to see you all at the next solstice gathering."

Parrish nodded back but Klud and Tomps both bowed, with broad grins on their faces. After all, how many plain, honest warriors of Dannu get to be spoken to as equals by a village Chieftain, let alone warriors *not* of that Chieftain's village?

"Be well Chieftain Barron, and the village of Cournan-Tullock." replied Parrish loudly, waving one arm wide to indicate all the people, and getting a mass bow in return from everyone in the crowd. "I hope to see you all there also." There was a pause. "But now we go. Take care, and go with Dannu."

And not even waiting for any reply, he spun on his heel and marched off down the entrance pathway towards the quietly waiting forest. Klud and Tomps fell in alongside, a blatant symbol of the three men's equality, and the trio moved away into the dull half-light, snow flurries swirling about them, giving their silhouettes an almost ghostly, ethereal quality. Someone in the crowd mentioned that it looked very much like Dannu's men were being swept into the Earth Goddess's realm and the snow laden gusts were her caring hands, drawing them to her.

Chieftain Barron just laughed and thought someone was imagining too much, but couldn't deny the strange sight as the warriors from the distant south moved away, blurring into the opaque landscape as they went.

"Back into the village then." he said brusquely. "Close the gates and everyone go back to whatever needs doing." And in a very Chieftain-like manner, Barron spun on his heel and marched away through the parting crowd.

Parrish and co knew nothing of the image they presented. Their thoughts were on the journey ahead and the prospect of finally returning to Dane-bre. But there was still a way to go and things still to be done.

Tomps asked if they were heading straight for the holy village of Avebury but Parrish replied that it would be rude not to at least let the people of Foinyah-Tullock know that the threat of wolf men attack was no more. No need to let their village live in fear any longer than necessary.

Klud wondered why a village that had no effect on Dane-bre should get any assistance, but he accepted without question that Parrish always went further than necessary for the people of Dannu's land. It was one of the things that made him great.

Parrish saw the pensive look on his friend's face.

"It is OK." he smiled. "There would be no need for you two to accompany me into another strange and very likely war-like village. No matter. I just need to shout the news over their wall. It is safer for us, plus I do not want to waste any daylight. We need to get back home, or at least to the holy village, before the weather closes in."

Klud had no intention of correcting his Chieftain's misunderstanding of his thoughts and he and Tomps simply nodded.

And so the three continued on their way, managing the two day walk southwards back to Foinyah-Tullock without mishap. The temperature stayed close to freezing but although the sky remained cloudy, the occasional snow flurries that swept across the forest as they travelled never laid deeply enough to become a hindrance. The ground was hard and the thin white cover over it was just enough to make their boots crunch as they walked but not enough to cause them wet feet.

Starting fires and building temporary lean-to's to keep the night snow falls off them took a little time, but they still made good time across the bare wooded landscape.

There was friendly chat around the fire at the day's end but the actual travelling was done in almost complete silence. The three were naturally on the lookout, and also listening out in the unlikely event they came across a wandering hunting party, or might perhaps encounter a wild animal that could provide some fresh meat. But all was quiet and the three friends were comfortable in their silence, Parrish leading the small patrol, at least for now with a quiet smile on his face while just enjoying the soldiering, and his two companions proud to travel with their friend and Chieftain, and following in the steps of Dannu's man.

*

Upon reaching Foinyah-Tullock the three did not blatantly walk out of the tree line onto the clear ground around the hillfort. They edged around inside the trees keeping out of sight, circling around from their northerly approach till they could see the south-eastern facing entrance of the village. Of course, the gate was closed and the soft dusting of snow all around showed there had been very little outside activity.

"I am going up to within shouting distance but no closer." Parrish briefed his two friends. "There I will call out the Chieftain, after all, he is the only one who has met me." he added with a wry smile. "If he turns out and is ready to listen, I will pass on the good word. But if the gates open and warriors come for me I will be legging it back this way quick as I can. So, I want you two to have your bows ready. If I come running, shoot some fast arrows over my head into the chasing men. Do not worry too much about aiming, but it should make them think twice about attacking and we can get away. With Dannu's blessing." he added, more in hope than in fact.

Klud and Tomps nodded, shucked off their equipment and reached for their quivers and drew out their bows. Parrish handed his longbow to Klud then turned and walked slowly out from between the bare trees into plain sight, with his empty hands away from his sides, and set off at a steady pace up the slope towards the main gate.

The two Danebury warriors watched their Chieftain as he drew closer to the closed gate, not missing the fact there was a flurry of activity from the watchers along the parapet wall.

Parrish stopped safely short of the reach of any well shot arrow and stood in quiet patience, appearing to watch without reaction the movement along the top of the palisade wall above him.

There was a protracted silence before the hillfort gate was pulled ajar and four men stepped sideways out into view. Klud and Tomps were not to know but the lead man out was Chieftain Raif. He had three warriors to back him up, one being the fisher man who had been humiliated by his earlier capture and his forced naked walk of shame back to his village.

Both Danebury men recognised this individual and Tomps started forward, his intention to rush to the defence of his Chieftain. Klud pulled him up short with a firm grip on the shoulder of his coat.

"But that man is the one we insulted before!" Tomps cried, turning to face his friend. "He will want revenge for the earlier insults and with three others there, Parrish is in great danger. Too many men even for him, also, he is unarmed."

"Not so fast, my young friend." said Klud knowingly, yet not for a single moment taking his eyes off the approaching group and the broad back of his Chieftain, facing up to them. "I think all is not as it seems."

"Huh?"

"All Parrish wants to use are words, so I have his weapon." He nodded to the wrapped bow. "But he is not so foolish as to be unready, I believe that somewhere with him is that black death giver he brought back from his visit to the gods." Tomps stared at his companion in sudden realisation. He had seen the terrible weapon before and seen what it did. "Have faith in your Chieftain, Tomps. Parrish knows what he is doing."

Tomps nodded at the wise words and relaxed, stepped back alongside Klud and turned again to watch what was about to unfold.

In truth it was all a bit of an anti-climax as far as the pair were concerned.

Parrish spoke with Chieftain Raif. The conversation did not take very long. He obviously told his counterpart what he had done, but nowhere near the whole story of how it had all come about. There was also a brief exchange of words with the fisher man while the other two warriors simply looked on in awe. Then Parrish nodded to the group. Raif nodded in return. The other three warriors bowed in respect and finally Parrish simply turned his back and walked away back down the slope.

Klud and Tomps watched fiercely until the Foinyah-Tullock group also turned and set off back to their village, then watched on in silence while Parrish re-joined them in the trees.

Collecting his bow from Klud he caught the questioning looks of his two friends and laughed.

"I just told the Chieftain the good news and he was grateful." he explained, to satisfy their curiosity.

"And the fisher man?" Tomps couldn't help himself.

"Ha! He just wanted to know why he had not been killed before. I told him that I had hoped he would get us entry into Foinyah-Tullock. When that did not happen, I used him to pass on a message. I explained that as long as he was useful, he was safe. Besides, a cold, wet, half frozen trophy is not much of a trophy at all. Where is the glory in that? I told him I bore him no ill will and he should just go about his business and not to think on it anymore." In fact, he didn't have the heart to tell the man he had forgotten all about him.

The two Danebury men's broad grins told him they were satisfied with the outcome. Parrish stepped between both men, clapped them simultaneously on the back and said over his shoulder as he walked on.

"Come on then. Let us be on our way. Next stop the holy village."

It sounded a simple enough thing to do but they all knew that place was still a full hand of days away to the south. And the sky overhead did not look very encouraging.

The Danebury pair shrugged, gathered up their kit, caught up with their Chieftain and again they set off together through the great forest.

24

The three pushed on south for the next four days. Initially crossing the hinterland of what would one day be the southern boundary of the city of Birmingham, making their way over the gently undulating vales that would be bisected by the M42 motorway in fifty five centuries time. Then down across the northern edge of the Cotswolds. They remembered the higher, rolling hills and valleys here. And all the time the grey skies hunkered over them. Occasionally dusted by snow flurries, the men pushed on through the never-ending forest, Parrish leading by example and keeping a good but not exhaustive pace. They travelled quickly by day, stopping to camp sometimes perilously late in the evening, putting their faith in the fact that they would be fortunate enough to find enough firewood to see them through the night. This was a risk. If the sky cleared and the temperature really plummeted, not having enough warmth to see them through till the dawn would bring the real threat of hypothermia, frostbite and even death.

But the weather held off from delivering its worst. Almost as if it were deliberately hanging back. The imminent severe weather was desperate to deliver its hardship to the earth but the grey, snow laden skies were almost reluctant to release their pent up snow and ice, as if silently urging the little group to get to their destination as quickly as they could. But the clouds could not hold out forever.

Yet by the end of the fourth day the three friends were almost within touching distance of Avebury. As the dull light began to fade they gathered up material to make a lean-to. This final one would have to be a slightly bigger single construction for three, but it would be a snug fit for them. Parrish didn't think they had time to make a pair. Oddly, suitable building materials were quite scarce in the half light of the forest and they barely managed. Almost as if the natural situation was forcing them to press together in a single small structure, keeping them warmer and thus safer. But two good trees of standing deadwood provided ample fuel for a long log fire across the mouth of the lean-to that would easily last the night.

Klud looked up at the grey dome of sky above them and sniffed the air. “Not far to go now, I am glad to say.” he said to no one in particular. Then he scanned the woodland around him. “And I think I recognise this place.”

“Yes.” Tomps nodded. “Me also. I think we walked through here with Luke. Before the end of the first day.”

Hmm, could be, thought Parrish. Didn’t the little man get his bollocking somewhere near here?

Everyone paused. Of all the events that had taken place in the twenty days since they had left Dane-bre, passing here as they’d set off on their adventure suddenly seemed a lifetime ago.

“I believe you are right.” agreed Parrish, breaking the sudden silence. “So, if we crack on in the morning, I think the holy village is less than a half days travel away.” About five or so miles, he thought to himself, allowing for the couple of miles cross country walkers always referred to as those ‘standing on end’. ie: the undulating contours of their route ahead.

There were nods of satisfaction and the men bent to their tasks. The fire was soon comfortably alight and the hastily erected lean-to was up, and it had a good layer of pine bough insulation on the ground beneath it. All this just before darkness closed in.

But as the men bedded down beneath their woollen cloaks, huddling close together and warmed by the burning logs just beyond the entrance of their shelter, and with the shelter doing its best to protect them from the light but cutting breeze and any precipitation, the sky above could contain itself no longer. As the night drew on and Parrish, Klud and Tomps slept, the silent snow began to fall. Heavily.

Coming to laying on his side, Parrish awoke to a chill, hushed morning. Opening his eyes, the first thing he saw were his two compatriots, both sitting up, hugging their knees to their chests and looking out into the day. Parrish pulled himself up into a sit also with a cold shudder, and he too looked out to see a piercingly white forest landscape. Someone of a romantic disposition would have called it a winter wonderland. Those with a more practical outlook thought very differently.

"Oh, crap!" he said quietly, thinking the same thoughts as his two silent friends.

Everything was blanketed in virgin snow. The long log fire still smouldered on in what was now an elongated pit in the snow before them. The forest floor beyond it was at least a foot deep in snow. Where the light wind had carried it, drifts had built up against the broad tree trunks and threatened to engulf the more dense bramble bushes or clumps of shrubbery dotted amongst them. Big, fluffy snowflakes were falling lightly from the heavens, seeming to disappear as they alighted on the surface of the snow, but slowly and surely adding to its depth.

At the sound of his voice Klud and Tomps looked to their Chieftain. Tomps looked particularly unhappy. He recalled a time when, as a youngster he had almost perished in a snow drift, only being rescued at the last moment by his tall friend.

"It's definitely over the cat!" Parrish said emphatically in English before reverting to the language of the people. "Humph! This will make it a bit harder to get to the village." he added rather unnecessarily. The two Neolithic men just nodded and all three looked back out at the snowscape.

Parrish took a deep breath. Time to re-assert his leadership. He leaned out of their now white roofed shelter, scooped a double handful of the light, cold snow up and rubbed it vigorously into his face.

"Well, we will not get there at all if we do not set off so…" he rubbed his palms together and leaned out again to inspect the fire, noting the still glowing embers deep within it. “Some food and a hot drink and we will be away.”

The smaller pair just nodded in resignation. They knew that travelling even short distances through deep snow meant they would soon get wet as the snow that encrusted their clothes would melt against them. And they somehow had to avoid too much sweating through over exertion lest it freeze and chill them when they stopped. But more importantly, was the threat of being overwhelmed by fatigue through the sheer effort of trying to move through the whiteness. No one went far when the snow lay deep.

“Oh, come on.” Parrish tried to put on a brave face, forcing a smile. “One last push and then good food and a warm bed wait for us at the holy village.” But he knew as well as his friends that these last five or six miles would need a real effort to complete.

Klud and Tomps just nodded again and the two men began to stoke the fire while Parrish reached for his mess tins to quickly melt some snow to drink.

Not long later they stood ready around the fire. Parrish had decided there was no need to dismantle the lean to or, more importantly, to carry the food or water bags. It was not the correct thing to do but he wanted to make sure his friends understood this was a ‘must finish’ hike. Thirst could be quenched with snow but there would be no long stops or camping out for another night.

His estimate of five or six miles did not seem very far but although he had never experienced it, he recalled while on training exercises in Norway that his instructors there had been very forthright in explaining the hazards of deep snow.

“If you lose all your kit and have to walk out in deep snow,” the huge, rugged looking Norwegian Sergeant instructor standing to the side of his whiteboard growled, “I can tell you that it will be very hard. For a start, there is very little grip to be had under foot, and you will be pushing through the snow every step of the way. Sure, it's soft and light I hear you say. But trust me, it’s very much like constantly wading through knee deep water and is basically resistance training every step of the way. You *will* tire and you *will* go slowly, very slowly. Falling over will be a constant interruption and just getting up time and again is awkward and difficult.

There have been recorded cases of people leaving cars stuck in snowdrifts knowing that the nearest houses are only a few miles away. And then being found frozen to death later because those few miles were just too difficult with no snowshoes, waterproof clothing or a decent level of fitness and determination.” He let that soak in to the classroom of suddenly very attentive squaddies seated in rows before him. “Do not underestimate soft, fluffy, deep snow. It looks pretty but it will kill you if you give it the chance!”

Whether or not Klud or Tomps knew it, Parrish was in essence gambling with his life and the lives of his two friends. But he knew his men. They were tough. They were determined and they were proud. It was a calculated gamble then, but he knew they would not let down their Chieftain, their friends or themselves. So, stopping short was not an option. Keeping all this to himself, he turned to the pair.

“One last warm of the hands over the fire, then next stop the holy village, OK?” he said cheerily.

Klud and Tomps just nodded back, rubbed their chilled palms together then pulled on their furry mittens and turned to the south. Tomps hitched up his precious sack of skulls over one shoulder as Parrish led off and they waded away through the almost knee high powder. Roughly six miles to go and Parrish was calculating in his head.

About half an hour after dawn before we kicked off, he thought. Dusk is around half four at this time of the year, so roughly seven and a half, maybe eight hours of daylight to do six miles. It's gonna be tight.

Looking back, he saw his two friends trudging steadily along in his footprints, with an unspoken trust that their Chieftain was doing the right thing.

Not for the first time, Parrish really felt the pressure of leadership.

25

The light was just beginning to fade as the head man of the village part of the holy village made his regular, end of day round of the place under his care. Last stop was to check the main gate.

Seeing it safely shut and barred, he made his way up onto the parapet walkway to the left of the main gate, gazing over its low wall to take in the uninterrupted view for a few moments and just enjoy the silence before he retreated to his warm hut and his warm wife.

Since the heavy snow had begun the night before, no one had ventured outside the village and the covering of white was still pristine, now very deep in places and beginning to drift up against the village wall and to fill in the defence ditch. But it did look incredible and the pureness of it made him mentally give thanks to Dannu for such a sight. Yet, he was as practical as everyone else here in the land of the young and he wondered how the people would cope. He had been told by the high priest only earlier this very day that the feeling was this cold spell was likely to last for three or perhaps even more hands of days. It was a concern but of course unavoidable and besides, his people had survived very cold and snowy weather for even longer periods than that in the past. It was just winter, after all.

Scanning the white scene one last time before descending, he caught a sudden movement out of the corner of his eye. Indistinct at this distance in the slowly fading light, he squinted and looked again to see trudging out from the tree line into the half-light a man. No two, make that three men, pushing slowly and it appeared with great effort through the depth of the day's unblemished snow.

As he watched and the three distant silhouettes continued to make their slow yet steady way towards the hillfort, he noticed with realisation that the lead man was undeniably taller than the other two. It could only be Parrish of Dane-bre. Then with a sudden sadness he really understood that when the same group had left Avebury, they were four. They were a man down.

Judging that the trio would still take some time to reach the gate, the Chieftain left the parapet walkway, dropping down onto the more hard packed snow within the village compound, and made for the nearest roundhouse.

Calling out the occupants, as per protocol, a warrior appeared in mere moments, surprise on his face as he bowed to his leader.

"There are men approaching." the Chieftain said briefly. "The Chieftain of Dane-bre returns." was all he gave as an explanation. "Go to their hut and get a fire going. And also make ready some food, drink and a good supply of blankets." He snapped out the orders, not caring how they were accomplished. He simply wanted it done and expected it to be done. Without another word he turned away and made his way back up to his observation point on the wall.

The warrior he had barked his orders at did not hesitate. If he was offended or rankled by his treatment, it did not show on his face. But he was excited to be the first man aware that the men sent out on a quest for Dannu were now returning. This he was more than happy to witness. He shot back into his home, barked orders at both his wives to gather blankets and food, scooped up some kindling and an armful of logs for fuel and dashed back out, heading for the small ancillary hut where the whole village had witnessed the little group lead off from after their discussion with the wisest of the wise ones.

After a brief while getting the fire to catch in the central hearth of the hut, he started to build up the flames with log sections. In short order the fire was dancing brightly and its heat rapidly pushing the cold out of the building. His two wives appeared with arms full of bedding blankets and then two other women followed in with water bags and carved wooden bowls holding cuts of meat, dried fruit and loaves of bread. Someone else had donated items at his order, but he cared not who. His eyes shone, and unable to contain his excitement he said to them all.

"Chieftain Parrish and his men return! They must have completed their task for the Earth Goddess."

The women's eyes widened at this impromptu announcement, but he did not notice. He pushed past the women and hurried out and away back towards the main gate, there to join his leader and have the privilege of being the only man other than his Chieftain to watch the return of the heroes.

The women just looked at each other, shrugged and set-to laying out four beds on the rattan covered floor, beyond the fire, furthest away from the door.

Back up on the parapet, the two Avebury men watched in snow dusted silence as the trio below drew nearer. It was plain to see that every step was an effort and during the time it had taken to organise a hut for them, they had still not quite reached the gate. The light was all but gone as they approached the entrance and the two watchers slithered back down into the encampment and lifted the locking bar on the gate. Fortunately the gate and its walls were lower than normal hillfort defences and it wasn't too much of a struggle for the pair to pull it open against the laying snow.

First up to the now gaping entrance was Parrish and he stopped at the threshold. Klud and Tomps laboured up behind him and the three looked through squinting eyes at the Avebury men. They in turn stared momentarily back, having never seen three warriors so close to the brink of exhaustion. The Danebury warriors were dusted with snow, with a white crust formed on the top of their hats and across their shoulders. Ice crystals encrusted their beards and eyebrows. The men began to shiver the moment they stopped moving and their faces were drawn. Even their heavy breathing seemed an effort.

"Permiss... permission to enter?" Stuttered Parrish quietly.

"Of course!" The head man jumped at the sound, even though the man's voice was quite soft, and the Avebury pair stepped aside. The three shuffled in before Parrish added. "I have news for the high priest..." he began.

"Yes, Chieftain Parrish, of course." came the Chieftain's interruption. "But the village sleeps now and surely your words can wait till the morning? We have a hut warming and ready for you. You are all clearly in need of rest."

Parrish would have smiled a thank you if he'd had the strength to spare. "You are not wrong there." he said under his breath in English. "Yes." He turned to his two companions. "Come on you two. Let us get warm and dry. And if I never see another snow drift, it will still be a day too soon." It was too much effort to laugh and Klud and Tomps did not even speak. They simply nodded, the action shaking a little snow from their hats in the process.

"Lead on." Parrish half raised one arm before it dropped back limp at his side.

"This way, this way." said the warrior who had set up their dwelling for the night, and he proudly led them slowly off into the village.

As the three shuffled off behind the warrior into the dusk, the Avebury Chieftain shook his head in amazement and headed off in a different direction, making his way towards the holy encampment at the other end of Avebury village. He needed to inform the Wisest of the Wise Ones that the Chieftain of Dane-bre and his men had just returned. Alive but barely able to stand up.

And without their holy man.

The three exhausted Danebury men trudged through the doorway into their old hut, the entrance blanket held back for them by the Avebury man.

Inside were the four women, standing quietly to the rear, the made up beds behind them. There was food and drink visible but the three warriors just stopped in their tracks with the realisation that the constantly stabbing, cold wind was gone. It was bright inside the hut with the cheery central fire and lots of hanging tallow lamps, but the warmth! It almost hit them like a physical blow, and the men closed their eyes and stood, swaying slightly, as the heat wrapped around them.

They had made it. Those last few steps into the hut had finally banished their merciless cold enemy. Almost as one they sighed and their shoulders slumped in tired satisfaction. Job done.

The warrior still at the door suddenly did not know what to do.

"Er... you." He pointed the women. "Help these men. Give them anything they need." And with that he ducked back out and the door blanket flapped closed behind him.

The women simply stared at the three snow encrusted, clearly physically drained trio.

"We should get these wet things off." said Parrish hoarsely and then began struggle with the fastenings of his clothing, but it was a great effort and his efforts were painfully slow. The women stepped forward, seeing the warriors struggle against their severe tiredness.

"We will help." One woman said bravely, stepped up and relieved the men of their equipment and weapons. The other three took her lead and went to the men, who were suddenly grateful just to stand there while they were quietly and efficiently undressed by helping hands.

In no time at all they stood naked before the ladies. There was no shame or embarrassment. Their entire bodies were soaking in the ambient warmth like sponges.

"Oh my." said Parrish with a sigh of pleasure.

"That is... very good." Tomps managed a grin while Klud simply nodded in agreement.

“Come, come.” said the lead woman, almost apologetically. The women wrapped the trio in scratchy, warm and quite wonderful blankets and led them across to the bedding. With minimal guidance they did as they were bid and slumped down gratefully down onto the beds. “And we have food here for you.” she added.

The four women returned to the edge of the fire, gathered up the food bowls, loaves and water bags and turned back to serve those under their charge. After a moment of surprise, soft smiles settled on their faces.

The three warriors were sprawled across their bedding, the odd naked limb poking out from folds in their blankets. All three were fast asleep.

26

Parrish came slowly awake and wriggled with delicious pleasure beneath the warm embrace of his blankets. A few twinges from his over exerted muscles of the previous day's efforts quickly reminded him where he was, and he sat slowly up and rubbed his eyes.

Klud and Tomps, already awake, had their backs to him, hunkered down before the central fire. A woman was tending to them, standing to one side clutching a water bag to her bosom, watching the pair who were obviously eating.

At the sound of movement, the men turned, and all eyes were on him. His friends grinned.

"You have slept well?" asked Klud through a mouthful of food.

"I should cocoa." said Parrish in English, and stretched, arms wide. His muscles again let him know that they had been sorely tried. "Ow! Yes." he added in the language of the people. "Feels like I slept the sleep of the dead. What is for breakfast?"

The woman snatched up a bowl with bread and dried fruit pieces on it, moved quickly to the Chieftains side and offered it out to him with a bow.

"Cheers." He took the bowl with one hand, grasped a big chunk of bread with the other and took a big bite. "Drink?" he said through his doughy mouthful.

The woman simply offered him the water bag after realising that there was no clay beaker to hand. The mortifying look on her face as she thought she had not provided properly for a Chieftain made the man himself guffaw.

"That will do." he chuckled, to the woman's obvious relief. "I'm starving. I could eat a whole sheep between two slices of bread! How are you two doing?" His attention turned back to his friends.

The woman's eyes bulged in surprise, unsure if the big man was speaking in jest, but Klud and Tomps both chuckled at their Chieftain's words.

"We are well provided for." Klud held up a partially eaten piece of meat and Tomps waved a crust of bread with fruit preserve smeared on it in his general direction.

"Good." Parrish approved. "Then once we have eaten our fill, we should find some dry clothes and get on with the day. We need to speak with the great Wise One." He turned to the still silent woman. "Can you let the holy man know that we wish to speak with him?"

She was once more astounded at the Chieftain's attitude towards her. Not an order, but a question. Yet she rallied and bowed again before finding her voice.

"He... The great one knows of your presence and has already made it known that he is ready to listen, whenever you are ready to talk."

"Fair play." A thoughtful look crossed Parrish's face before he turned again to his friends. "Eat up men, drink, get dressed and comfortable and then we will go and have a chat with the old so and so."

The woman was mortified at Parrish's casual disrespect towards the high priest of the Earth Goddess. Klud and Tomps just nodded again and returned their attention to the food in their hands. The man himself took a swig from the water bag, winked a smile at the gaping woman and turned his attention to his own food.

*

The meeting with the Wisest of the Wise Ones went almost as Parrish had expected, but at the end he wasn't the only one to deliver a surprise.

The men were called out of their hut and led away through the snow to the great shine hut. They walked in silence down through the gently sloping access tunnel and out onto the central floor at the base of the huge Earth Goddess statue.

Parrish had done this trip several times, but his friends were completely in the realm of the unknown.

Directly across from the trio sat the Wisest of the Wise Ones, on the bottom row bench seat of the internal amphitheatre. Seats that went up and back in regular increments all the way to the far wall, curving around and encompassing three quarters of the huts internal circumference. The other section was filled with the huge Goddess statue, more than five metres tall. It towered over everyone, especially the three men who had emerged from the access tunnel which exited into the shrine hut beneath her feet, placing her worshippers below her.

There was no central fire but the place was not cold, and it was well illuminated with dozens of tallow lamps hanging from long string baskets, their securing points hidden way up in the dark rafters of the thatch high above everyone.

Of course, no one cared about such a trivial thing. On the rising and receding benches sat dozens of holy men, all peering silently down at the three warriors in the pit below the Earth Goddess's feet.

Perhaps the place is heated by religious fervour? Parrish thought briefly before being hailed by his old friend.

"Come. Come and sit." crackled the unmistakable dry, rustly voice. "You and your fine friends. Sit." And he patted the hard surface beside him with his left hand.

Parrish crossed the open area and sat as indicated, now immediately facing the great statue. Klud and Tomps dutifully followed and sat to their Chieftain's left, on the opposite side to that of the high priest. Yet because of the curvature of the bench, they were all clearly visible to one another.

Then, to the hungry ears of every holy man there, Parrish told of the events to the north of this part of Dannu's land. Klud and Tomps were initially unsure that they should even be in such exalted company, but their Chieftain was insistent. As far as he was concerned, they were as important to the eventual successful outcome of their recent adventure as he was. As he told the amazing tale to the revered old man the two Danebury warriors added snippets of information when asked and by the end were helping to explain aspects of the mission that Parrish was either not sure about or was deliberately omitting through modesty. At these parts the two warriors were quite boldly interrupting their Chieftain, determined to make sure their great friend got all the credit due him for his efforts, skills and accomplishments.

The grey-haired old man could not contain his smiles whenever the two warriors proudly spoke out, occasionally correcting Parrish's less than boastful moments, or to add details or enlarge on a particular event or crucial moment. They wanted the great holy man to know just how great their own Chieftain was, and how great was their love and respect for their leader and friend.

There was no denying it *was* an astounding tale and the high priest of the Earth Goddess and every other holy man there bowed emphatically to them all when they were finished. Parrish took this mark of respect in his stride, but Klud and Tomps were quite stunned by the accolade.

"And this white wolf man?" The old man asked finally. "He believed he was possessed by the spirit of the creature he killed?"

"He had been badly injured." Parrish tried to explain without appearing to condone the man's actions. "His mind was broken. You can see his skull if you wish."

"No need." The high priest paused. "Well, it is a great tale, well told and well done. Dannu and I could not have asked for more. I must say though, I find it quite a surprise to hear that a holy man, no less than one from this very temple, has a trophy. This is not something I would expect or perhaps approve of."

This time the wise old man managed to hide his smile of satisfaction as the three heroes opposite him immediately leapt to their friend's defence.

"He saved my life!" barked Klud on the instant.

"He has also taken charge of a lost village." added Tomps with a fierce pride.

"He saved all our lives." Parrish followed on. "There cannot be another holy man in all of Dannu's land who has done so much for the Goddess. Luke has taken a head, which I am sure he regrets every day, and he carries a battle wound. And I can think of no one more worthy of our respect."

"Yes!" exclaimed Tomps sharply.

"He is a brave man." said Klud more evenly. "And he is our friend."

"I understand." said the holy man, knowing that a bond formed in battle is as close as that between brothers, and also that these two honest warriors of Dannu had just come as close as they dare to actually criticising their religious leader. He offered them both a disarming smile then turned again to Parrish, considered for a long moment then spoke.

"It was well done, my son. And we are all in your debt. But there is now another matter to be taken in hand."

"Huh?"

"There is someone here you need to see." The Wisest of the Wise Ones said evenly, all evidence of mirth dropping from his face. The sudden, deadly seriousness in the old man's eyes made Parrish's heart sink. He had seen that look before.

After bowing a goodbye to the high priest, which received a massed bow from all the holy men in return, the three men made their way back up through the access tunnel and out into the crisp, cold, snow laden air. They were accompanied by one of the old man's personal assistants, one of the pairs that seemed to go with him everywhere. In truth, the Wisest of the Wise Ones would have liked to walk with his tall friend, but the old man had no desire to risk injury or ill health through unnecessary exposure to cold and possibly treacherous ice, so offered the man as a guide.

"He will take you where you need to go." was the high priests mysterious, disturbingly vague parting comment.

The silent guide bowed again to Parrish once they had emerged into the dull daylight, took the lead and strode boldly off, up over the raised walkway and back into the Avebury village proper. The Danebury trio followed him through the eerily quiet compound in silence, and they all weaved their way Indian file between silent, snow shrouded roundhouses until they came to a stop outside one, as non-descript as all the others. It was almost the nearest hut to the entrance gate and on the edge of the village.

Parrish, Klud and Tomps just waited in the chill with bemused looks on their faces while the aloof holy guide called out the occupants of the building.

A young man ducked out and straightened. A stunned, surprised look froze his features.

In contrast, a smile burst onto Parrish's face and his companions grinned too.

"Hew!" he exclaimed. "Well, what a surprise."

The holy man simply turned to leave, catching Parrish's eye as he did so. The Chieftain's eyebrow rose in silent query. Was this what the wise one had hinted at, he wondered.

The departing holy man clearly understood, almost imperceptibly shook his head and just walked away.

"It is good to see you." said Klud with a broad grin.

"You look well." added Tomps with a cheery smile. "I trust you are in good spirits?"

A troubled look had replaced Hew's initial surprise and, unaccountably for Klud and Tomps, he ignored the pair and bowed formally to Parrish.

“Chieftain. If you would please...?” he indicated the entrance to his house and Parrish smiled again to his young friend as he passed him and ducked inside.

Klud and Tomps followed their leader in but almost physically bumped into his back once they entered as the Chieftain stood erect then stopped dead in his tracks, just inside the entrance.

All those inside the hut had risen to their feet as he had entered. But one of them only had a single foot.

“Gant!” Gasped Parrish and couldn't stop the English words tumbling from his lips. “What the fuck are you doing here?!”

27

Gant bowed to his friend and Chieftain. It was difficult to explain but even before anything had been said, Parrish somehow felt the apology in the gesture.

Klud and Tomps stood at Parrish's back, stunned to see their friend in this stranger's hut in a strange village. Their thoughts were as one and the question, so who is in charge at Dane-bre, ran through their minds.

Parrish was much more succinct.

"What has happened?" His voice, somewhere between anger and puzzlement, cut through the bafflement.

"That... that is what I am here to tell you." blurted Gant, his usual confidence and calmness nowhere to be seen. "And to give you warning."

"Warning?" Parrish's face began to darken, puzzlement giving way now to more open anger. If Gant was here at Avebury, it didn't take a genius to figure out something had gone badly wrong at Danebury.

The calm voice of reason, trying to defuse the rising tension, came from a totally unexpected quarter.

Mara stepped forward and spoke, even as she was bowing to the terrifying giant that had just appeared in her house. She knew who he was though, easily recognisable from her son's descriptions.

"Please, Chieftain. Come. Come and sit by the fire. I have food and we shall eat and then perhaps everything will become clearer to you."

Klud and Tomps were shocked at this bold and unforgivable interruption by a female, Gant not so much, having spent several days in her company. Parrish turned slowly to face down the approaching female, only to be interrupted by Hew, darting quickly in between the tall man and this outrageously forward woman.

“Yes. Please.” he said hurriedly. “Please sit.” Hew desperately wanted to try and save his mother from what looked like an imminent beating. Parrish ignored the youngster, sweeping him roughly aside with an arm and towered over his diminutive mother.

“And you are?” he growled flatly, glaring down at her.

“I am Mara.” Came the reply. The woman’s colour began to drain from her face but she heroically stood her ground. “Hew is my son, and you are in my house!”

There were more gasps. Such effrontery! Such an insult! How dare a mere female reply so boldly to a man, let alone a Chieftain? There would surely be severe retribution now.

Parrish bristled momentarily, but then something seemed to leave him. His natural equilibrium appeared to return and his shoulders relaxed. He exhaled forcibly and looked Mara in the eye. It was then that she looked hurriedly away, knowing she had gone way too far, his stillness frightening her more than his bluster. She cowered to take the first blow but the giant before her simply bowed his head in apology.

“You are right, of course. Look at me. I come straight in here and act like it is *my* house and I can do as I please.” Mara’s eyes came up to look at him and he laughed out loud. “I can see who runs this house. I apologise for my bad behaviour.” He straightened and nodded to the woman barely two thirds his size and less than half his weight. “I am Parrish, Chieftain of Dane-bre and I thank you for inviting me into your home.” he said cordially. “These are my two friends and if there is enough food to go around, I would be grateful if you could share it with us all.”

Hew stepped up a second time, as amazed as everyone else by Parrish’s sublimation, and bowed to his friend.

“This is my mother,” he said proudly, “and this,” He pulled a small girl out from behind Mara, where she had been all the time clinging to the back of her mother’s skirt. “This is my sister, Mimi.”

The little girl's eyes looked ready to fall right out of her head they were so wide, her head tilted right back so she could look up at the huge giant towering over her. And she had Parrish right there and then. Anger instantly gone, his voice dropped and he knelt down to Mimi's level.

"Hello little one. I am pleased to meet you." He said softly. The girl did not utter a sound. "I am the Chieftain of a village called Dane-bre, but you can just call me Parrish."

Mimi remembered herself then and managed a half decent bow before retreating part way back behind her mother's legs. "I... I am honoured... to meet you. Parrish." she finally squeaked.

Parrish laughed again and rose back up to full height.

"Right." he said back to his usual, Chieftain-like demeanour. "Now everyone knows everyone, let us all sit." He nodded to Mara as if silently asking permission, who nodded respectfully back. "And we can get to the bottom of this mystery." He eyed his one-legged friend, who looked stressed and rather forlorn. Gant wasn't looking forward to telling his Chieftain that his beloved village was lost and *he* was to blame.

*

By the time the full story of the fall of Dane-bre had been told, dusk had come and gone and another cold, cloudy and snow laden night had begun.

Mara had supplied food and drink during the pow-wow, all the while listening in silent amazement to the story of the unfolding events at a village to the south she had never even heard of. Mimi too had kept very quiet, only occasionally putting another log on the central fire around which all the men sat. Parrish did notice though that the girl always seemed to slip carefully back around behind the group and unerringly ended up beside Gant. It was obvious to him the girl was staying close for moral support. The mere slip of a thing had clearly taken a shine to his one-legged friend and was feeling his pain. The man himself was the only one who spoke, relaying the events that led up to where he now sat, and the impossible position he felt he had put Chieftain Parrish in. Gant told the tale to him and his friends and fellow warriors with pain in his voice and anguish in his eyes. He was damned from his own lips. He knew he had let down his Chieftain, his friends, family and village. He had no doubt Dannu thought ill of him too. His honour was gone and he had no excuse. It was a wonder his friends and his Chieftain could even bear to look at him as he sat there in disgrace.

The silence that fell as he finished was complete and heavy. Everyone just stared at Gant now the full story had come out. Gant stared at the ground before him, now unable to look anyone in the eye. And the silence dragged on.

"Well." said Parrish finally, breaking the hush. All eyes turned to the tall man as he leaned back from his contemplation of the news. "It looks like everything has gone seriously pear shaped back home!" He rolled his eyes then erupted loudly. "What a real shit that Shimon turned out to be!" he spat.

Gant looked up then.

"I am sorry, my Chieftain. I know I should have stayed and died with honour, but I thought you should know before..."

"Quite right." Parrish interrupted. "And do not be sorry. What you did was right. A lesser man would have not seen past his own honour. Even more so as a village Chieftain. You did the right thing, even though it was the hardest choice. Anyone can give their life for their village. But their honour is another matter. It is what makes a man a man. Add to that the agony of leaving everyone behind to be at Shimon's mercy," He scoffed. "and knowing you would not be there to try to protect them all, Gant, what you did was one of the finest acts of bravery I have ever heard of. Speaking as one Chieftain to another, you know now as I do, that the right decisions are sometimes the hardest ones. I honour you for it, my friend." He made a decent seated bow of respect to his one-legged friend.

Klud, Tomps and Hew were still seated, motionless as the two men spoke, mouths open as Parrish laid out in no uncertain terms their friends predicament. When he bowed to Gant the Danebury pair seemed to come back to life.

"You are in the right of it!" blurted Klud as he now saw his great friends reasoning and understood Gant's dilemma.

"Yes. I could not see it till you explained." added Tomps. "A lesser man would have just attacked and died honourably."

"It is what I would have done!" interrupted Klud.

"But it would have been a hollow victory." Tomps continued and turned to Gant. "I am sorry to have felt ill will towards you, my friend. You are a wise and great man."

Gant finally allowed a small smile to cross his lips, looked up to the Dane-bre warriors, who bowed back, then he looked again to Parrish, this time gazing directly into the tall man's eyes.

"But I feel I could have, should have done more."

"I understand." Parrish nodded, and he truly did. "But there was no more you could have done, trust me. Dying back at Dane-bre would have only given Shimon a Chieftain's head as a trophy, a victory to show everyone there and more power to control the villagers with. But instead, you are here. With friends, brave warriors and with information that is of great use to me." He paused and looked at everyone around him. Klud and Tomps, both keen and brave, Hew was still in stunned amazement, likewise Mara, still motionless and open mouthed, the bowl of food momentarily forgotten in her hands as she stared at the Chieftain of Dane-bre. Even little Mimi was staring at him, now sat beside Gant and clinging on to his arm.

Parrish looked at them all then stared into the fire for a few moments, took a deep breath and, summing up everything in his mind said to no one in particular.

"Dane-bre is in peril. Wives and families are at a bad man's mercy and we are at least three days walk away, with winter biting hard."

“Yes.” said Gant, still as practical as ever and seeing the total futility of their situation. “The snow is much too deep for travel. And the holy ones say this weather could last for perhaps three hands of days or even more. And every village settles in and waits the winter out. It is the way of things. It is set that we will be here till the spring!”

There was a long silence. Parrish could feel them all looking at him even though he continued to stare into the flames.

Klud of course was the one to break the spell.

“So, there is nothing to be done? We just wait here till the weather gets better?” There was a tang of hopelessness in his voice.

“Fuck that!” snapped Parrish and his head swivelled until he looked his oldest friend in the eye. The hard, pitiless gaze made the Neolithic man suddenly gulp. He had seen that look before and it frightened him. And there was a moment when he almost felt sorry for the Chieftain of Olann-bre. He did not know it but the wrath of Dannu was in her man and his gaze was looking in Shimon’s direction.

“I will not stand idly by while some Stone Age shit tries to take my village.” growled Parrish slowly and with determination. “His time will come.” Then he sat up straight. “But that is for later. First, I have three words for you all. Tent, sledge and snowshoes.”

28

Parrish asked Mara and Hew if he and his men could stay the night in their house. The pair could hardly refuse but it was a nice gesture on Parrish's part and much appreciated by those whose house it was.

Klud and Tomps braved the cold night air and quickly returned carrying three sets of bedding from their original ancillary hut.

Once everything and everyone was settled, Parrish took centre stage and by the dancing light of the central fire and the hanging tallow lamps he preceded to explain his scheme for the next day. Or two days at the most, he did not intend to hang about.

Everyone would make a pair of snowshoes. He would show them how. Describing the deep snow defying footwear as looking like cheap and nasty tennis rackets didn't help much, but they would understand once he had demonstrated.

And he wanted a sled built. Sturdy, at least the length of two men with a long central platform to carry the load, runners the full length beneath the sled with curved up front ends and a sturdy foot board at the rear just behind a waist high handrail. Everyone would chip in with its construction and he would lead the way if there were any confusion.

Then he wanted Mara and Mimi to organise as many loose animal skins as they could and sew them together in such a way that they would wrap fully around his final piece of equipment. He wanted eight poles, at least fifteen feet long, which would be tied together at one end then stood up with the other ends splayed out on the ground. With one huge, segmented skin covering wrapped around the structure, with the top foot or so open to allow smoke to escape, he would have himself a wigwam. His thinking was having a single structure that would be quick to erect at the end of each day, weatherproof and big enough for everyone on the journey in one overnight shelter.

The sled would carry the poles tied to its sides. It would also carry all the bedding, other necessary equipment and food enough for five days travel, although Parrish expected the thirty five mile journey to take no more than three days. And it could also carry Gant if, as he suspected would be so, it was simply too difficult to fit a snowshoe to a wooden stump or for the man to use it. With three body strap harnesses roped to the front of the sled he estimated it should not be impossible for three men, perhaps only two at a time if the ground wasn't too steep or obstructed, to pull the sled. It was his hope to complete at least ten miles a day. But of course, only time would tell.

Snowshoes first, then everyone would have some time to practice with them while gathering materials and construction of the transport could begin. The wood for the sled and wigwam could be gathered from the forest. As for the pole covering, Parrish assured Mara that he would speak with the holy village Chieftain. If every home in Avebury gave just one skin, there should be enough to make a wigwam covering and no family would be so inconvenienced as to make their own lives difficult. Also, enough rattan matting would be needed to cover the wigwam floor to insulate its occupants against the frozen ground.

It was at this point that Hew spoke up.

“I have been thinking.” The lad began cautiously. “I have spoken with my mother, and although we do not know what you intend when you reach Dane-bre, it is sure to be dangerous. I think you will need all the help you can get. So, I would like to go with you, my friend.”

Parrish was charmed by the gesture but did not agree with it.

“I do not think so.” he said quietly. “Even if we all live, it will be difficult for you to get back here to your family. So, it would be more likely you would have to remain at Dane-bre till the spring. What would then happen to Mara and Mimi here? Who would look after them then? And provide fuel and food? No, I do not think so."

"Then we shall come along too." said Mara in a very matter-of-fact tone, hugging Mimi to her side. "There would be nothing and no one for us here anyway. It was just so when Hew left for Dane-bre the first time."

"But if you come, and are not killed," said Parrish, "you would have to remain at Dane-bre too."

"As you once said to me." interjected Hew with a wry smile. "It is a fine place to be."

He had the tall man there.

"Yes, I did." Parrish thought fast. "But that was before that shit Shimon made his move. I know not what is going on there now or what condition my village and its people are in." It hurt him to say those last words and he worked hard to suppress the sudden dread he felt for his own family.

"True," Hew nodded and waved an arm towards his mother and sister. "But we would still be together as a family, and you will have our support, no matter what."

Parrish wasn't overly pleased but could not deny the logic of the lad's answer.

"I am grateful for your offer and another man at my side would be a help, but this decision is on your own head, Hew. I do not know what Dane-bre will be like when we get there. I do not know if any of us will live long enough to find out. I cannot promise that we will even live to make it all the way home in weather like this. I can make no promises but that I will do everything I can to make things right. I offer no more than that."

Hew looked at Mara and Mimi. His mother nodded firmly. Mimi simply clung to her mother's side watching, wide eyed. Hew turned back to Parrish.

"We are with you, my Chieftain." he said firmly.

There were cries of appreciation from the Danebury men and Gant clapped the young warrior on the back.

There was a pause before Parrish sighed in resignation.

"OK." He nodded acceptance to these fine people of Avebury. "Good man. And I am grateful. Anyway," he smiled, suddenly changing the subject. "Well, at least that is the issue of the floor mats solved. We will take the ones we are sitting on. After all there will be no one here to use them once we have gone!"

After a moment's stunned silence, the hut rang with laughter and Parrish clapped his hands together, grinning. "Glad that is sorted anyway. Now, let us all get a good night's sleep. A lot to do on the morrow."

*

The following day started with Parrish and his people wading out through more fresh snow into the forest, gathering a good selection of willow and hazel wands and then retiring back to their roundhouse to weave and knot together what in essence Parrish had previously described as 'rubbish looking tennis rackets'.

Despite the cold there was some fun to be had as everyone learned and perfected the wider legged, short pacing technique used to master snowshoes. Bouts of falling over in the snow, waddling around and watching others learn at their own pace kept the seriousness of what they were soon going to attempt a little lighter.

But Parrish eventually called the group back to the task at hand and, using their new found skill and footgear, a more determined foray was made back into the quiet forest for materials. They sought out the correct shaped sturdy, straight limbs with curved ends, the various lengths of timber for the bed and rails of Parrish's never before heard of sled. Plus the long poles for the wigwam. Aided by their new found ability to move across snow that was sometimes thigh deep, the rough wooden assemblies were transported back to their roundhouse. With some shaping and scraping smooth where needed, notching and tying, the sled soon began to take shape. Everything went smoothly and Parrish was pleasantly surprised. He had genuinely expected it would take more than a day to get his never before heard of 'load carrying over soft snow thing' made.

But he had forgotten about his good friend. Gant the organiser. His logical, instinctively planning brain came into its own. He organised the warriors to fell and carry the long lengths, the women to collect skins and sew. He even had Mimi gather items Parrish had requested as what he called 'extra kit'. The girl was more than happy to follow Gants guiding commands and cord and rope were swiftly collected. She made small brush brooms to sweep off accumulations of snow and to clear the ground for the wigwam after the shoulder blade shovel she also collected would have removed the bulk of the snow from the prospective campsite.

The whole team were busy the entire day, working outside their roundhouse while Mara, between sessions of joining together the wigwam skins, called them in periodically for reviving warmth, food or hot drinks to keep their energy levels up.

Parrish was pleasantly surprised just how fast they all gelled together and the speed at which the work progressed. But what really surprised him was the fact that nobody else in Avebury village seemed remotely interested in their endeavour.

The place was like a ghost town. The only other people seen during the day was the occasional woman who would appear from some random roundhouse, mine an undisturbed nearby snowdrift for clean snow to fill their buckets, and then quickly retreat back into their huts, no doubt to melt the snow for water. No men appeared at all. Not even the village Chieftain. Perhaps they simply did not care? Maybe they thought it was none of their business. They might not have even been aware of what was going on if their wives, who obviously were not permitted to speak out of turn, simply didn't tell their warrior husbands of the busy builders outside in the cold.

Whatever, Parrish just shrugged and worked on with everyone else, under his guiding instructions and pitching in where necessary. To his utter amazement and complete joy, the sled was completed before dusk that day. They even had time to tie off the ten feet long tow ropes to the front of it, looped the wide leather straps around their shoulders and the men had a dry run towing the sled around inside the village. The curved runners worked well enough and on flat snow even with the pullers still quite new to their snowshoes, two men could easily move the empty sled. Parrish knew that loaded it might be a different matter, but he had four able bodied men to do the work, plus Gant who could push or scoot a little at the rear of it. Mara and even little Mimi were on hand and could push too if it really came down to it.

I mean, he thought. This is just a few days across a snowy southern England. Not Captain Scott trudging to his eventual doom near the South Pole.

Leaving the new sled outside as dusk fell, everyone retired for the evening and in the warmth of the roundhouse they rechecked their equipment, foodstuffs and any personal items Hugh, Mara and Mimi might want to take away with them. Finally everything that they could think of to do was done. Everyone sat around the fire and looked in silent expectation to the Chieftain of Dane-bre. Parrish was not sure how the next few days would unfold but he was as confident as he could be about their little expedition.

"I believe we are ready." he said firmly to his people, who nodded in agreement. "We load up at first light. Last thing we do is cut up part of this floor." He grinned. "If there is anything else you can think of that you might want," he looked to Hew and his family, "Now is the time to gather it. As soon as everything is strapped onto the sled tomorrow, we set off for Dane-bre."

“Should we not load up the sled now and be ready first thing in the morning?” said Hew tentatively, not quite sure if he should question the Chieftain.

“No.” Parrish thought it was a reasonable assumption and explained why not. “If we load up now and leave it all outside it will freeze solid during the night. It will be that much heavier and harder to move first thing.” There were nods around the group at their Chieftains wisdom. “So,” he scanned the faces before him. “Get a good night's sleep. Up with the dawn and we will load up and set off towards Dane-bre as soon as we are sure everything is ready.” Another grin spit his features at that. Finally, he was going home. Klud and Tomps nodded firmly in agreement.

The Avebury people were not quite so certain, but just as determined.

29

Nervous anticipation ensured everyone was up before the dawn. Mara had everybody fortified with bowls of a hot, coarse porridge and as soon as it was light enough the loading began. Mimi was secretly pleased that the very first items used was one of her little hand brooms, to sweep the light overnight dusting of snow off the bed of the sled. It really didn't take that long to load. Things needed last went on first, and those needed first on last. The wigwam parts were laid on top of the covered bedding rolls and finally the men's weapons were secured on top of everything else.

Mara was the last one out of her roundhouse. There was no real regret at leaving her home. Some other family would move in sooner or later. She kicked at the patch of bare earth in the flooring, hid a small smile then stepped out into the cold.

Everyone was well wrapped up. Parrish looked at her for a moment then swept the rest of the band with his gaze. He had to stop himself from laughing out loud. A bunch of Eskimo pirates wasn't too far from the mark.

“All ready?” He didn't really wait for a reply. “Then let us go.” Klud, Tomps and Hew looped their straps over their shoulders. Gant stood ready to push/scoot and Mara and Mimi stepped up beside the long sled. “Forward!” Parrish did his best US cavalry officer wave and led off towards the main gate.

Once Gant had rocked the sled to free its runners from the nights ground ice, it lurched and moved forward with surprising ease and the three men yoked to it began to realise their hope that this journey might not be as big a trial as they feared. Parrish had said that over flat ground he thought two men would be enough to pull the sled. And that the pairs would take it in turns to do the work. But for leaving the encampment, everyone agreed that the Chieftain should be seen to lead the way, not pulling a load plus, with three people pulling the sled, it would appear to any onlookers that their task was almost effortless.

But it was only as they reached the main gate did they see any other people out in the cold. A tiny delegation of just two holy men waited at the entrance. They did at least heave the gate open and as Parrish waved his people on through, saying he would catch them up, he stopped to talk with the men. They both bowed and before he could speak, one piped up.

"The Wisest of the Wise Ones begs the pardon of the Chieftain of Dane-bre but he fears the cold and snow would not be good for him. He sends his best wishes and says to go with Dannu, my son. He also says he feels things will unfold as they should now."

The last sentence in particular made Parrish smile. It bolstered his hopes for a brighter outcome in whatever lay ahead. After all, the holy one was not given to making wildly inaccurate statements.

"Tell him I am grateful for his words and wish him well through these cold days. Tell him also that I look forward to seeing him at the next solstice gathering, if it is the will of Dannu."

"It will be done." The pair bowed to him again and one man looked out to where the sled party were making their way off down the gently sloping open snowfield that led towards the great stone circle. "Take care, Chieftain. And go with Dannu." He said it like he expected them all to be dead of exposure before the next morning, but he meant it all the same.

Parrish nodded in acknowledgement. "And you." was all he said in reply then turned and set off after his party.

The two holy men swung the gates shut without a word, shrugged and set off back to the great shrine hut to inform the holy one that the tall man and his group had left. And also, to warm up.

Once they were out of sight, Parrish pulled Klud off sled duties. He felt it only fair to explain that not only did he do it to see if just two men could manage, but if they could, then he was putting together matching pairs. He and Klud were the old hands while Tomps and Hew were his two young fire eaters. This caused grins all round and the two youngsters bowed in their harnesses.

"We will not let you down." They said, almost as one.

"I do not doubt it for a moment." said Parrish and returned the bow.

With fresh grins on their faces the pair leant into their task and pulled away manfully towards the great stone circle at the head of the monolith lined avenue that led away to the gathering point.

Parrish watched them closely as Klud and the two females walked alongside. Gant did his best to scoot and help on any shallow inclines. His occasional glance at the Chieftain told Parrish that his friend was not happy at being basically excess weight for the pullers, but his common sense told him there was no other option. Parrish nodded and smiled at his friend to indicate he understood and the quiet agreement between them seemed to be enough.

Once they had push/pulled and otherwise walked through the varying depths of snow up and over the low ridge beyond the gathering point, the expedition was into the Vale of Pewsey. Steadily travelling southwards, the day became a silent trudge, quietly weaving their way between the widespread oaks, beech and hazel trees, with the ever present cold and the undulating, unblemished, virgin snowdrifts their only companions.

The pulling pairs traded places at regular intervals, the relief from the unhitching pair palpable every time. It was not unduly hard, but it was relentless work.

By the middle of the day Mimi was flagging and really beginning to struggle, only to be suddenly scooped up by Parrish and plonked atop the sled just in front of Gant.

"I... I can walk." she whispered in a high squeak to the friendly giant towering over her.

"I know." Parrish whispered back with a smile at her tiny act of bravery. "But I need you to keep Gant company. He is not happy all alone there on the back. After all, no one likes to be last man."

"Oh..." She turned to look at her friend, who smiled back then nodded in gratitude to his Chieftain.

"Thank you..." his voice low also.

"Do not thank me." Parrish interrupted still speaking quietly. "Tomps and Hew are still pulling and have not noticed yet." He grinned, winked to the pair and walked away, his heart warmed by the incident. It was so Army to sneakily add some load to another squaddies pack and watch their faces when they realised what had happened. Happy days, he thought and for a moment saw his friends Chris Dunn, Bunny Rabbett and the rest of B squad in his mind's eye, all pissing themselves laughing. And it did not matter at all that he and Klud would have to haul the same extra weight later.

The men continued to swap places on a regular basis, Parrish trying not to push the pace too hard or punish the pullers any more than necessary. 'Marathon not a sprint', were the watch words from the Army instructors when he was one of the many soldiers training in Norway.

The distance across the ground from Avebury to the northern edge of Salisbury Plain was a little over ten miles. The group made it with some daylight to spare. This same route, but in reverse, from Dane-bre heading northwards and up and out onto the plain involved no more effort than a gentle incline, until the plain opened up before everyone, a great, almost treeless expanse. But after crossing the plain, descending from the northern edge down into the Vale of Pewsey was by a steep decline, dropping down into the wooded valley. Parrish always knew this topographical change would be the stiffest obstacle on their journey back and would need everyone's determination and maximum effort. Parrish's dilemma was should he either, push everyone and struggle up the steep slippery hillside after an exhausting day or camp overnight under the lee the escarpment. It would hopefully be easier to tackle the slope in the morning when everyone was fresh, but then the risk was not getting right across the plain the next day and finding themselves exposed on a windswept and desolate plateau with no fuel and shelter bar what they had with them. He knew the Plain was about twelve miles across. If they tackled the hill fresh just after first light and did not take too long to reach the crest of the escarpment, they could hopefully move more swiftly across the open, unobstructed area ahead of them and make the southern edge with its forests, fuel and shelter, by dusk. The approximate area he was aiming for was where one of his old Army stamping grounds, Tidworth, would eventually be built, far off in the future. He knew there were low hills and streams there, so a much better place to stop. Especially if it continued to snow, or the bitter wind happened to pick up.

Looking at his tired men and feeling it himself, he knew hours of slow weaving between the mighty oaks had taken it out of them all.

OK. Hill in the morning then, he decided, and bank on an untroubled crossing of Salisbury Plain tomorrow, if it is the will of Dannu.

The escarpment rose into view, and everyone began looking at it with a growing sense of trepidation, and could not take their eyes from it as they drew nearer.

Calling a halt, Parrish stood with hands on hips, looking up at the obstacle before them. They were not to know it, but everyone was standing almost exactly at the base of what would be marked on a modern Ordnance Survey map as Redhorn Hill. It wasn't a cliff or in any way a dangerous climb, but still a punishing, steep and relentless up slope to its summit on the northernmost lip of Salisbury Plain at six hundred and ninety feet above sea level.

“That will take a bit of effort.” said Parrish rather nonchalantly. Everyone turned to him. “But not today.” He smiled at their grim faces. “An early camp tonight I think, then we will have a bash at it fresh in the morning.” There were poorly disguised expressions of relief all round.

The wigwam went up easily enough. Gant had the two young men set off to find fuel for the night. Klud and Parrish shovelled the snow out from inside the span of the wigwams spread legs then shovelled it back over the foot of the skin covering around the base once it had been fitted to the framework, to make a waterproof and windproof seal. Mimi brushed the remaining snow up against the inside edge and helped Mara lay down the rattan matting, leaving a central area of bare ground for a small hearth. She was preparing food as the two young warriors returned with armfuls of felled standing deadwood and Gant soon had a small central fire going as Mimi laid out the bedding around it. It was fairly snug inside, but everyone could at least lay out without putting their feet in the flames. By the time dusk fell and the temperature really began to plummet, everyone was inside, snug and warm. With eight bodies, well seven and a half with Mimi, their natural heat and a small fire was more than sufficient. So, there was fuel enough then to last the night and everyone was well fed.

Lots of tired limbs had a final stretch then sleep came quickly to the occupants of the only wigwam in Neolithic Britain.

30

With no fresh overnight snow, it was a slightly brighter start to the morning, at least weather wise. For the seven people standing at the bottom of the hill, looking up at its bleak, snowy steepness, not so much.

Everyone was fed, warmly wrapped and ready. The sled was loaded just as the day before, but Parrish could have sworn it looked heavier than yesterday. He chuckled at his silliness, causing his companions to shoot him puzzled glances.

"Right. Let us be off. The sooner we get this done the better."

There were nods and everyone bent to their tasks. All four fully fit men were strapped into harnesses now. Parrish and Klud were the inside pair, with Tomps and Hew as wing men. The two females were set to push. No one expected anything of Gant. They all knew he had a struggle of his own to deal with. To lighten everyone's load he had earlier insisted that he would make his own way up the incline. In the deep snow, everyone knew it was going to be difficult for him. The other three men had earlier voiced their concerns to their Chieftain, but Parrish answered quietly.

"He feels he must do this. He sees it as a point of honour. But, if we get to the top before him, then we will go back and help him up." That settled the others and now they were ready.

Parrish signalled to start and up they all went.

Everyone was determined there would be no stopping. The quiet descended again, with no talking and no looking up and away to the summit. With light but very sparse snowflakes beginning to drift gently down around them, Parrish set a slow, steady pace and with heads down the men pulled while Mara and little Mimi pushed as best they could. Parrish's one fear was that if they did stop, or more than a couple of them lost their footing at the same time, they might all start to slither backwards, but no one paused or failed. The distance over the steep ground was less than a mile but it did not take long before their breaths became ragged and their chests heaved, yet they did not stop. It seemed that the top remained stubbornly as far away as ever, but they did not stop. And finally, just when everyone thought their hearts would burst, they felt themselves slightly speeding up and it was as if their load had strangely lightened. Like everyone else, Parrish had just been looking at the snow in front of him, planting one foot doggedly in front of the other, and he looked up in surprise to discover that they were now on level ground, a bleak but beautiful snowy expanse spreading out before them.

He called a halt and just stood leaning forwards, palms flat on his thighs, panting. Everyone slumped into the snow and there was a grateful silence while they all regained their breath.

Parrish gave everyone a few more moments then turned to face them.

"Right-oh." he said shucking off his straps. "I am off back for Gant..."

"No, my Chieftain." said Tomps boldly. "We will go." and he helped Hew who was already clambering to his feet.

"Yes," agreed his young friend readily. "Everyone rest, and we will soon be back." He smiled at his mother, who stared proudly back. Before Parrish could even reply the two youngsters had turned and set off back down the slope.

Gant was indeed struggling up through the drifts, but he had done well, and the two descending young warriors found him almost three quarters of the way to the crest. Without a word they went to his side, looped an arm each over their shoulders and with Gant half hanging between them by his armpits, the three paddled their way steadily up to the summit.

"This way, my friend." Tomps could be heard to say as they began to come back into view of the others. "Your sled awaits." And the two youngsters laughed, setting the rest of the troop off, and as they crested the escarpment in the fresh tracks of the others, the youthful cheer seemed to cap off everyone's achievement.

Parrish enjoyed the merriment but while the rest were still chuckling, he looked away to the southeast across the snowy plain, the smile dropping from his face as he knew what must be done next. It was crucial to cross this before night. Apart from the odd snow mounded up lumps of scrub, the scene reminded him of arctic tundra. His earlier thought of Scott of the Antarctic walking slowly to his doom suddenly didn't seem quite so far-fetched.

After giving the others their moment of success, he called them all back to the task at hand.

“Right.” he said again but in a lighter tone than before. “If we can get off this Plain before dusk, one more day of effort should see us home, yes?” They were happy nods of agreement, the others missing the hidden threat to life and limb in the beginning of his sentence. “OK. Everyone as you were, and we will be off.”

And Parrish’s earlier assumption was right. The going was somewhat easier over open, more-or-less level ground. Especially without the need to constantly dodge trees. Everyone quickly fell into the routine of the previous day and pushed on. Around mid-morning the very light snow stopped falling and shortly after, the clouds began to break. The sky never fully cleared but occasional bouts of wintry sunshine on the faces of the travellers lifted the people’s spirits. The wind remained light and for a short while, the cold seemed just a little less cold.

Parrish thought it was a stroke of good fortune, just when they needed it. Others in his little band thought the Goddess was smiling on her man and they were fortunate to feel its benefits also.

Shifts regularly changed on the harnesses and everyone knew they were doing well, but by the end of the day the clouds had reformed into a solid mass from horizon to horizon and as the light began to fall, so once again did the temperature. It was keenly felt on the people's exposed cheeks.

Even so, the little patrol found themselves dropping down into the edge of the great forest just as the light began to go.

Using the knowledge gained by their previous days assembling of their camp, the wigwam went up expertly and in quick time. It was almost dusk by the time the warriors returned from a quick forage in the woods for some fuel, and everyone found themselves safely inside their shelter as the winter night pressed in. Parrish was not going to mention it, but he felt sure everyone else knew they had reached their safe camp site just in time.

"Back home this time tomorrow." he said as they all sat on their bedding, surrounding the fire. Everyone looked at him, hearing no mirth or joy in his tone. No one wanted to ask the crucial question, what happens then? No one there knew the answer, apart from perhaps their great Chieftain. And he wasn't telling, because Parrish let the unspoken words hang in the air.

In truth, the Chieftain of Dane-bre also had no idea, which just left the great Earth Goddess. And she wasn't telling either.

By the time noon had passed the next day Parrish and his people were steadily closing in on Dane-bre. Those that lived in the hillfort knew the area and were beginning to spot the occasional landmark, recognising a certain weathered tree or natural hollow or watering point. Even in the deep snow. Parrish estimated they were no more than five miles from home, and still with no idea what to do, when they pulled steadily into a shady yew grove and came across what might loosely be described as a small encampment. It looked deserted. A slightly spread cluster of five sorry looking battered wickiups, each perhaps a third buried in freshly drifted snow, despite them being under the spread of the evergreen trees. It was clear that there had certainly been no activity, at least in the last day, the virgin snow around testament to that.

But Parrish was taking no chances. He signalled his people to remain silent and those in the harnesses stepped free and everyone collected their weapons from the sled. Then Parrish had his men spread out and move slowly forward before calling out.

"Hello the camp!"

The weighty silence dragged on. Klud was just about to declare the place deserted when snow was carefully pushed out from the covered entrance of one of the wickiups and a rather haggard, heavily bearded face peered out.

In an attempt to appear threatening but coming across as slightly pathetic, a stone club was waved through the gap.

"Who is there?" came a gruff voice. "I warn you, I am armed."

Klud instantly recognised the voice.

"Bryn? Is that you?"

"Klud?"

"Yes. And the Chieftain is here." Klud added quickly, remembering his manners. The reply surprised everyone.

"Which one?"

Stunned, there was a moment of silence before Parrish said flatly.

"I am Chieftain Parrish of Dane-bre. Now show yourself!"

And the sled party watched in complete hush as one by one the snow encrusted doorways of the wickiups fell away and nine haggard, tired, half feral looking men crawled slowly out and rose to their feet. To their credit they still clutched axes and clubs, but Parrish had never seen such a sorry looking sight.

"Wait. I know these men!" blurted Gant suddenly. "They are the hunting party I sent out the day before Shimon attacked!"

The raggedy men waded slowly through the knee-deep snow and finally stood in a loose group before their tall leader. His own group were close behind him and they all took in the wild looking warriors before them. Dirty, raggedy, sunken cheeked and most likely very hungry.

They all bowed to the Chieftain. He nodded back and immediately took charge.

"Let us get a good fire going. No smoke though. I think we are quite close to Dane-bre, and I do not want to attract any unwanted attention. You men look like you could do with some food, yes?" There were eager nods in reply. "Well, we have plenty." He tilted his head back to indicate the sled behind them. Mara and Hew exchanged amazed looks. How could Parrish possibly have known they would need the extra food when they set off from Avebury? Parrish continued. "Mara, Gant, get the wigwam set up. This is now the campsite for tonight. Everyone keep an eye out in case we have any unwanted visitors, although I doubt anyone will be wandering around in this weather. When Gant's hunting party is fed and more comfortable, I want to have a good talk with them. I think they have given me an idea about Dane-bre."

Everyone glanced at each other. It suddenly seemed like the Chieftain had a plan. Klud and Tomps exchanged knowing glances and grinned together. Things were starting to look up.

"Right. Let us be about it, my friends. Lots to do before dark." Parrish's eyes had a more determined look now. This he could turn to his advantage. At least now he thought he was in with a shout. The half starved ruffians before him didn't look up to much, but for him it was as if the cavalry had just arrived at the eleventh hour.

*

The hunting party immediately felt better coming under someone of command and everyone set to their tasks. In short order the men were warming themselves by a good fire and food was prepared.

Parrish had his back turned when he heard the sharp smack of fist on cheek. He spun to find Mara sprawled on the ground and one of the raggedy men standing over her.

In a flash Parrish pushed between the prone woman and the warrior with the raised fist.

"What goes on here?" he barked.

"How dare a woman approach, speak and ask a question without permission!" snapped the man loudly.

Parrish had nothing to say to that. He looked down again at a repentant looking Mara then back to the 'insulted' warrior.

"You are right." he agreed, somehow managing not to bite his tongue as he said it. "Forget her. I will deal with this." and curtly dismissed the man by turning his back on him.

'Honour' satisfied, the man nodded in agreement. The Chieftain would put this female in her place.

Parrish grabbed Mara roughly by the bicep, hauled her to her feet and half dragged, half marched her around to the far side of the wigwam and out of sight.

Once there he let her go and she just stood in silence, staring submissively down at the ground. Parrish gently cupped her chin in his hand and tilted her face up towards his. A large red welt was already glowing over her left cheek bone.

"Are you alright?" he asked quietly, obvious concern in his voice. "I am so sorry about that."

The confusion on Mara's face was clear but she nodded. "It is as always. But I forgot myself and took what was due me. Do not apologise to me, Chieftain Parrish." She said very formally.

"No. The fault is mine not yours. I should have remembered. This happened once to my wife." He paused. "And it cost me a son." he added quietly. It took him a moment but he shook off the bad memory and picked up. "You are just as my wife. In the house she is free to ask questions but must remain on her guard everywhere else. You are a fine woman, too Mara. Do not change, but please be more careful. I will not always be there to protect you."

"I... I understand." she replied, although she did not fully. "I will not dishonour you."

Parrish grinned and brushed snow particles from her shoulders. “You honour me by being you and not being afraid to speak plainly to me when I need it. You and my wife are I am sure going to be great friends. Now,” He leaned in close. “Look like you have been properly punished, and please be more guarded around this bunch of ruffians.” With that he smacked his hands together loudly twice.

Mara grinned briefly at the deception, then in a flash the smile dropped from her face. She nodded and walked slowly, with head bowed, back around the wigwam and went to pick up the items she had dropped when she was struck.

“Good girl.” Parrish said quietly under his breath.

The remainder of the daylight hours were spent making the ‘miracle’ snowshoes that stop a body from sinking up to the waist in deep snow. The hunting party spent some jolly time flattening the snow around the campsite as they got used to using the footwear, while periodically coming back to the fire to warm themselves.

By the time dusk had come and gone the hunting party had been well fed and watered. Their recovery after that, back to something close to their previous rude health, was quite remarkable. The big, warming fire in the middle of the little encampment had long been extinguished and the light from the small fire inside the wigwam was hidden from the outside world. Inside, the big conical shelter was packed. People sat cheek by jowl with barely room to move. The smell wasn't too good either, but it was ignored. Everyone there was all ears and there was total quiet as the sled party listened to the hunting party’s tale.

With no outright leader amongst the group all of the men chipped in as the story unfolded. Of how they had returned, unsuspecting, to their home after a successful hunt only to be chased away by Olann-bre men. One of their number had been killed by arrow shot and another wounded who managed to escape with his compatriots but died later from his wounds.

Parrish winced at that, knowing it would not have been a pleasant end for the poor individual.

And so, the hunting party had been forced to survive in the great forest. They were of course accomplished hunters and outdoorsmen and were managing, despite having to be ready at a moment's notice to move on from one camp place to the next, being doggedly pursued by bands of Olann-bre hunters. The nine men were proud to say they used their Chieftains stag method to keep watch during the nights but were still surprised one night and lost another man while they made good their escape.

But then the snows had come. The game disappeared and the remaining nine men had to hunker down to wait the weather out, only the deep snows and severe cold persisted. It was clear they were now all somewhat the worse for wear and struggling to survive. And it was only now, having been found by Parrish and his band, the nine felt that they were saved.

Saved by their Chieftain, the great Chieftain of Dane-bre. And Dannu's man.

And now he was plotting their revenge.

31

"Right! This is what I am thinking." Parrish looked around at the faces before him, glowing in the reflected firelight. Well, he thought. I've been in worse places for a combat briefing and at least this lot look keen.

Everyone understood that what the Chieftain thought, because he was now going to explain it to everyone, was what he *expected* to happen, if everyone did their part and it was the will of Dannu.

Parrish nodded in Gant's direction. "We are going to do to Shimon, what he did to us." A wicked grin crossed the one legged man's face. Parrish continued. "We are going to get into our village just as he did. Straight in through the main gate. Only this time it will be *before* dawn tomorrow." The swiftness with which he wanted to execute his plan surprised everyone.

"Er... So soon?" asked Klud carefully. "Do we not need to rest first?" No one else would have dared to question a Chieftain but Parrish and Klud had their almost telepathic understanding of each other so there was no offence meant or taken.

"No." Parrish sounded certain. "Our new friends here have waited long enough. We have travelled more than far enough, and besides, we have eaten all the food today. Plus, the snow helps us. No one will expect anybody to approach with it this deep." Several eyes glanced towards the stacked snowshoes against the wigwam wall behind their Chieftain. "We will all be at the gate a short while before daylight starts to show. The darkness will help hide our approach but it is of no matter. We can cross the snowfield and get to the gate, but everyone knows someone just on foot would struggle very badly. And I am hoping that because it is colder than usual, it will keep them in their beds till after dawn. So I do not expect any lookouts."

There were several nods.

"Klud and I will gain entry to Dane-bre from the north side of the wall. Again, I expect no lookouts there." Klud grinned at the prospect of going into action with his tall friend and gave Tomps beside him a small shoulder barge. Tomps remained po-faced. Parrish appeared not to notice. "We will open the gates and let you all in."

"What about me?" Gant wiggled his prosthetic limb. "The snow…"

"I know." Parrish gave him a friendly grin. "We will pull you on the sled to the gate. We have lots of strong backs," he glanced around. "And also, I have a task ahead just for you. But more of that later." Gant just nodded.

"Once through the gate, and while it is still dark we will start entering the roundhouses. I want at least two men to each hut at first. Grab any Olann-bre men you find sleeping there and tell them that if they make any noise they will be killed. Give any clubs and axes you find to the Dane-bre warriors and allow them to take charge. I know there are more of my men than Shimon's, so as we do the sweep through the village we should soon take back the hillfort as our numbers grow when we free our warriors in the huts."

He paused. Next came the tricky bit.

"Now hear me, and hear me well. And it is important that you pass this order on to every Dane-bre warrior you free or meet. There is to be no killing. Hear me now. NO killing unless there is no other way. I know you all, and I have no doubt *all* my warriors will want revenge and the chance for trophies. But trust me, if the killing starts, those men of Olann-bre will see they have no choice other than to fight for their lives. Then," and he paused for effect, "the village of Dane-bre would run with blood. If a full battle does happen, fighting would carry on down to the last man of one village or the other. And then it would not matter who lived through it. Dane-bre would just be a place of dead men, women without husbands, and fatherless children. There would be no village of Dane-bre or Olann-bre left to carry on. So, I say again, NO killing. OK?"

The nods were slightly reluctant but no one could deny the Chieftains logic and no one would disobey his orders. "Now," Parrish continued. "As we sweep through the village it is my plan that we should be able to hold all the Olann-bre warriors in the huts until they can be gathered together once it is light enough. Then I want them all herded to the open area just inside the great gate. There we can check that we have every man, and there also I can speak to everyone together, to tell them their place."

"And the women?" Tomps asked.

"They will go where their men go." Parrish was blunt. "Mara and Mimi will stay safe here in the wigwam and will be sent for when it is over. Then I shall decide what to do next."

All the men nodded at that. The Chieftain's words were great, and his plan was bold. But what to do after? That was beyond their reasoning.

"And me?" Gant asked his tall friend again.

"Ah." There was a pause and a wicked grin crossed Parrish's his face. "As the men go from hut to hut, gathering up the sleeping warriors of Olann-bre as a small girl might walk through a meadow picking up wild flowers," There were wide grins then. Parrish nodded slowly. "I want you, my friend, to lead a few good men and head straight for the Chieftain's hut. I am sure that is where Shimon will be, and fast asleep I hope. I want you to have the honour of taking the village back from him. Perhaps Tomps might like to go with you?" The young warrior grinned broadly and returned Klud's shoulder barge to his friend.

A cheer erupted at that but Gants face remained serious. He bowed deeply to his Chieftain, even in his sitting position. "I thank you greatly." he said with a catch in his voice, stifling the sudden rush of emotion. Parrish clapped the man on the shoulder.

"He took Dane-bre from you, my friend. It is only right you take it back. But remember, no killing. Trust me, taking back the village and taking his power of Chieftain away will hurt Shimon much more than a knife in the ribs."

"You are a wise man." said Tomps with a satisfied smile.

"It is a great plan!" said one of the hunting party.

"Yes. But only if it goes to plan." added Parrish firmly. "Now. We should make ready. We will set off shortly. I think that the forests edge to the north of the village is within easy reach. There we will wait till just before the dawn. Klud and I go first. Everyone else get to the gate. We will open it and, as quietly as possible, you can all be about your work." He eyed the men sternly. "And remember. NO killing."

Another cheer went up. Parrish caught the only concerned eyes in the house and winked at Mara, hoping to convey to her that, with a little luck, this would be a totally bloodless coup.

*

It was still dark. Parrish and his men peered out from the tree line. The hillfort in the middle distance was dark and quiet. Between it and the trees the snow lay open and bare, softly glowing with that eerie blue tint the night time seemed to imbue it with.

Parrish gave the signal and he and Klud moved out of the protection of the trees and into the open. To the soft swooshing of snowshoes on snow the pair headed straight for the ditch and wall ahead of them, about half a mile distant.

At that same signal the rest of the men angled out from the trees and away towards the left end of the hillfort silhouette, southeast towards the entrance. Parrish glanced to his left to observe them and witnessed quite a stirring sight. A group also in black silhouette against the blue/white snowy background, all moving with focused intent towards their target. In the late twentieth century these men would have been military special forces, armed to the teeth, well trained and bristling with intent.

Parrish cocked his head to one side. Beggars can't be chooser's but he was not complaining. They looked plenty scary enough to him. The group were steadily moving away, Tomps leading. Parrish approved. The rest were slightly spread out behind him. Four men had ropes gripped in their fists, pulling behind them the sled, now empty apart from its lone passenger Gant. He was hanging on for dear life, the towing warriors not giving him any special consideration. They just wanted to get at those inside Dane-bre. The slim outline of Hew could be seen moving alongside the sled, keeping pace. Parrish approved of that too. He allowed himself a satisfied grin. They were all good men. Things were off to a good start.

Klud knew nothing of this. He just did his best to keep up with his long-legged friend and together they crossed the snow the shorter distance to the edge of the ditch that separated them from the north wall of Dane-bre.

Both men were quietly proud of how well kept the defences of Dane-bre were, but now, as they stood at its snowy lip, it looked particularly steep and deep. Barely hesitating, the two men slithered the almost twenty feet down to the bottom and started to clamber up the other side. The snowshoes stopped them sinking in, a blessing not fully realized until the pair had to resort to using all fours to help them scramble up the incline. Their arms were plunging elbow deep into the snow. At least the disturbed snow that tumbled down in tiny avalanches behind them to the bottom of the ditch was silent.

Then they crested the top. Both men kicked out of their snowshoes and waded through the knee-deep snow the few steps to the base of the wall. Klud turned, pushed his back against the unyielding timber façade, cupped his hands together in front of himself and flexed his knees. Parrish was about to put his boot into Klud's stirrup when he paused, then looked up at the parapet above him, cocking his head to one side. Klud looked at his Chieftain in sudden confusion.

"It looks to me," Parrish whispered suddenly to his friend, "That all I seemed to be doing this winter is sneak into hillforts."

Klud nodded, snorted a short laugh through his nose then offered out his cupped hands again.

"Right." Parrish whispered back with a wry smile, planted his foot in his friend's grip and lunged up for the lip above him. Klud heaved up with all his might and Parrish easily reached the top, hauling himself over. He disappeared for a few moments then leant back over the parapet and reached down with an outstretched arm. Klud reached up. They gripped each other's wrists and with Parrish heaving and Klud's boots initially scrabbling against the trunk wall, the Neolithic warrior made the top and was half hauled and half clambered over the lip.

The pair crouched on the walkway, readily expecting to be jumped on by a band of marauding Olann-bre warriors, but all was quiet.

There wasn't much to see. The rising ground in front of them blocked their view of the rest of the village. The only building visible, in silhouette on the brow against the cloudy night sky, was Parrish's log cabin. But it did somehow did not look right.

Quietly, pushing through the snow, the pair made their way up to the cabin and it soon became clear what had happened. Shimon, or someone on his orders, had slighted Parrish's house.

To the invading Chieftain, the unique building was a blatant symbol of the previous one and Shimon wanted it gone. His first thought was to burn it to the ground, but even a madman would not deliberately set fire to a building in the middle of a village mostly made of straw! So, he had done what the parliamentarian army of the English civil war would do in many centuries time to castles and other fortifications used against them by the royalists. They broke, wrecked or destroyed them. This was known as *slighting* the castles so they could not be used against them in any future conflict.

Both men stared in silence at the cabin. The roof had been deliberately and thoroughly collapsed in. The wooden window shutters had been torn away. Lumps in the snow, when the whiteness was brushed away with the hand, revealed the smashed remains of the furniture that had been inside.

Klud saw his Chieftain's mouth set in a firm line.

"I am sorry, Parrish." He said quietly.

"No problem." Parrish growled, but ground his teeth in silent fury. "It can be fixed. Which, is just what I am going to do to Shimon." he added with real venom in his voice. Turning his back on the destruction he looked Klud in the eye with a steely stare and said coldly. "Right, my friend, let us get that gate open and we can sort this crap out once and for all."

Klud did not know what 'crap' meant but he understood his Chieftain well enough. The pair turned to face the sleeping snow-capped village, moved silently down and vanished into the darkness between the huts.

32

The walkways between the village roundhouses were well-trodden and after all the deep snow, Parrish and Klud found the going much easier. They moved quickly and silently towards the main gate, the open area before it also widely flat and well-trodden. This subtle indicator that there was still plenty of activity within the village and thus no mass deaths, was lost on the pair. It did however mean that Parrish was right in his assumption that all his warriors were still alive.

The pair lifted off the heavy locking bar and as they pulled back the gate Tomps' war party flowed silently in and bunched up in front of their Chieftain.

"Start with the nearest huts." he said quietly. "Get the Olann-bre men under your control then either wait till you are relieved or if there are Dane-bre men there, pass the control over to them and move on to the next hut. Keep it quiet and this whole mission will not take too long." There were barely seen nods in the darkness, although the faintest of pre-dawn glows went unnoticed as it started to illuminate the eastern horizon.

Parrish turned to Gant and Tomps. "Away you go." And his two friends moved off directly towards the Chieftain's hut, two more men at their backs. Everyone watched them for a moment before Parrish looked back at the remaining seven men. "And you too." he said. "Dannu be with you."

And the little troop split up into two groups of two and one of three as they readied to move away.

"Come on Klud." Parrish smiled a humourless, determined grin. "Pick a hut." And hope no one dies in the next few minutes, he thought to himself.

They move swiftly away to their right as the rest of his men broke left.

Klud stood to the right of the first door blanket, Parrish to the left. Apart from not clutching a firearm to his chest, Parrish had trained for this many times. He nodded then shouldered his way through the ice encrusted door blanket, Klud only one pace behind.

A warrior was asleep to the left side of the hut, everything softly illuminated by the low burning central hearth fire. He was an Olann-bre man. Parrish saw this, firstly because he did not recognise him and he knew all his own men, at least by sight. But also because, ignoring the four women to the right, two Danebury men was sleeping huddled under their capes at the rear of the hut. The interloper however had a full bed and several blankets to himself. So that was how it had been for his people since Shimon took over, Parrish realised. All this the two-man assault team took in on the instant. Just as the Olan-bre man began to awaken Parrish crossed to him, Klud alongside, and stopped at the bedside, momentarily unsure quite how to proceed. But Klud intervened. Without hesitation he drove his boot firmly into the still prone man's midriff.

“Oof!!” the half-asleep man blurted as the breath whooshed out of him.

Parrish almost grinned at his friend’s action and felt his satisfaction. The man curled into a loose ball, clutching his stomach. Parrish put his own boot on the side of the man's neck and hissed.

“Make a sound and you die!” There was no reaction. He pushed down on the man's neck a little harder and a strangled squeak came from the man's throat. “Yes?” he insisted.

“Ye... yes.” The man under his boot managed a hoarse croak.

Parrish lifted his foot off and stood menacingly over him while Klud bent, snatched up an impressive looking flint axe from beside the bed, and handed it to one of the Danebury warriors, who were now both on their feet.

“Watch him.” Parrish instructed the pair and they nodded in return. He looked them both in the eye. “No killing him when we have gone.” he warned. “I want these men for later.” They nodded but Parrish wasn't convinced. “NO killing.” he repeated. “If I find out later he died at your hands for revenge, I will *not* be very happy. Understand?”

“Yes, my Chieftain.” They said in unison, some alarm at the threat showing readily in their faces.

Parrish smiled then. “Good men.” he said. “And it is nice to have my men back with me.” The two grinned back. “Do not kill him but keep him quiet. If he needs a little reminding of that, well...” he cocked his head non-commitally to one side. “Come on.” He turned to a grinning Klud. “On to the next hut.”

*

Just as his friend had done, Tomps burst in through a doorway, this one being the Chieftain’s hut, closely followed by the other two warriors. Gant held back a moment to let them do their work then stumped in like he owned the place.

There were no Danebury warriors inside, Shimon wasn't that trusting that the men he knew all resented him would all keep to their pledge of loyalty to him while he slept. But there were two other Olann-bre warriors there as well as the Chieftain and four women crouched off to one side. To their credit Shimon’s two bodyguards almost managed to get unsteadily to their feet before they were knocked back to the ground by the two Danebury hunting party warriors, who delivered stunning blows to the chest and neck and they both fell gasping to the floor.

Shimon leapt to his feet. “What the...!” he started loudly before Tomps silenced him with a punch to the solar plexus and a clubbed fist to the side of the neck. The man crumpled back onto the bed.

“Silence!” The young warrior hissed before stepping back to allow Gant his moment.

The former Chieftain of Dane-bre stepped up to the gasping Chieftain laying on his side on the floor before him. Shimon had a close up view of one booted foot and a wooden stump before he looked up at the warrior standing over him.

"My name is Gant." the one legged man introduced himself. "You will have heard of me, I think." He looked down his nose at Shimon. "You have my village, and I am here to take it back." Shimon went to open his mouth to speak but Gant cut him short. "And if you say one word, I will have you killed here and now, even if Chieftain Parrish wants to speak with you later on."

The two Danebury hunting party men gasped at his declaration of willingness to disobey his own Chieftains direct order. Tomps looked on passively, not giving away the fact that even he wasn't sure if Gant was bluffing.

Shimon struggled to his feet, gasping for breath, and tried to stand tall and impose his position as leader on the situation. Tomps moved in close with a look that would have frightened even the toughest warrior and any words he was about to speak remained unsaid.

Gant just looked Shimon in the eye and said evenly.

"No noise, and you may live a little longer, *warrior* Shimon." thoroughly enjoying emphasising the man's demotion in position. And though the Chieftain of Olann-bre's eyes burned with undisguised fury, he could do nothing.

At that moment Tomps could not have been more impressed or proud of his great friend.

Similar hut invasions were going on all across the village of Dane-bre. Some of the huts had more than one Olann-bre warrior in but all of the huts had many more Danebury men. As Parrish had predicted from the start, he alone knew Olann-bre's full complement of men was less than forty. There were more than sixty Danebury male adults and as the men led by Parrish cleared each hut, the extra Danebury men formed into additional teams and began their own attacks.

But Parrish's orders were passed on and despite the fact that upon their Chieftains return they considered themselves released from their oath to Shimon, *and* that there was serious animosity towards the occupying Olann-bre men, no one was killed. Several men needed gentle persuasion to obey their new masters and to keep quiet. A few bruises and the odd black eye were apparent when the men were finally gathered together at the open gate area. But to Parrish's satisfaction and admiration of his own men's control in response to his order, no one actually died. He could imagine how his people must have been treated but he was greatly impressed with their restraint and said as much.

As the sun finally rose over the horizon, the overnight clouds very slowly starting to break up, it threw its watery light on the amazing scene of Danebury warriors herding all the interlopers from Olann-bre towards the gate courtyard and the ever-larger gathering there. Women from both villages followed on behind in a tight and growing cluster as more of them spilled out of the huts. Even the smaller children braved the cold dawn to witness what was happening.

It was patently obvious to everyone as they gathered that the Olann-bre men looked healthy and well fed, while everyone else looked undernourished, slightly haggard and scruffy. Clearly recent times had been tough here for the folk of Danebury and it doubled Parrish's appreciation of his people's restraint in their handling of their antagonists while fuelling his anger at how his people had been treated.

Finally there was a hush over the gathering at the entrance to the great gate of Dane-bre. The courtyard was full of people. More people than had ever been seen there before.

Parrish stood centre stage, Klud on his right, shoulder to shoulder. Tomps stood to his left just as close. Gant stood the other side of Klud and Hew outside of Tomps. A couple of paces behind Parrish, where he had long ago learnt to stand when there was likely to be trouble, stood the Danebury holy man. Behind this formidable line up were the bulk of the Danebury warriors.

Directly opposite Parrish, just a few paces distant stood Shimon and behind him a tight group of all his thirty five Olan-bre men.

Everyone at the gathering who had come from one hut or another had a blanket or cape wrapped about them for protection against the crisp cold air. Shimon himself sported a large, finely worked blanket that hung over his shoulders, down over his back and wrapped around him, the edges held closed together over his chest by his one visible hand. Parrish in contrast just wore his outdoor clothes, as did his escort and it was they who were starting to shiver as the earlier adrenalin began to fade and the cold made itself felt. Behind the tight Olann-bre group was a line of Danebury men enclosing them in a semi-circle, all armed and keeping a wary eye on their prisoner's backs, while trying to ignore the cold too.

To one side of the great gathering, keeping back out of the way but not wanting to miss anything or any words, the women clustered together, some holding children against their fronts.

Shimon visibly bristled at everyone while Parrish just stared boldly back, confident now of his position, having successfully reclaimed his village from the villain he saw opposite him.

Everyone was waiting for him to speak and they heard him inhale deeply.

"You have invaded my village." Parrish finally said evenly. "Taken lives, food, goods, and anything else you wanted. You have moved into other people's homes and treated them with no respect at all. Every day you have been here is the greatest insult to my people." This got no verbal response from Shimon but his eyes blazed with misguided indignation. "And now see what has become of your own people. Their lives and yours are at the whim of me and my men. I had to persuade them all not to kill you to a man, as soon as they had a chance. You attacked Dane-bre when everyone slept, and have now almost brought your own village to ruin. What say you to that?"

“I care not what you say.” Snarled Shimon, the anger and frustration in his voice was almost palpable. “I am a Chieftain, and you will treat me as an equal!”

Tomps scoffed at that and Shimon’s furious gaze darted to the young man. “I should kill you where you stand for that!” He hissed.

Tomps just stared back and in a quiet voice that shouted out self-belief said simply.

“You could try.”

The other Danebury men nodded but Parrish held up a hand. Shimon’s acid stare returned to him, his threat to Tomps seen by everyone else as just another hollow gesture.

“Any one of my men would relish a fight to the death with you.” Parrish quashed the man’s diminishing power even more. “And still you do not see, or do not care to see, that what you say and do next could save you and all your people’s lives.”

Shimon began to shiver now. But not with the cold. His fury could barely be contained. As his self-control completely ebbed away his stare became almost manic and his teeth were now gritted.

Parrish tried one more time.

“And not just you and your men.” he said evenly. “What about your own village’s women and children…?” He turned his head and looked to the big group of women off to his left at the edge of the gathering, all standing silently there between the warriors and the big gate. At the front of the group was a face he instantly recognised, and a broad grin swept onto his face. His wife was safe and appeared well. Thank the Goddess! Juli saw his reaction and waved an arm in return.

It was Parrish's unintentional, innocently happy grin that was the final straw for the man before him and as his head turned and he lost eye contact with Shimon, the Chieftain of Olann-bre completely lost control. He dropped his blanket to reveal the flint headed axe he had been concealing, held unseen behind his back. In a blur of motion he lunged forward one long step and with an insane cry of fury and before anyone else could react, swung the axe with all his might, aiming for his victim's heart.

The weapon hit Parrish squarely on his chest, just left of centre, right over the heart, charged with the full power of a furious madman. As it bit into the front of Parrish's combat jacket there was a muffled, dull '*chang*' sound and the flint head shattered into a myriad of black, glassy fragments. Parrish was still standing square on to Shimon and the anger, weight and drive behind the blow rocked him backwards and he fell. Instinctively flinging his arms wide in an attempt to keep his balance, he caught both Klud and Tomps across their chests and the three men all sprawled on their backs.

Shimon stared in amazement at the bare axe shaft with its missing head, then looked down at Parrish. Unbelievably, the tall man was not dead! Shimon shrieked in fury, hurled the axe handle aside and, pulling free a flint dagger that was tucked into the rear of his belt, leapt at his opponent.

Klud and Tomps were still flat on the ground either side of Parrish and everyone else just stared on in stunned amazement.

But Hew was still on his feet and, as everyone knew, he was fast. Very fast. Even as his friends fell back, he burst into a run. The distance was less than half a dozen paces and even as Shimon lunged forward to finish off Parrish, dagger poised, Hew hit him side on, clasping his arms around Shimon's body just below the armpits in a textbook rugby tackle. It knocked Shimon sideways and they both fell to the ground. Once again Shimon was denied the satisfaction of killing his arch enemy. Still raging, he stabbed Hew in the back as best he could while in the awkward position of being on his side on the ground with the young man hanging on, arms clamped around his middle. The clumsy stab went in through the back of Hew's winter coat, pierced his skin below his shoulder and stopped as the flint head jammed up against his shoulder blade. Deep, but not fatal.

Hew rolled away with a painful cry and, fortunately for the lad, Shimon had no interest in finishing him off. He leapt back to his feet just as Klud and Tomps were doing likewise. Parrish was still flat on his back, gasping for breath against the sharp pain of what was most likely a couple of cracked ribs. The Danebury holy man, who was in the act of kneeling to attend to his Chieftain, looked up as Shimon once again stood tall. Totally out of control, the wild eyed Chieftain of Olann-bre tried to rally his own warriors, still grouped closely behind him.

"Now my warriors!" he cried. "Kill them. Kill them all!"

All the reaction he got from his men was a moment of stunned silence. It was blatantly clear to every Olann-bre man there that he was demanding they all die here and now just to satisfy his furious blood lust for revenge. And yet he was still their Chieftain, and instinctively reacting to his order, they all quickly produced flint daggers from under their capes and blankets. But the indecision was there and they hesitated.

All the Danebury men had their weapons drawn now as well, but they were loyally waiting for the word from their own Chieftain.

Instead, words came from the kneeling holy man.

"To raise your hand against Parrish is to raise it against Dannu!" He proclaimed loudly.

Shimon ignored the cry.

"Kill them!" He screamed again.

Shimon's men were already hesitant to die uselessly on the order of their leader, but to be ordered to go deliberately against their Goddess was too much. Their leader had clearly lost his reason. In the Olann-bre group many arms holding daggers were suddenly raised high, yet to every Danebury person's surprise, no warriors advanced towards Parrish.

The first downward stab struck Shimon in the shoulder. The next one cut into his back.

"No... No!" He shouted, spinning to face his warriors, who briefly registered the shock on his face before they all crowded in around him and then all that could be seen were dozens of daggers plunging down, pulling back dripping with blood before plunging down again.

Shimon's screams were loud but short lived and everyone else watched in shocked, opened mouthed silence as the warriors of Olann-bre continued their frenzied stabbing until everything was silent. Then they all stepped quietly and respectfully back and looked to Parrish, who was now being helped to his feet. The bloodless slash through the front of his jacket the thing everyone was staring at.

"Drop your weapons." Came a quiet voice of authority to Parrish's left and everyone looked to see Gant, momentarily taking charge. "I said, drop your weapons." He repeated.

At first in ones and twos, and then en-mass the warriors of Olann-bre let their daggers drop to the blood splashed snow at their feet.

Gant nodded then looked to Parrish, now being held up by Klud and Tomps. The Chieftain held his hand to his bruised chest.

"Shit!" He gasped. "Did no one search Shimon?" He looked in disbelief at his men. "Did you not search anyone?" He added in amazement.

"He... He was a Chieftain." said Tomps sheepishly, as if that explained everything, now realising how badly things could have gone.

"And knives are just... knives." added Klud quietly.

Parrish tried to gather his wits. Everyone was looking to him.

"OK... OK." He puffed and took a few calming breaths. "Right...."

He scanned about him, taking in his armed and poised Danebury warriors, and the sheepish, resigned looking Olann-bre warriors. Now completely unarmed, they just stood, shoulders dropped and eyes downcast, knowing now they were at the complete mercy of those around them. Parrish avoided looking at the women and straightened, winced at the sharp reminder of his sore left side ribs, and tried to sound as Chieftain-like as he could. He needed time to think.

"OK." he repeated, nodded to himself then spoke loudly and clearly. "People of Dane-bre. My people." He couldn't help but smile at that. "Everybody as you were. Go back to your homes. I know they have been taken from you, and even damaged, but now they are yours again. Broken things, losses and bits to be replaced can be dealt with later. For now, just go home. Keep warm and do what you can."

As he looked at the crestfallen Olann-bre men, out of the corner of his eye he caught Klud and Gant helping Hew gingerly to his feet. The youngster's face was contorted with pain but at least he was up. Returning his attention to those in front of him he adopted a stern tone.

"You men gather your families if you have them. Every one of you then go to the shrine hut. There is room for you all in there. Stay inside and settle yourselves." He raised his voice so everyone could hear. "Everybody now just calm yourselves. I will consider and decide what is to be done." Turning back to the Olann-bre people he said calmly. "Do not fear." and glanced down at the bloody, mutilated corpse at their feet. "You have my word of honour that you will be safe in the shrine hut." He again scanned the faces of his own people to be sure that they all got the message. There were several nods amongst the crowds. "Good. Now, everyone back in the warm." He spun to his friends. "How is Hew?"

All the Olann-bre people abruptly felt as if they had been dismissed. They immediately began to move away en-mass back into the heart of the village. The people of Danebury just let them go. They all remained, standing about, just looking at their great, victorious Chieftain. Parrish's attention was now on his young friend. "How is he?" he repeated.

Hew was being supported by Klud and Gant. Tomps moved up beside his Chieftain, also concerned for his young partner.

"He is injured but not badly." said Klud, trying to make light of it but Parrish could see the occasional red flower bursting on the white ground behind Hew as drops of blood dripped from his coat end and splashed on the ground.

Women began to appear and 'Parrish's girls' were suddenly there along with Mara, who gratefully accepted her son's right arm from Gant, Klud understood and stepped back as Anna moved in close to take Hew's left. Klud's first wife stepped forward and bowed to Parrish. He smiled warmly down at her.

"Can you take him somewhere warm and comfortable to treat and heal his wounds?"

She did not openly smile back but her eyes twinkled at his unnecessary question.

"Of course, my Chieftain. Come, come with me." Turning away from the tall man she did her own wagon master wave, and the cluster of women bustled a wincing Hugh away.

"You will be OK." Parrish called after him. "I would trust these women with my life." Have done, he added under his breath.

Juli stepped up behind her husband. Parrish offered her a warm smile then looked around him. He had expected the crowd to have thinned but apart from the departing Olann-bre clan, everyone else was still standing. Just waiting.

"What?" Parrish was confused.

"They want to know." said Klud in a serious tone. "Everyone wants to know."

"Know what?"

"Why you are not dead!"

"Huh?"

Klud pointed to the slash in the front of his friend's jacket. The slash over his heart. The deep, open and completely bloodless slash.

"Oh." Parrish took a deep breath, winced again, then simply reached inside his jacket with his right hand and pulled out the black Beretta 92 handgun that had been nestling in the pocket there. Across the weapons slide was a bright, metallic silver diagonal slash against the usual gunmetal black finish, the streak of damage done by Shimon's flint axe strike.

There were gasps from the watching crowd. Everyone recognised what he held. Dannu's Black Death Giver! And this time it had protected her man. It was clearly the will of the Great Goddess!

Everyone bowed deeply.

Parrish just shrugged, examined the pistol briefly then thrust it back inside his jacket as if it were nothing. His people still just watched.

"Well, that was a bit of luck, eh?" he said with a wry smile.

No one believed him for a moment and there was an awkward silence before Gant coughed and stepped forward.

"We are all finished here." He again briefly took command. "So everyone back to their homes now." He stood and crossed his arms, letting everyone know he would brook no dissent.

Parrish nodded approval and, curiosity satisfied, his people started to disperse, all more eager now to get back to their reclaimed homes, keen to get back to some sense of normality. No one said, but everyone wanted to do their bit to help return Dane-bre to the happy village it was before. They would do what they could and, now he had returned, trust in their great Chieftain to do the rest.

In no time, all that remained at the place where a remarkable event had just happened in this humble Neolithic village, was the small group of Parrish, his wife and his best and trusted friends. And the twisted corpse on the blood spattered icy ground before them.

The low sun, now clear of the horizon, and the slowly dissipating cloud cover did nothing to improve the gory sight and there was a cold stillness before Klud, who else, asked the question.

“What about Shimon?” They all knew that certain rituals should now take place. After all, he was a Chieftain.

Parrish stared momentarily off into the distance. He hated everything about the dead man for what he had done to *his* village by his unfeeling, brutal and self serving actions. He did not even want to say the man’s name.

Without giving the corpse a second glance he turned to the holy man.

“Wrap that up and put it somewhere out of the way. I will deal with it later.”

The holy man bowed in acknowledgement but Parrish had already turned away.

33

The day passed and the people of Danebury spent their time repairing the village. Lots of things got burnt in the fires outside the huts. Parrish never asked or went to see what those things were, but it appeared to him as a sort of 'spring clean'. It seemed very cathartic to his people and in the same vein but also to keep out of the way, the man himself walked up the hill and stood, hands on hips, just staring at his ravaged cabin for a long time.

Juli had kept busy throwing things out of the Chieftains hut, their official and as of now temporary home, anything she thought Shimon had touched, slept on or otherwise used. A symbolic but very real cleansing of the prestigious roundhouse. Yet she found time to join her husband outside their vandalised home and it seemed a few moments before he realised she was there beside him.

"I have never been so angry as when I watched that man order his men to do this." she said suddenly, pulling Parrish out of his dour thoughts.

"No matter." he lied. "It can be put right. But we will have to wait till the spring for fresh thatch." He reached out and pulled her to him. Her arm snaked round his waist and she did not care who might be watching from below. They hugged side by side and then she stepped away, as was proper. Parrish turned and together they looked down at his village, as he had done countless times from the same spot.

The sun was out and the clouds were thinning to nothing. It would be a fine end to the day and it appeared a thaw was beginning to set in. It would however be a clear and cold night to come.

"What they are doing is because of something bad, but it is still nice to see the people busy." he said, watching his people.

"Everyone is back as families and back as a village." Juli finished what her husband was thinking.

Yes." he paused and abruptly changed the subject. "How is Hew?"

"Klud has him being cared for in his own home."

He would, thought Parrish. He liked the lad from the very start. And he knows I owe that boy big time, so would want to make sure everything possible was being done to aid his recovery.

"Good." was all he said though. "I hope the lad will be able to attend the shrine hut tonight. I want everyone there if it is possible."

"No one will miss that." Juli said emphatically. "Everyone wants to know what you have decided."

Parrish grinned and tapped the side of his nose.

"No spoilers." He chuckled then laughed at his wife's frown of confusion at his words. "You will have to wait and see. But there is plenty to sort out."

"Yes." And we all know you will, she thought to herself, but just nodded. "Well. You and your son will need to be fed before then, so, with your permission?"

"Of course."

And as she turned and made to move off back down the slope, he slapped her playfully on the behind.

"Oh... you." she laughed and without turning back walked away and left her husband, her Chieftain, to return to his silent pondering.

*

There appeared to be no sign of life from the shrine hut, at least when viewed from the outside. Inside, the entire remaining villagers of Olann-bre were simply keeping quiet and out of the way. Despite all they had done or been forced to do by their now deceased Chieftain, Parrish still had some of the Danebury women deliver food to those occupying the hut stalls in the late afternoon. The warriors of Dane-bre thought they should be left to go hungry, especially as the village itself was by now very low on food, but they obeyed their Chieftain. He always had a reason for his actions and instructions, and no one was going to question it. As far as Parrish was concerned, it was simply compassion for a group of warriors and their families who now found themselves in their current position because of the greed of one bad Chieftain.

Now the briars burned bright around the outside of the shrine hut, doing their best to hold off the approaching night while calling the villagers to what would surely be a most unusual gathering. The second such in just one day. This was indeed a day like no other and sure to be talked of around campfires for a long time. Everyone would of course be there. Chieftain Parrish was going to announce the fate of the people, from both camps, now inside.

Gant had been in earlier and instructed the Olann-bre clan to occupy just one side of the hut. So now all the stalls to the right of the great central hearth between the entrance and the huge Dannu statue were full of confused and concerned people.

As night fell everyone from Dane-bre entered the shrine hut and naturally gravitated to the left side of the hut. The stalls there were even more crowded, with their extra numbers to squeeze in. Parrish had offered his double sized Chieftains stall to the families of his friends and along with Gant, Tomps and Klud's people, Hew's were also there, the boy himself sitting at the entrance, leaning against one side support pillar and favouring his injured shoulder.

Parrish, his wife and son were the last to arrive. He stopped just outside the entrance to the shrine hut, turned and scanned his deserted village. It looked silent and dark beneath the clear night sky. Stars began to twinkle in the heavens and the fore-glow of the imminently rising moon was starting to softly lighten the north eastern horizon. He grinned to see just how peaceful it looked, then turned back to the job at hand.

There was complete hush as he appeared in the mouth of the entrance passageway and led his family across to the Chieftains stall. Stopping briefly to see Juli and Chris settled, he nodded to Hew and the others then strode back out and took command of the floor. The holy man stood beside the Dannu statue on its plinth as Parrish moved in front of it and looked about at the people before him, lots of people, and all looking with a mixture of expectance and trepidation back at him.

He wanted to put on a beaming smile, tell them everything was great and they would all live happily ever after. But it wasn't and he could not. This was not the time to be polite and pussyfoot around. And although he hated to act the dictator, he was Chieftain, so this is how it was going to be! Standing tall, he tried to look as business and Chieftain-like as possible, and spoke clearly to the two sided crowd.

“OK people, this is how I see it.” He launched straight in. “The constant threat of attacks with two villages living so close together has got to stop.” He scanned the crowded hut with a stern eye. “But it is clear to me that Dane-bre cannot keep and feed so many people, and even if it could, because of what has already happened, there would be disagreements, fights and killings. We cannot all become one big village. So, the people of Olann-bre must return to their own village.” There was no disguising the looks of glee on the faces of *his* people and the looks of fear in the eyes of the Olann-bre contingent. He continued.

“But not right now,” he nodded to the people on his left. “As soon as the snow goes, so must you. But we will keep you till then. Coming back to the fighting though, and how to stop it from happening is my main concern. It is my order here and now to have a bridge built across the east river between our two homes. And I want a proper, solid bridge. Timber built and big enough for two people to cross walking side by side.” More than a few faces on either side of the hut thought, why? “And both villages will be working on its making.” That got everyone’s attention. “Now, I need someone who can see my vision, organise the people to do it and get the bridge built. And only one man springs to mind.” He turned to Gant. “Can it be done, my friend?”

It was posed as a question but as a Chieftain, Parrish's words were really a direct order.

“Yes. Yes, my Chieftain.” Gant was rather stunned but answered promptly. He thought for a moment. “But, it will take time and many men.”

Parrish pointed to the warriors of Olann-bre.

“Here is the bulk of your workforce.” The men in question looked startled. “But I do not want them worked to death, especially while they are fewer in numbers than Dane-bre and their village is struggling. What I want is someone who can organise the building of this great bridge, using men from *both* villages, but without upsetting the day to day life of either village too much. And to organise Olann-bre village so it can become safe, strong and able to live on as a proper village in its own right.” His expression turned slightly grim. “I have thought long on this and though I am not happy about it, and I think some others will be unhappy also, but I see no other way. When I say these are your workers,” he pointed again to the people of Olann-bre, “I mean these are your people. My friend, What I am offering you now is the village of Olann-bre, as its Chieftain!”

There were gasps right across the hut and a hubbub of discussion immediately broke out.

“But... Parrish...” Gant was staggered.

“I know.” Parrish did not smile. “And believe me, I want you to stay here. Your friends would want you here too. What you do for Dane-bre I am very unhappy to lose, but it is because you are the only man able to do what you do, that I ask you to help put right the problems at Olann-bre plus pull everyone together and build a link that will bring both our villages together. So again, I offer you the position of Chieftain of Olann-bre!”

Gant opened his mouth, shut it again without speaking then stared down at the floor for several long, silent moments. Parrish had to hide a smile then. This was his great friend Gant, doing what he did best. The thinking man, the organiser, running through the scenarios in his mind.

Finally, he looked up and stared into his tall friends eyes. He understood now how building a bridge and putting a Dane-bre man in charge of Olann-bre would help the villages form a bond. It was a clever thing the Chieftain was doing. He could see how it would save lives and make everyday life for *all* the people safer and more secure. And he also saw the sacrifices his Chieftain was making for himself, his friends here and what it would cost Dane-bre once he had left.

"I understand and, I would be honoured." he said finally.

Parrish nodded back.

"Then my last instruction to you as a warrior of Dane-bre is to use every man here wisely to build the bridge. And my first words to you as a visiting Chieftain, is to honour you to our place of worship." And with that he bowed deeply to his friend. Gant simply stepped forward and held out his hand. Parrish reached too and they gripped each other's forearms.

"You have made me a Chieftain, twice. But whatever happens," Gant said quietly. "You will always be my friend, Parrish."

"And you." Parrish's eyes glowed with pride. He knew his friend would step up to the mark.

They both turned to face the people of Olann-bre, who stared back, shocked and amazed at what had just happened.

"Well?!" growled Parrish.

"Chieftain Gant!" came back the expected chorus and all the people of Olann-bre bowed to their new leader. Their new, one legged leader!

"Right. Now that is sorted, next." Parrish moved across to face his own people and stood outside the Chieftains stall. He smiled warmly at them all, each stall down this side of the hut brimming with people all the way to the entrance passage, every face looking in his direction.

"Gant will have the bridge building work parties fairly arranged. We will not be too overstretched. I will arrange hunting parties and work parties for any village repairs. Then we can put all this," he waved his hand in the air above his head. "behind us." He turned to look at Hew, who had struggled manfully to his feet. Parrish could smell the heavy odour of the healing poultice that he had no doubt Klud's first wife had applied to his injured back.

He addressed the lad directly.

"I saw what happened this morning. I owe you my life and I am in your debt. So, I have decided I have a gift for you, your mother and little Mimi."

"Huh?" grunted Hew, briefly forgetting his manners before a Chieftain.

"When we left the holy village to return here, you said you would be glad to live in Dane-bre." Parrish recalled the youngster's words. "But we cannot just take in any old wandering boy and his family."

Hew's face fell and Mara and Mimi gathered in close behind the young man.

"But as you helped me, so I shall help you, and my village too. Anna!" He called out. The girl emerged from a group two stalls down and walked sheepishly up to her Chieftain. Hew instantly recognised her as the kindly girl who had given him his travelling cape. Parrish knew the girl originally from Olann-bre had been keeping out of the way and suppressed a grin as she drew near. "You lost your husband at the start of all this. Well, I give you to Hew here, a gift from a grateful Dane-bre and its Chieftain." Both boy and girl looked mortified. Parrish carried on. "I know you are alone in your own house and it is a struggle. Hew has no wife and has nowhere for he and his family to stay. So now I offer him a fine female and a house in the village here.

He gets a home and a wife and the village gets one more complete family. It was meant to be!"

There were open mouths on the Dane-bre side of the hut now, before the stunned silence was broken by Klud bursting out laughing, Tomps and the others began to join in. Hew and Anna still looked shell-shocked but Mara looked to her new Chieftain. She understood and gave him a discreet, grateful nod. Parrish winked back then gently pulled Anna up alongside Hew. "Meet your new wife." He leaned in and said quietly to the young warrior. "It is for the good. And thank you again for saving me from Shimon, at great risk to yourself."

Hew accepted everything then. He was not about to argue with Dannu's man, *his* Chieftain now and those final words made him feel proud. The tall man was right. It was a good arrangement.

Parrish straightened up and mocked rubbing dust from the palms of his hands.

"And I think that is just about everything." he said with a satisfied smile.

"Er... great Chieftain Parrish." came a stammering voice from across the floor.

Parrish turned.

"Yes?"

A burly looking bruiser of a warrior from Olann-bre had stepped out from the group. He didn't look bright enough to be Chieftain material, Parrish assessed him instantly, but he felt pretty sure he would be a good man in a scrap. The man spoke.

"I... we were just wondering, what about Chieftain Shimon? I mean, his body?"

A few soft gasps came from the Dane-bre contingent. Everybody knew it was not wise to ask Chieftain Parrish, Dannu's man, to explain.

Parrish waved them all to silence. His face darkened and the man involuntarily took a step back, suddenly thinking that he had seriously offended the Chieftain, but Parrish's anger was not for the living.

"That man was a bad man, but he was your Chieftain, so only for that reason will I tell you what is going to happen to him. He was a very bad man." He repeated to emphasise the point. "People have died for no good reason because of him. He threatened to kill every man, woman and child in *my* village. Someone like that, Chieftain or no, does not get to sit in the great shrine hut of the Earth Goddess among the other warriors there, after they are dead. My holy man here will set his body on a trestle on the knoll in the east as usual. But when the sky spirits have taken his soul from his frame, I am going to gather up all his bones and bury them at the foot of the entrance pathway up to this village. His two halves of body and spirit will never be joined again and every person who walks in or out of Dane-bre, if they know it or not, will walk over the remains of the man who threatened all my people and my village. No one does that and escapes my wrath, alive or dead! And if anyone objects to this course of action," He spun to face everyone. "Then you are free to come and talk to me about it!" The look he gave dared anyone to say anything.

At that moment no one wanted to look him in the eye and there was some uncomfortable shuffling of feet at their Chieftain's sudden anger. He turned back to face the burly man and just fixed him with a stare.

I... I understand." The man bowed and backed away into the Olann-bre crowd, as shocked as anyone at the severest of punishment the tall man was meting out to their former leader.

"Good." said Parrish bluntly. And besides, he added to himself with a mental grin, it will blow the minds of any archaeologists who dig up those random bones in a few thousand years time.

"Right then. If there is nothing else and everyone here is fed and happy with my arrangements, I am away to my bed." He knew Gant and Klud could handle anything else that might arise after he left. He held out his arm towards the Chieftain's stall and Juli scooped up Chris and crossed to her husband's side. Together they crossed the open middle of the hushed shrine hut, negotiating the big central fire, and vanished into the entrance way passage. All to complete silence from the watching crowd almost two hundred people strong. Everyone just stared after them.

As Parrish and his family stepped out of the hut and into the fresh, cold night air, the world about them looked at peace and somehow magical. The still laying snow held a soft glow, the clear night sky was filled with stars and the moon had now risen, fat and full, hanging low above the shadowy horizon. Its glowing light seemed to cast a beam onto the roofless cabin atop the slope of the north west quadrant of Dane-bre, catching Parrish's eye.

He stared up at the forlorn looking building for a long moment before turning to gaze at the full moon. He recalled leaving the cabin and setting off for Avebury not too long before the winter solstice. Suddenly he grasped that that moment had happened more than twenty days earlier and realised that far ahead in the twentieth century, the new year would now be considered well into January.

He laughed.

"What? What is it?" ask Juli, seeing her husband's sudden amusement.

"Oh, it is just, back where I come from, the first full moon in Jan... er, after the winter solstice, is often called the 'wolf moon'."

The irony of it was lost on his wife but he hugged her to his side, kissed the top of her head and ruffled his son's hair before the three turned their backs to the glowing orb and headed off towards the Chieftain's hut.

EPILOGUE

Gants construction of the bridge had begun. After the mini thaw when Parrish had returned to Dane-bre from his adventures in the north, the weather remained cold but not freezing cold. To the hardy peoples of Neolithic Britain, it was considered quite bearable and not much more than a persistent inconvenience.

So, Chieftain Gant of Olann-bre had thought hard then set the people, *his* people and the people of Dane-bre to starting the building of Parrish's commanded bridge. He had of course talked it over with the great man and together they had worked out a schedule/rota to maximise the building work force yet minimize the disruption to both camps. It did mean the work was slow but it had now begun.

Rotating the work parties between the men of each village in groups of five, or one hand of men from either camp, did not upset the village routines unduly. More men from each camp could have sped up the construction but Gant also had to manage the resurrection of Olann-bre village, sort out food and water supplies there, plus erection of a proper security wall around the village and still somehow gain the trust of the people there who were unsure of their newly appointed leader. A leader not chosen by them, a man not of Olann-bre at all but another village, *and* appointed by that village's Chieftain. And to top everything, the man only had one leg! It was a lot to swallow and the warriors of Olann-bre, while not openly hostile to their new leader, were less than welcoming.

If Chieftain Gant was enraged, upset or offended by his people's attitudes, he did not show it. He ordered the people about, set different people different tasks according to their village status and what he estimated as their levels of ability, and let them get on with it, *expected* them to get on with it, as ordered by their Chieftain. And all the while he remained calm, steadfast and resolutely determined.

Every day, after first setting tasks for his warriors and expecting the women to attend their men, when necessary, Gant stumped his way down to the river to oversee the starting of the bridge construction. He explained what he wanted done and *expected* to be done on that side of the river. The small group there's task could including gathering up materials, felling trees if and when necessary, preparing the trunks and supervising the start of construction. After all that, he would move away upstream the several kilometres to the shallow crossing point. It was the first safer place to cross the east river. The flowing water was still a chest deep wade for the Neolithic population and a risky exercise every time. It was there that Gant had supervised and helped build a simple crossing for easier access to the far side. Because the water was not deeper than one and a half metres he had been able to create a walkway by having pairs of long stakes driven into the riverbed at angles, each pair forming a large wooden 'X' with its cross point only a foot or so above the rivers rippling surface. These crosses were lashed together, sited no more than two metres apart from each other, then rough-hewn planks laid on top spanning from cross to cross and also secured by ropes. This created what was in essence a rough, long trestle type raised foot wide walkway above the clear, flowing water enabling people to cross in single file without the risk of imminent drowning. It was basic, simple, did the job and provided a safe and dry passage from one side of the Test Valley to the other. But this single lashed together planked walkway would not do where the water was deeper, wider and just as fast flowing.

Meanwhile Gant, once across the river, would then stump his one footed way back down along the Danebury side of the valley back to where the bridge was to be built, and continue to supervise the start of its construction there also. And there he would stay for most of the day, organizing from the riverbank and shouting any necessary instructions across to his people on the Olann-bre side if he felt they needed it.

But his one real pleasure of the day, if it happened, was his favourite visitor. Not always, but most days he would receive a visit, which was a welcome break from the relentless work Gant had tasked himself to do.

This particular crisp, cool day, Chieftain Gant had brought two Olann-bre warriors with him around to the Danebury side of the river. The first man was a particularly well built, thickset warrior powerful enough to wield the big, barrel-headed solid oak mallets which we used to drive in the wooden cross stakes of the plank walking design footbridge. Gants intent was to start with 'cross walkway' footbridges leading out into the flow and then begin constructing the main bridge from there. But right now he needed two muscular men to drive in the early posts and so, the first big warrior had volunteered his friend, who was also a beefier than average Neolithic man.

This second man, resplendent with a jet-black beard and wild mass of hair had no issue with been told to go with the Chieftain to help with his bridge but, as long as he was out of earshot of his leader, was quick to voice his unhappiness at the man himself.

"Stumping around like he owns the place." He grumbled to his oppo as they leaned on their mallet handles during a break for water and to gather their breath. "Ordering us around without saying why."

"Well, he *does* own the place." Came the quiet reply. "And since when did you expect a Chieftain to tell you, or anyone else, his thoughts?"

"But he just stands there and points. Do this, do that... I do not see him doing that much himself."

"Just like before then." The first warrior was surprised to find himself defending his new, universally distrusted leader. Now that he took a moment and looked closer at just what the one-legged man had been doing since his elevation to Chieftain, he came to realise that it was no different to when Shimon was in charge. Except that Gant was not nasty with it, or vindictive or appearing to be lining his own nest or making his life easier at the expense of the others in his village. The more he thought about it the more the new man seemed genuinely straightforward and honest!

"Yes. Well." came Blackbeard's retort. "And he always has a face like the great stones at the Temple. Never smiles. Never frowns. Never gets angry. It is not right. No one can tell what the man is thinking or what he will make us do next."

Mmm… Better than some other Chieftains I can think of, was the first man's thoughts, but just as he was about to speak to them out loud he spotted a diminutive figure coming down the slope from Dane-bre hillfort towards the little group of riverside men.

"Ah, you know nothing, my friend. But watch and learn. Now you will see your all-serious Chieftain smile. Here comes the young woman from Dane-bre he gets regular visits from."

"Eh?" Queried Blackbeard and looked up to see this mysterious young woman that approached. In truth he had not worked on this side of the river before and was completely in the dark as to who the person might be.

Young woman indeed! He saw the joke and smiled. A small girl was drawing near. In one hand she carried a wooden, three legged 'milking stool' no more than a foot or so high and in her other hand a clay pot half wrapped in a section of cloth. Over her shoulders was slung a food satchel and a water bag. Both were miniatures of normal food and water bags, perhaps half the regular size. They had obviously been made to suit her small form. She looked no more than seven or eight summers old and strolled steadily down the hill and boldly approached Chieftain Gant directly. There was no respectful bowing or lowering of the gaze. She looked the man in charge straight in the eye, her head tilting back as she drew close and looked up at him. This was not how a female, of any age, approached a warrior.

Then unbelievably to the two watching warriors, she grinned. An open-faced grin! Such disrespect! To their further amazement Chieftain Gant just grinned straight back.

"Hello little one." he said, using the nickname his friend Parrish had given to her.

At that Mimi nodded.

"I have come to look after you." she said in a serious tone.

"As always." Gant smiled back. "And pass my thanks on to your mother."

"I will as always." said Mimi in reply. "Now, please sit. We must always take care of your poor leg."

The two Olann-bre warriors watched in stunned amazement as little Mimi, blatantly ordering a Chieftain about, unceremoniously plonked the three-legged stool on the ground in front of Gant, and he duly sat. Unbidden he stretched out his stump leg and pulled back his leather trouser to the knee, revealing the leather cup and its attached strappings that held his prosthetic in place. He undid the straps and Mimi grasped the wooden end. A very brief tug of war ensued before the false limb pulled off Gant's stump with a soft plop!

Mimi fell back on to the cold earth into a sitting position and waved the prosthetic triumphantly aloft and both participants laughed. Then Mimi examined his stump. As usual it looked a bit raw and red.

"Mother says you always do too much, and this is not good for your leg."

"Well, I will not tell her if you do not tell either." Gant smiled.

Mimi gave him a reproachful look then unslung the bags.

"She also says you must eat and drink to keep your strength up. Please eat while I tend to your leg."

And handed over the food bag to Gant while the two Olann-bre men continued to stare on. It wasn't till then that Mimi appeared to first notice the pair. “Oh, hello.” She did not seem the least bit intimidated by or frightened of the two powerful looking, big, mallet wielding warriors from another village. “I have enough food for everyone. If you would like some?”

The two were speechless. They glanced from the girl to their Chieftain then back again.

Gant broke the silence.

“Yes. You have been hard at work. Come. Sit and eat.”

A direct order from their leader could not be denied. They moved across and squatted beside him, all three now at the same level and looking across at the small girl.

“Eat.” She said then paid them no more attention and after examining the end of Gants footless leg for a moment, rubbed her palms together to warm them. Dipping her fingers into the clay pot she scooped out some of the heady smelling healing poultice it contained and began to apply it onto the tender red stump.

Gant appeared not to notice and bit down on some jerky, while holding an apple ready in his free hand. The two men just held their broken off pieces of flat bread in their hands and watched the small girl as she rolled and massaged the thick poultice around on her patient’s stump.

“But… my pardon, my Chieftain.” said the first warrior quietly, unable to contain his curiosity any longer. “Does… does it always hurt?”

Gant smiled secretly at this first small breakthrough between the men of Olann-bre and himself. And who would have thought it would come about through one little girl.

“The foot does not.” He laughed. “But the stump can sometimes be a little soft. And…” The man pointed with the remainder of his jerky at Mimi. “My young friend here learnt to do that when we were at the holy village together.”

The two warrior's eyebrows went up at that. So, this mere slip of a girl was someone special. It was clear now that she had holy connections with the priests of Dannu.

That... that sounds most interesting." Blackbeard finally spoke, like his friend, now beginning to grasp that he was learning more about his new leader with every minute.

"Just wait till he tells you all about the time we rode on a sled together across the deep snows of winter." Mimi piped up. "And we were pulled along by the bravest men in all of Dannu's land!" she boasted and almost squealed with delight, the moist poultice making slathering sounds as she continued to apply it across Gant's scarred skin.

"Yes, but perhaps not now." Gant reigned in Mimi's obvious enthusiasm.

"Yes," the first warrior agreed, suddenly feeling that it was all becoming a bit *too* familiar and some respect should still be maintained towards the Chieftain. "But we still have work to do, so, with your permission?"

"Well said." Gant nodded, which made a surprise rush of warmth well up in the warrior, who was instantly pleased by the unexpected approval from his Chieftain. "But food first, and make the most of it. Mimi does not always come along to take care of her old friend."

"Oh, you." Mimi giggled and smacked him with a wet handed slap higher up on the shin.

Gant smiled but his men found the familiarity and unbelievable boldness of the small girl he allowed very uncomfortable to them. They sat down on the cold earth and as suggested, turned their attention to their food, looking sideways at each other as they ate, both men now thinking the same thought.

Perhaps not quite such a stern faced, cold and considered man after all?

Perhaps not such a bad Chieftain after all?